Toward a Common European Union Energy Policy

Toward a Common European Union Energy Policy

Problems, Progress, and Prospects

Edited by
*Vicki L. Birchfield and
John S. Duffield*

TOWARD A COMMON EUROPEAN UNION ENERGY POLICY
Copyright © Vicki L. Birchfield and John S. Duffield, 2011.

All rights reserved.

First published in 2011 by
PALGRAVE MACMILLAN®
in the United States—a division of St. Martin's Press LLC,
175 Fifth Avenue, New York, NY 10010.

Where this book is distributed in the UK, Europe and the rest of the world, this is by Palgrave Macmillan, a division of Macmillan Publishers Limited, registered in England, company number 785998, of Houndmills, Basingstoke, Hampshire RG21 6XS.

Palgrave Macmillan is the global academic imprint of the above companies and has companies and representatives throughout the world.

Palgrave® and Macmillan® are registered trademarks in the United States, the United Kingdom, Europe and other countries.

ISBN 13: 978–0–230–11319–0
ISBN 10: 0–230–11319–2

This book is printed on paper suitable for recycling and made from fully managed and sustained forest sources. Logging, pulping and manufacturing processes are expected to conform to the environmental regulations of the country of origin.

Library of Congress Cataloging-in-Publication Data
    Toward a common European Union energy policy : progress, problems, and prospects / edited by Vicki L. Birchfield and John S. Duffield.
      p. cm.
      ISBN 978–0–230–11319–0 (hardback)
      1. Energy policy—European Union countries. I. Birchfield, Vicki L., 1965– II. Duffield, John S.
HD9502.E82T69 2011
333.79094—dc22   2011002898

A catalogue record of the book is available from the British Library.

Design by Newgen Imaging Systems (P) Ltd., Chennai, India.

First edition: July 2011

10 9 8 7 6 5 4 3 2 1

Printed and bound in Great Britain by
CPI Antony Rowe, Chippenham and Eastbourne

Contents

List of Illustrations		vii
Foreword		ix
Preface		xi
Introduction	The Recent Upheaval in EU Energy Policy John S. Duffield and Vicki L. Birchfield	1

Part I Developments in Key Policy Areas

One	EU Internal Energy Market Policy: Achievements and Hurdles Per Ove Eikeland	13
Two	Foreign Policy and Energy Security: Markets, Pipelines, and Politics Richard Youngs	41
Three	Common Rules without Strategy: EU Energy Policy and Russia Jonas Grätz	61
Four	EU Emissions Trading: Achievements and Challenges Jørgen Wettestad	87
Five	EU Renewable Electricity Policy: Mixed Emotions toward Harmonization Måns Nilsson	113
Six	Energy Savings and Efficiency Jørgen Henningsen	131

Part II National Perspectives

Seven	French Energy Policy within the EU Framework: From Black Sheep to Model? Sophie Méritet	145
Eight	Germany and EU Energy Policy: Conflicted Champion of Integration? John S. Duffield and Kirsten Westphal	169

Nine	The UK and EU Energy Policy: From Awkward Partner to Active Protagonist? *Francis McGowan*	187

Part III Cross-Cutting Perspectives

Ten	Rethinking European Climate Change Policy *Arno Behrens and Christian Egenhofer*	217
Eleven	The Role of EU Institutions in Energy Policy Formation *Vicki L. Birchfield*	235
Conclusion	Taking Stock of EU Energy Policy: Problems, Progress, and Prospects *Vicki L. Birchfield and John S. Duffield*	263
Contributors		277
Index		283

Illustrations

Figures

5.1	Growth in renewable electricity generation (in twh per year)	114
5.2	Renewable energy use and goals for 2020 in the climate and energy package of 2008	118
7.1	The French energy mix in 1973 and 2008 (in percent)	150
11.1	Key developments in EU policy formation	251

Tables

5.1	Summary comparison of FIT and TREC	116
7.1	Primary energy consumption in 2008 (in mtoe and in percent)	151
9.1	Energy production and supply in the UK	190
10.1	Simplified summary of climate change impacts in Europe and their intensity	219
11.1	Energy policy initiatives and legislative actions	253

Foreword

Of the challenges that the European Union faces, ensuring a secure, competitive, and sustainable energy supply is certainly one of the more complicated ones. There are few areas of EU policy that energy choices do not impact heavily or at least impinge upon. Climate change, the EU's increasing dependence on imports, the strain on energy resources, and access to affordable energy require an ambitious response, and the benefits or even the need for a more integrated EU energy policy aimed at delivering a low-carbon economy are becoming ever more evident.

For that reason, we are fortunate to have this timely, thorough, authoritative contribution to the study of EU energy policy. Professors Birchfield and Duffield have assembled a first-rate team of experts to examine recent developments in EU energy policy and to explore the prospects for future progress in this critical area. This book will be essential reading for scholars of the subject and will provide a very useful reference for practitioners and policy analysts.

GÜNTHER OETTINGER
European Commissioner for Energy
Brussels
May 2011

Preface

This volume, like its subject matter, was a complex undertaking, It involved the collaboration of scholars from 12 different countries and the coordination of two universities to host a symposium out of which the manuscript developed. The idea for the project originated with a grant proposal to the European Commission and was supported by the award of the European Union (EU) Center of Excellence at Georgia Tech and supplemented with a conference support grant from the Georgia State University Research Foundation. Other material and financial support came from the European Union's Delegation to Washington, D.C., the Atlanta Regional Commission, the Georgia Institute of Technology, and Georgia State University (GSU), for the use of its conference facilities.

The editors wish to thank William Downs and Kenya Walker, of the GSU department of political science, for help with conference arrangements and Allison Smith and Ansley Hynes of the EU Center of Excellence at Georgia Tech for logistical and administrative support. Deserving of special recognition are the invited discussants who attended the conference and offered incisive comments and constructive feedback on the research papers presented by the contributors to the volume: Dr. Paul Baer, Dr. Marilyn Brown, Dr. Jay Hakes, Dr. Charles Hankla, Dr. Wilfrid Kohl, Dr. Janelle Knox-Hayes, Ms. Luisa Ragher, and Dr. Adam Stulberg.

We also gratefully acknowledge Shane Tomashot, for research assistance and help with the conference, and Matthew Schipani, for research and editorial assistance. A tremendous debt of gratitude is owed to Lauren Kretz who provided skillful research and editorial assistance as well as invaluable help with the final manuscript preparation. Finally, the project would not have been possible without the excellent contributions of the authors. Their wide-ranging knowledge and individual expertise strengthened our collective enterprise, and the collegiality enjoyed among virtual strangers in Atlanta, Georgia during the symposium in November 2009 and throughout the project is a testament to the power and attraction of common purpose.

The project was envisioned around the time the Irish initially rejected what eventually became the Treaty of Lisbon. The actual conference took place on the eve of the Treaty's ratification and the nomination of the EU's new leadership team as well as the approaching Copenhagen Summit on Climate Change. And now, we complete the manuscript just days after the European Commission unveiled a new energy strategy paper that calls for one trillion Euros in investments over the next decade "both to diversify existing resources and replace equipment and to cater for challenging and changing energy requirements." A summit meeting to consider the Commission's proposal was held in February 2011, and in the words of the EU energy commissioner, Günther Oettinger, "It's all a matter of national political will...We will be asking heads of state, Do you really want this, or is this just something for speeches?" (As reported by Joshua Chaffin, *Financial Times*, November 11, 2010: 2). While this study shows that sometimes ambitious rhetoric exceeds the will to act and major obstacles to the construction of a truly common energy policy for Europe certainly persist, when the various elements of such a complex, multifaceted policy are disaggregated, it become clear that substantial progress has indeed been made. Despite the pitfalls and remaining challenges, we believe readers will find in this volume reasons to expect that energy policy may in fact be the next big integrative engine in Europe.

VICKI L. BIRCHFIELD AND JOHN S. DUFFIELD
Atlanta, Georgia
November 2010

Introduction

The Recent Upheaval in EU Energy Policy

John S. Duffield and Vicki L. Birchfield

Although two of the three original treaties on which the European Union (EU) is based explicitly concerned sources of energy, the EU and its predecessor institutions have exercised relatively little competence in the area of energy policy over the years. During the past decade, however, the EU has arguably made unprecedented strides toward the creation of a common energy policy, as exemplified by the European Council's adoption of an ambitious and relatively comprehensive energy action plan based on the European Commission's communication "An Energy Policy for Europe" in 2007 and the subsequent approval by the Council and the European Parliament of a number of concrete measures to implement the plan. In late 2009, energy policy per se became a formal competence of the EU with the entry into force of the Lisbon Treaty.

This book takes stock of these important recent developments. In particular, it addresses the following questions:

- How much progress has actually been made toward the establishment of a common EU energy policy?
- What conditions and events explain this recent progress?
- What remains to be done before the EU can be said to have a truly common energy policy?
- What obstacles stand in the way of and what are the prospects for creating such a policy?

This introductory chapter sets the stage for our analysis by first describing the evolution and limitations of EU energy policy from its origins in the first European communities. It then provides a more detailed overview of the recent developments in EU energy policy that serve as the impetus for this volume. A third, brief part summarizes the limited existing literature on the subject and the approach employed here. A final part lays out the organization of the volume and of the individual chapters.

Historical Background: The Long-Standing Absence of a Common EU Energy Policy

In the beginning, energy policy was at the heart of the institutions out of which the EU eventually evolved. Indeed, it could be said that the EU began with a common energy policy. With the passage of time, however, these initial institutional arrangements became less and less relevant to the energy needs and concerns of the Member States, and for many years they were never replaced or supplemented by more relevant arrangements. This marginalization of energy policy stands in stark contrast to—and is especially puzzling in light of—the considerable progress that was made toward European integration in other policy areas, especially the closely related common market. Until and through much of the 1990s, energy policy remained largely an orphan of the integration process.

The European Union traces its origins to the establishment in 1952 of the European Coal and Steel Community (ECSC). At the time the Schuman Plan was proposed in 1950, coal accounted for more than 80 percent of the energy consumed in what became the original six Member States, with oil a distant second at 10 percent, and most observers expected that coal would remain the most important fuel well into the future. With its entry into force, the treaty establishing the ECSC created a common market in coal (as well as steel) almost overnight. With just a few exceptions, it required the immediate elimination of all restrictions on trade, including import and export duties, quantitative restrictions (quotas), discriminatory prices and transportation rates, and state subsidies. To facilitate the achievement of the common market, the treaty also endowed the High Authority of the community with unprecedented supranational powers. The High Authority could break up cartels, impose fines, guarantee loans, influence investments, and, in certain circumstances, fix prices, limit output, and allocate supplies (Diebold 1959).

In 1958, the ECSC was complemented in the energy field by the creation of European Atomic Energy Community (Euratom). At the time, the atom was expected to become a major additional source of energy, especially after the Suez crisis cast doubt on the reliability of

Middle East oil supplies. Thus Euratom was intended to promote the growth of the nascent nuclear industry. Nevertheless, within its area of application, the powers of Euratom were much more modest than those of the ECSC, being largely limited to the financing of some common research programs and a common supply policy carried out by a Nuclear Supply Agency based on the principle of equal access. For the most part, the Member States were otherwise left free to promote national nuclear industries as they saw fit (Black 1977; El-Agraa and Hu 1984).

At about this time the ECSC began to be less relevant to the energy needs and concerns of its members. The institutional limitations of the ECSC were starkly on display during the coal crisis of 1958/1959, when the recommendations of the High Authority for addressing an acute excess of supply were blocked by the Member States. More fundamentally, the ECSC was increasingly marginalized by the rapidly rising use of oil. In 1960, coal's share of energy consumption among the six Member States had declined to 60 percent while that of oil had risen to more than one-quarter. By the middle of the decade, oil had surpassed coal as the most important fuel supply. And by 1970, the shares of a decade earlier had been almost exactly reversed, with oil accounting for 60 percent of primary energy consumption and coal for just 25 percent, with natural gas rapidly catching up.

Yet the institutional powers of the evolving European communities were never updated to reflect this tectonic shift in the energy mix. In particular, the community institutions were never given any explicit jurisdiction over oil and, later, natural gas, not to mention any general competence in the area of energy policy.

This lacuna was not the result of a lack of interest in the matter or a lack of trying. Every decade from the mid-1950s and to the mid-1990s saw at least one effort to establish a general European energy policy, but none of these came to fruition. The issue of bringing about integration of the conventional energy sector was raised at the 1955 Messina conference, which was intended to revive the integration process after the failure of the European Defense Community the previous year, but it was quickly dropped in favor of a narrow focus on atomic energy (Diebold 1959, 646). In the early 1960s, the Member States tasked an Inter-Executive Working Party on Energy with defining a community energy policy, but the resulting memorandum on the subject was not translated into explicit policy (Black 1977, 181). Then in 1968, the recently merged Commission, on its own initiative, presented its "First Guidelines for a Community Energy Policy," which laid out the case for such a policy and offered a number of concrete measures for creating a common market in the energy sector, but the Council of Ministers could agree on only a set of general principles (Black 1977, 182–83; CEC 1968). Thus, according to one assessment, "by the mid-1970s, efforts to establish a comprehensive energy policy [had] resulted only in agreement in principle on what the parameters ought to be, without any agreement so far on a set of substantive policy instruments "(Black 1977, 165).

This lack of authority greatly limited the ability of the Community to deal collectively with common energy problems, especially those posed by the oil shocks of the 1970s. Prior to the first oil shock, the community had adopted the requirement that members maintain at least 65, and later 90, days of oil stocks. The European response to the 1973 Arab oil embargo and production cutbacks, however, played itself out largely within the framework proposed by the United States (US), and all the community members but France would subsequently rely primarily on the International Energy Agency's emergency oil sharing mechanism. And although, following the first oil shock, the community adopted ambitious long-term goals for energy production, consumption, and imports, it was never able to agree on concrete measures for achieving them.

Similarly, the following two decades saw several proposals for but no concrete actions toward the establishment of a common energy policy. In the early 1980s, the Commission drew up several communications that indicated the need for more joint action in the field of energy (CEC 1983). During the negotiations over the Treaty on European Union in the early 1990s, the inclusion of a new chapter on energy was proposed but not acted upon. Also in 1995, the Commission prepared a White Paper on energy policy that contained a number of detailed guidelines. Once again, the initiative languished in the face of indifference by or opposition from Member States.

Instead, as new challenges and opportunities arose in the energy field, the Community actors were forced to take a piecemeal approach, making use as best they could of the powers they did possess in related areas, especially for market liberalization but also increasingly in the environmental realm. Employing these imperfect tools, the EU was able to make some noteworthy progress, especially with regard to the creation of a single internal energy market. Following the adoption of the Single European Act (SEA), the Commission presented a first set of draft directives and regulations meant to apply the principles contained in the SEA to the energy market, although it took a decade for the Commission's efforts to culminate in the adoption of directives to open up first national electricity and then gas markets. In addition, some progress was made in the environmental arena, with a 1990 agreement to stabilize CO_2 emission, a program to promote energy efficiency, and a 1997 White Paper for promoting renewable energy sources. But the principal proposal to reduce the environmental impact of energy use, a carbon/energy tax, was dropped in the face of strong opposition by Member States.

Recent Developments: Upheaval in the 2000s

The EU's relative neglect of energy policy underwent a profound change in the first decade of the twenty-first century. Those years saw a veritable explosion of proposals, directives, and regulations that touched upon almost every aspect of energy policy. The decade concluded in 2009 with the adoption of an energy chapter in the Lisbon Treaty, which brought energy policy for the first time fully within the competence of the Community organs.

The first part of the decade saw continuing efforts to create a single energy market. The high point of these efforts was the adoption of a second package of directives calling for full opening of the gas and electricity markets for all customers in 2007 and legal unbundling of supply and transmission functions. On the environmental side, during these years, the EU also adopted directives to promote electricity generation from renewable sources, biofuels, and greater energy efficiency in buildings, and to establish a path-breaking emissions trading system intended to reduce greenhouse gases. With regard to the external dimensions of energy policy, the EU initiated an energy dialogue with Russia and negotiated a treaty extending the internal energy market to southeastern Europe.

In the middle of the decade, these somewhat scattershot efforts were replaced by a more integrated approach to energy policy. In 2006, at the invitation of the national leaders, the Commission prepared a Green Paper that laid out a comprehensive general strategy for obtaining "sustainable, competitive, and secure energy" (CEC 2006). The following year, the Commission presented a more detailed energy policy action plan that was adopted by the heads of government that March (CEC 2007; Council 2007). This plan established three ambitious goals: to reduce greenhouse gas emissions, to increase the share of renewable energy in EU's overall energy mix, and to reduce overall energy use in the EU all by 20 percent by 2020. Then based on the action plan, the Commission developed an "energy and climate package" of specific measures designed to achieve those goals which was presented in 2008. These initiatives on the part of the Commission were largely matched by the efforts of the Council and the Parliament, which adopted numerous implementing directives and decisions between 2006 and 2009. Those years saw, among other things, a revision of the ETS and a third package of energy market liberalization measures, as well as other concrete policies to promote renewables, energy efficiency, the construction of energy infrastructure, reductions in greenhouse gas emissions, and the security of energy supplies. While much remained to be done, this flurry of activity was capped by the ratification and entry into force in late 2009 of the Lisbon Treaty, which for the first time brought energy policy explicitly into the remit of the EU. Although energy policy remained a shared competence between the EU and its Member States, no longer could initiatives by the Commission be questioned as lacking a legal basis.

The Scholarly Study of EU Energy Policy

Given the renewed significance of energy to the economic well-being of industrialized and industrializing countries as well as its increasing importance to the environmental fate of the planet, it is vital to take stock of these developments and to explore their implications. How much progress has in fact been made toward the establishment of a common EU energy policy? What factors account for this recent progress? And what are prospects for further movement toward a truly common EU policy in this area?

Despite the importance of the subject, surprisingly little has been written on EU energy policy, perhaps reflecting the limited formal competence that EU institutions enjoyed in this area until very recently. To be sure, the 1950s and 1960s saw a number of studies of the ECSC and Euratom. But the only comprehensive single volume in English on the subject since then, Manne Haaland Matlary's *Energy Policy in the European Union* (1997), appeared more than a decade ago and thus does not address the important developments of the 2000s at all. David Buchan's recently published *Energy and Climate Change: Europe at the Cross Roads* (2009) represents a welcome corrective to this general neglect of the topic, but it still suffers from some limitations. Primarily a journalistic account, it is not grounded in the broader literature on European integration and contains few citations to other scholarly works on various aspects of EU energy policy.

In addition, we contend the subject consists of too many often highly technical topics for any single individual to cover it with authority. Hence the approach employed here: to bring together in a single volume a number of scholars with in-depth expertise in each of the main policy areas as well as the energy policies of the leading EU Member States. In this way, we are able to offer a thorough scholarly analysis of how much, or how little, progress the EU has made toward the construction of a common energy policy in the past decade and what obstacles remain to be overcome. In seeking to offer the most comprehensive empirical analysis to date of this most complex of subjects and to answer as fully as possible our set of guiding questions, we deliberately avoided imposing a common theoretical framework across the various chapters, nor did we attempt to test different explanatory or analytical models of EU integration or policy-making. Instead, our approach is empirically grounded, policy analytic in nature, and comprehensive in scope as we examine both the internal and external dimensions of the EU's emerging energy policy as well as the supranational and intergovernmental processes that are shaping its development.

Organization of the Book

The core of the book consists of 11 chapters divided into three parts. The first part examines recent developments in six key policy areas: market liberalization, external energy policy, EU energy relations with Russia, emissions trading, renewable energy, and energy efficiency. Each chapter in this part addresses to varying degrees the following questions:

- What actions have been proposed and what actions have been taken by the EU and Member States?
- How much progress has the EU actually made in this issue area? What are the limitations of what the EU has done? How far is the EU from having a common policy in this area?
- Why were these particular policies proposed? What obstacles has the EU faced in making progress? What considerations have motivated EU bodies and Member States in both furthering and impeding the creation of a common policy in this area?

- What are the prospects for further progress in this area? What obstacles remain?

The second part contains national perspectives on recent developments in EU energy policy. It focuses on the three states that have traditionally been most important in the promotion or hindrance of the development of common EU policies: France, Germany, and the United Kingdom (UK). Each of these chapters addresses the following questions:

- What has been the country's general attitude toward a common EU energy policy?
- What energy issues has the country sought to address through the EU, and how has it sought to do so? What energy policy initiatives has it resisted and why?
- What have been the underlying determinants of the country's policy toward a common EU energy policy?
- What are the implications of the country's domestic politics for the development of a common EU energy policy?

The third part of the book evaluates recent developments in EU energy policy in terms of how the inherent crosscutting nature of the policy arena itself contributes to or impedes the achievement of the traditional functional goals of energy policy: security of supply, environmental sustainability, and economic competitiveness. One chapter focuses exclusively on the EU's climate change policy examining both the internal and external aspects of EU policy-making in this area and the challenge of balancing domestic competitiveness and global leadership in environmental sustainability. Another chapter offers an analysis of the policy-making process at the EU level with a goal of teasing out how each of the core EU institutions has contributed to energy policy formation and its relative coherence (or lack thereof), given the varying degrees of competence and authority, dimensions of intergovernmentalism and supranationalism as well as competing institutional interests and policy preferences. These two chapters also address the following broad questions:

- What particular challenges does the EU face?
- To what degree do the policies adopted so far address those challenges?
- What more needs to be done to advance EU interests?
- What further policy developments are feasible or realistic?

A concluding chapter, coauthored by the editors, provides an overall assessment of the progress that has been made toward and the future prospects for the development of a common EU energy policy. Drawing on the insights of the individual chapters, it considers both the internal and external dimensions of this strategic policy area. Our focus is on the tensions and the complementarities between national policies and the efforts of the EU to produce a coherent energy policy as well as to assert itself as a global leader in addressing the problem of climate change. As such, we hope this volume will serve to advance both the scholarly literature and inform ongoing policy debates.

Works Cited

Black, Robert A., Jr. 1977. Plus ça Change, Plus C'est le Même Chose: Nine Governments in Search of a Common Energy Policy. In *Policy-Making in the European Communities*. Ed. Helen Wallace, William Wallace, and Carole Webb. New York: John Wiley & Sons.

Buchan, David. 2009. *Energy and Climate Change: Europe at the Crossroads*. New York: Oxford University Press.

Commission of the European Communities (CEC). 1968. *First Guidelines for a Community Energy Policy*. Memorandum presented by the Commission to the Council. Bulletin of the European Communities, Supplement to No. 12-1968. COM (68) 1040 final (December 18).

Commission of the European Communities (CEC). 1983. *Community Energy Strategy: Progress and Guidelines for Future Action*. COM (83) 305 final (June 2).

Commission of the European Communities (CEC). 2006. *Green Paper: A European Strategy for Sustainable, Competitive and Security Energy*. COM (2006) 105 final (March 8).

Commission of the European Communities (CEC). 2007. *An Energy Policy for Europe*. Communication from the Commission to the European Council and the European Parliament. COM (2007) 1 final (January 10).

Council of the European Union. 2007. *Presidency Conclusions—Brussels, 8/9 March 2007*. 7224/1/07 REV 1 (May 2).

Diebold, William. 1959. *The Schuman plan: A Study in Economic Cooperation, 1950-1959*. New York: Published for the Council on Foreign Relations by Praeger.

El-Agraa, Ali M., and Yao-Su Hu. 1984. National versus Supranational Interests and the Problem of Establishing an Effective EC Energy Policy. *Journal of Common Market Studies* 22(4) (June): 333–349.

Matlary, Janne Haalan. 1997. *Energy Policy in the European Union*. New York: St. Martin's Press.

Part I

Developments in Key Policy Areas

Chapter One

EU Internal Energy Market Policy: Achievements and Hurdles

Per Ove Eikeland

It is now more than 20 years since the European Commission (hereafter: the Commission) issued its first Green Paper on the internal energy market in Europe in 1988 (CEC 1988). The major idea was that *free and fair competition* between energy companies across the European Community would lead to large efficiency gains, lower and more similar prices for consumers across the community, increased competitiveness for energy-using industries, economic growth, and increased welfare. An important part of the proposal was a "common carrier" system for gas and electricity, which meant that European electricity and gas infrastructure should be operated and further developed by agents that were independent from the production- and supply-interests (Eikeland 2004; Lyons 1992). Such independence would allow consumers to purchase energy from any supplier in the internal energy market, regardless of who owned the grid. The visionary concept emerging was nondiscriminatory *third-party access* to the grid.

Internal market policy has since gone through distinct stages ending with revision of legislation aimed at bringing speed to market opening. These are now called the first, second, and third internal energy policy packages, denoting clusters of directives and regulations targeting different aspects of liberalization of the electricity and gas markets. The first package took several years to negotiate and ended up with the 1996 Electricity and 1998 Gas Directives as major outputs. The second package was enacted in 2003 and contained revised Electricity- and Gas Directives as well as specific regulations to harmonize trade and operation of infrastructure across national borders. The third package was finally enacted in July 2009, containing further revisions of the Gas and Electricity Directives, the cross-border regulations as well as an additional regulation establishing an independent agency for boosting cooperation between national energy regulators.

Gas and electricity supply in Europe were historically organized as separate businesses. Most European Union (EU) countries evolved with self-sufficiency in electricity supply. In natural gas supply, however, only a few countries, notably the United Kingdom (UK) and the Netherlands, had sufficient resources to cover their own demand. Most countries became dependent on imports from the main surrounding gas producers Russia, Norway, and Algeria. Until the deregulations of the 1990s, gas and electricity supply were organized in entities enjoying exclusive rights to supply all customers within a specifically defined area. Wholesale supply was in most countries operated by public utilities. These figured as dominating national electricity producers and gas importers, with monopoly control also over national transmission lines or the major gas pipelines. Private ownerships were allowed in some countries but still kept under governmental control in exchange of exclusive monopoly rights. Lower levels of supply (electricity and gas distribution) enjoyed similar monopoly rights, but here, the evolving ownership structure differed significantly across the countries.

The UK had chosen a model of two major public utilities responsible for all generation, transmission, and distribution within the electricity and gas sector, respectively. A similar structure evolved in France. The German electricity and gas sectors evolved with mixed ownership—several major private generators and wholesale suppliers, and a great many distribution companies owned mainly by the regional and municipal governments. The Scandinavian countries (Norway, Sweden, and Denmark) evolved with major state-owned electricity generators and wholesale suppliers, but with considerable parts of the business owned by lower governments or private shareholders.

Irrespective of ownership, the structures evolving entailed strong vertical linkages in the electricity and gas supply chains, in the form of vertically integrated companies or vertical chains established through long-term supply contracts between foreign producers and gas utilities with exclusive rights to import. An important part of EU's efforts at establishing an internal energy market was to restructure energy supply—abolishing de jure and de facto monopoly rights. Since electricity and gas grid operations would still have a natural monopoly character, separating these from the commercial businesses (electricity and gas sales) became paramount to avoid anticompetitive practices of cross-subsidization and grid access discrimination. The Commission admits that these efforts have partly failed and that the

European electricity and gas markets are still characterized by structures that hinder free and fair competition. Its January 2007 final report from the energy inquiry instigated in 2005 identified serious shortcomings in the electricity and gas markets, including inadequate levels of unbundling between network and supply interests and too much market concentration in most national markets (CEC 2007a).

Instead of a common internal market, the EU has developed into regional and local markets characterized by different market structures and competitive conditions. Some member countries, notably the UK, made a full transformation of the electricity and gas industries—abolishing legal monopoly rights and splitting up and privatizing the gas and electricity industries to reduce market concentration. Full ownership unbundling was mandated for electricity and gas transmission companies. Similar ownership unbundling was carried out swiftly in Scandinavia. Other countries, notably Germany and France, lagged behind and did not implement ownership unbundling, a strategy shared by many of the Eastern European countries that got access to the EU in 2004 and later. In 2007, the Commission concluded that wholesale electricity market concentration was *very high* in seven member countries (including France), *high* in nine countries (Germany included), and *moderate* in seven countries (including the UK and Spain), (CEC 2007a, 12). The situation in the wholesale gas market was no less worrying. Here, ten countries appeared with very high concentration (France included) and five with high concentration (Spain included), (CEC 2007a,17). In parallel, horizontal and vertical mergers and acquisitions have created major energy conglomerates doing business in both electricity and gas supply, something that may have aggravated the initial market concentration problems in many countries (Domanico 2007).

Given this long history and background it would not be unnatural to discuss how far the EU has come in establishing an energy policy that adheres to the principle of free and fair competition. Free competition should mean that energy consumers are free to choose service from companies across Europe, whereas the suppliers in turn should encounter no barriers to transport of electricity and gas across Europe's national borders. While necessary, securing such freedom of choice is far from sufficient for competition to be fair. This would depend on market conditions free from dominant actors as well as harmonized governmental regulations across national contexts; the latter is important to ensure that companies in one country do not enjoy far better opportunities at home than other companies, with the competitive advantage this would also give in the greater internal market.

The remainder of this chapter is structured in four parts. The section "Brief History of EU Internal Energy Market Policy Development" provides a brief historical description of EU internal energy market policies, highlighting the most important parts and how the situation was evaluated before the most recent round of policy-making (the third package). The section "The Third Internal Energy Market Policy Package" focuses on the third and hitherto final package of internal energy market policies, the proposal of the Commission, and what was finally adopted by the European Council. Specifically, we look at the Commission proposal to mandate transmission system operators (TSOs) to separate by ownership the operation of transmission grids and that of other commercial production and supply businesses (mandatory ownership unbundling—MOU) and why this was not adopted in the final directive. We place this European Council decision within the long-term context of internal energy market policies and apply a historical-institutional framework to answer the question. This framework looks at the development over time (shifts) in coalitions supporting and opposing the idea of a free-market solution to European energy problems. We identify the key stakeholders, their positions, and how these positions have changed or remained stable over time. Particular focus in the explanation is on the evolution of the relative power of Member State governments and EU institutions, especially the Commission and the Parliament.

The section "Evaluation of Progress in Completing the EU Internal Energy Market" evaluates the progress made in the course of the years and how far the EU still is from realizing the vision to create a common free energy market characterized by fair competition between the suppliers. The evaluation discusses the development over time in several indicators, information disclosed by the Commission in annual benchmarking reports on national implementation of internal energy market policies. The last section "The Road Ahead—Prospects for Free and Fair Competition in the European Energy Market" rounds up with a discussion of future prospects for the internal energy market. Here, we show that EU internal energy market policy is more than the directives and regulations provided by the successive packages. We explore three different procedures pursued by the Commission in pursuit of a free and fair energy market. In addition to directives and regulations, these include application of the general EU treaty competition legislation and more bottom-up methods of coordination initiatives (coregulation).

Brief History of EU Internal Energy Market Policy Development

Toward the First Policy Package

In 1987, the EU Council adopted the Single European Act revitalizing the *general principles* guiding community cooperation—removal of barriers to trade and movement of capital across the Member States as a means to increase growth and welfare in the region. It strengthened supranational authority in a number of EU policy areas, allowing for greater use of qualified majority voting in decisions on EU-wide market rules and thus removing blocking votes of Member States skeptical of increased harmonization of national policies.

Although energy was not initially part of the reform program, the general drive toward common internal market rules created a new dynamic where energy market actors became more active in redefining traditional energy policy issues (Andersen 2000). European enterprises also argued for deeper integration of national energy markets, as a way to make energy supply more efficient, to align and cut energy prices across the region, and thereby to increase global competitiveness of European industry. From 1986 onward, the Council of Ministers discussed greater integration of the domestic energy markets (Stern 1990; Andersen 2000), and the Commission set out to identify procedures for the creation of an internal energy market.

The 1988 Commission communication *The Internal Energy Market* envisioned the electricity and gas grid in Europe as a "common carrier" system across the Member States. Any consumer should be able to purchase energy from any supplier across the community without discrimination in access to grids, regardless of ownership of the grid structures (CEC 1988).

The electricity and gas sectors were viewed as particularly challenging, characterized as they were by nationally dominant, vertically integrated utilities (Lyons 1994, 6–7). Dismantling these structures was viewed as pivotal for free and fair competition to prevail in the internal energy market. The Commission again discussed different *decision procedures* for restructuring these sectors specifically. One was the application of EU competition rules (then Articles 85 and 86 EEC—European Economic Community) against the utilities to dismantle dominant market positions. Another was to initiate infringements procedures according to Article 169 EEC against the Member States. It also acknowledged the need for specific directives for the electricity and gas sectors, which could either be formulated unilaterally by the Commission based on Article 90 (3) EEC, or on the basis of Article 100a EEC-Treaty, a consensus-based procedure allowing other EU bodies to participate in deciding the pace and scope of the liberalization package (Eising 2002; Lyons 1992, 23).

Acknowledging that energy was widely regarded as a public good within European Member States, with dominant public utilities a normal structure in energy supply, the largest part of the Commission (including its energy policy service), the Member States and the European Parliament preferred a consensus procedure (Article 100a) to allow for *incremental* change (Eising 2002). Directorate General for Competition (DG-COMP), on the other hand, opted for a faster breakup of monopoly structures by using competition rules and Article 90 for pressing forward Gas and Electricity Directives (Eising 2002). In fact, the Commission allowed DG-COMP to start up proceedings against gas and electricity import/export monopolies and sent letters to Member State governments asking them to justify their national monopolies, warning that the Commission would act aggressively in order to achieve a single market in energy (Lyons 1992, 23). DG-COMP was inspired by a March 1991 judgment by the European Court of Justice (ECJ) upholding that the Commission could use such procedures to force greater competition in the *telecommunications* sector (Lyons 1992, 13).

Intense lobbying of commissioners by national governments, energy industries and the European Parliament, however, sent clear signals to DG-COMP to keep its hands off the internal energy market. And, in 1994, the ECJ formalized this lesser role of DG-COMP with its rulings in the so-called *Almelo* case of Dutch electricity distributors asking for dismantling the exclusive import and export rights granted to the electricity generators (Lyons 1998, 34). The ECJ found that Articles 85 and 86 of EU competition rules had been breached, but that Article 90 offered the companies opportunities for derogation if operating under public service obligations (PSOs). It did not make any judgment on whether the obligations necessitated the monopolistic behavior in the specific case, however.[1] DG-COMP was therefore unwillingly constrained in playing any active role in EU energy market policies during the decade. To be sure, the Commission continued to remind European politicians that an option existed under European Community (EC) Treaty rules to apply general competition rules, which was used to press Member State governments' adoption of the first liberalization package (Lyons 1992, 24).

The main procedure adopted for internal gas and electricity market policy development was therefore Article 100a, the development of directives through deliberation and consensus-seeking. The process of getting directives adopted became thorny and lengthy, and only toward the end of the decade, after long deliberations with the Commission, and with active mediation from the European Parliament, did the Council adopt the 1996 Electricity Directive and the 1998 Gas Directive. These were heavily watered-down versions of the Commission's initial plan of a common carrier system for Europe. They entitled only a limited number of high volume gas and electricity consumers the right to freely shift suppliers. The Electricity Directive set quantitative goals and a deadline for the reforms whereas the Gas Directive left open for the Member States to decide (Stern 1998).

To ensure a de facto right for these entitled consumers, the Commission sought to establish harmonized terms of access for third parties to existing networks and gas pipelines. This effort largely failed, however. True, Member States were instructed to ensure that the TSOs kept separate accounts (unbundling of accounts) for activities subject to competition (production and supply) and those considered a natural monopoly (operation of transmission grids). No agreement was reached, however, on uniform rules for how TSOs should facilitate access by third parties. In the end, the directive merely listed different options: grid owners could openly list access terms, such as tariffs for using the grid and capacity of the grid (called a system of *regulated* third-party access), leaving traders with information in advance of striking new deals. They could also choose the less transparent system of *negotiated* access (allowing the TSOs to negotiate separate deals with each eligible customer). The Commission also had to accept that Member States could restrict trade across national borders with a "single buyer" system adopted, allowing a single national firm to retain full control over imports. The failure in providing for invariable instructions as to how owners of power lines and gas grids should secure access for alternative suppliers meant that vertically integrated companies were still left with great opportunities to obstruct access for competing power supply businesses.

Toward the Second Policy Package

EU decision-makers acknowledged that there were additional barriers to the creation of an internal energy market that were outside the scope of the new directives. The directives therefore instructed the Commission to go on reporting on *additional* needs for harmonizing national regulations to remove barriers to trade and physical flow across national borders.[2] In the first communication report on the Electricity Directive, which came in 1998,[3] the Commission addressed the problem of reconciling the community's environmental policy with the goal of creating an internal energy market. More specifically, the report discussed the need of ensuring that provisions in the 1997 White Paper on renewable energies[4] were not at odds with free and fair competition in the internal energy market. The Commission concluded that the existence of various schemes for the promotion of renewables in Member States would most likely lead to trade distortions. The Commission concluded that further analysis of existing national support schemes for electricity from renewable energy sources would be needed, and announced plans for a directive on the harmonization of national schemes by the end of 1998.[5]

New follow-up reports in 1999 on the Gas Directive and in 2000 on the Electricity Directive addressed these issues and concluded that great variation in transmission prices, congestion management systems, and outright lack of cross-border transmission capacity across the Member States restricted cross-country trade (CEC 1999; 2000a).

Acknowledging the limited success of the top-down legislative approach applied for the Electricity and Gas Directives, the Commission this time chose another strategy—to involve a broad range of stakeholders in a bottom-up process to identify and seek consensus on the harmonization of cross-border transmission system rules and technicalities. Organizing these processes, stakeholder forums (the Electricity Regulatory Forum of Florence—the Florence Forum and the Gas Regulatory Forum of Madrid) involved participation by national regulatory authorities, Member State governments, the Commission, TSOs, electricity traders, consumers, network users, and power exchanges.

While giving high priority to these bottom-up processes, the Commission also continued to push Member States on implementation of the Electricity and Gas Directives, with benchmarking reports used as a major new tool. A 2001 benchmarking report concluded that large asymmetries in implementation had jeopardized the process of creating a level-playing field in the internal market for energy. While some Member States had over-fulfilled their obligations under the directives, ensuring third-party access through a system of full ownership separation of infrastructure and production/supply businesses (*ownership unbundling*), other countries maintained systems that seriously deterred consumers from changing suppliers in the market (CEC 2001). The 2001 Gothenburg European Council Summit agreed on this diagnosis and asked the Commission to prepare a second energy liberalization package. When adopted by the Council in June 2003, the new Electricity and Gas Directives required full electricity and gas market opening for nonhousehold consumers by July 2004 and for all consumers by July 2007 (European Parliament and the Council 2003a; 2003b). To prevent discrimination by TSOs in transmission system access issues, the directives mandated organizational separation of units operating transmission activities from those operating generation and supply activities *(legal unbundling)*. Full ownership unbundling had been proposed by different agents but the Commission failed to include it the proposal due to great opposition by many Member States.[6]

In addition, the directives instructed Member States to set up national regulatory agencies with well-defined functions and greater transparency was called for in that the directives mandated publication of network tariffs by the TSOs (regulated access) instead of case-by-case negotiations. A separate Regulation sought to strengthen the bottom-up processes by establishing a separate EU-level committee, the European Regulators' Group for Electricity and Gas (ERGEG), constituted by Member State regulatory authorities, with the mandate to develop guidelines for harmonization of technical and market factors constraining access to cross-border infrastructure and cross-border trade (such as rules for inter-TSO compensation, national transmission tariffs and on allocation of cross-border interconnection capacity (European Parliament and the Council 2003c).

The Third Internal Energy Market Policy Package

The Commission Proposal

Despite this new second package, energy consumers continued to voice dissatisfaction, allegedly experiencing higher tariff levels than before and discrimination in access to grids from vertically integrated companies. In June 2005, the Commission launched gas and electricity sector inquiries, with a preliminary report adopted in 2006 concluding that flaws in access to energy infrastructure in many Member States had caused unnecessarily high energy prices in Europe and the loss of welfare opportunities for European energy *consumers*. Vertically integrated energy producers had constrained competition through discrimination of others in the use of infrastructure and held back on new infrastructure investments, causing problems for independent producers of electricity and heat. This was also viewed as a barrier to producers of indigenous renewable energy and hence to the alleviation of climate change and security of supply concerns in the EU. These new concerns made the Commission in March 2006 propose that a new energy strategy for Europe should be developed, aimed at creating greater coherence between the Member States and consistency between policy measures dealing with the three primary objectives: competitive energy for European consumers, security of supply, and environmental improvement of EU energy systems (CEC 2006a). This strategy was approved at the European Council Spring Summit 2006.

January 2007, the Commission adopted the strategic energy review as part of an energy and climate package that also included the full energy sector inquiry (CEC 2006b; 2007b). The package proposed new quantitative goals, tabling the so-called "20–20-20" goals: a 20 percent unilateral reduction of climate gas emissions by the EU, a 20 percent share for renewable sources, and 20 percent reduction in energy use compared to "business as usual"—all to be attained by 2020. The action plan proposed to achieve the larger energy and climate policy goals had listed further measures to ensure access to and investments in new infrastructure as top priorities.

The review concluded that European gas and electricity markets remained national in scope and had maintained from the preliberalization period a high level of concentration and scope for exercising market power (CEC 2007a). Lack of access to infrastructure was highlighted as a major barrier to free competition, causing, together with higher primary fuel costs and environmental obligations, significant rises in gas and electricity wholesale prices (CEC 2006b).

The review elaborated in detail on vertical integration between network and supply interests as a mechanism causing negative repercussions for market entry and incentives to invest in networks, despite the existing legal unbundling provisions. Vertically integrated operators of the networks (in gas, also storage and liquid natural gas terminals) were suspected of favoring access to their own affiliates (discrimination). Operation and investment decisions had been made on the basis of own supply interests. Vertical integration of generation/import and supply activities had reduced incentives to trade on wholesale markets and thus a lack of liquidity in these markets, in turn an entry barrier. The review also added insufficient or unavailable cross-border transmission capacity as a barrier to integration of national markets together with lack of transparency, reliability, and timeliness of information on network availability (electricity interconnections and gas transit pipelines).

Based on this description, the Commission proposed to go forward with a *third legislative package*. The proposal included many different measures, with ownership unbundling of network and production assets placed at the top. An alternative Independent System Operator (ISO) was proposed as a fallback position, the latter retaining joint ownership with returns on network operations regulated and operation, maintenance, and development of networks no longer decided by the vertically integrated owner. The long list of proposals included the following:

- measures to harmonize the levels of powers and independence of national energy regulators from industry and government;
- strengthening the EU-level regulatory function with a new body that could beef up governance required for satisfactory progress in the work of harmonizing standards facilitating cross-border trade across the Member States;
- instead of the *voluntary* cooperation approach pursued by ERGEG, the Commission envisioned new EU-level powers to develop binding standards;
- new harmonized minimum standards for transparency of information provided by the TSOs and generators to facilitate market-access by new entrants and prevent price manipulation;
- measures to beef up planning and approval of priority trans-European gas and electricity networks;
- the setup of a new Office of the Energy Observatory to monitor the demand/supply balance in Europe;
- the development of an Energy Customers' Charter to ensure PSOs; and
- the setup of a solidarity mechanism assisting Member States particularly import dependent and vulnerable in the supply for oil, gas, and electricity and other measures to improve the security of supply within the EU.

The European Spring Council in 2007 endorsed the integrated energy and climate package and the 20–20–20 percent goals set for energy efficiency, renewable energy, and climate gas reductions in the EU. They also consented to a third internal energy policy package but asked the Commission to come up with more specific drafts for the Energy Council meeting in June 2007. This meeting showed that a blocking minority rejected full ownership unbundling as a mandatory measure, while still acknowledging "the need for action on...unbundling of network operations from energy production and supply activities."[7] The Energy Council also rejected any EU-level arrangements that would interfere with Member States' exclusive right to decide on their energy mix, such as the idea of an EU Energy Observatory. Energy Commissioner Piebalgs, attending the meeting together with Neelie Kroes, the Competition Commissioner, admitted that the "majority of the countries did not support 'ownership unbundling' legislation" and that the Commission would have a very difficult time ahead in putting together a new energy liberalization law.

Despite the signals given, the Commission had not abandoned "ownership unbundling" as the preferred mandated option in its September 19, 2007 proposal. To be sure, the "Independent System Operator" was retained as a fallback-option. Another last minute "reciprocity clause" was included, specifying that would have barred companies from nonmember countries from exercising decisive influence on transmission assets, unless a bilateral agreement on mutual market access to transmission assets in the investors' country of origin had been concluded (Grätz 2009, 77). This was aimed at preventing the takeover of transmission systems by vertically integrated companies from outside the EU, with Commission powers to intervene in acquisition matters.

The Final Output

Nearly two years of negotiations followed. In July 2009, the European Council finally adopted the third internal energy policy package: new Electricity and Gas Directives And new regulations for harmonization of cross-border trade in electricity and gas as well as a specific regulation providing for the establishment of the new regulatory body ACER (Agency for the Cooperation of Energy Regulators).

The new Electricity and Gas directives did not provide for MOU but allowed the TSOs to choose two other unbundling methods: the ISO model that had been proposed as fallback position by the Commission and the Independent Transmission Operator (ITO) model that had been proposed by a group of eight Member State governments, led by Germany and France, during the negotiations. Under the ISO model, big energy companies would retain ownership of the transmission lines, but hand managing control over networks to an entirely separate operator not sharing any shareholders with the parent company. The ITO-model also foresees a parent company retaining ownership of transmission networks, but owned by the same set of shareholders. To compensate for the continuation of shared ownership, the model envisages supervision by a national regulator. Among other things, there will be a mechanism preventing top management from moving freely between a company's production and transmission wings. An executive involved in the transmission business will not be permitted to work three years before and four years after in the parent company. In addition, the national regulator will examine the transmission operator's development and investment plans and may require changes.

There were few changes to other proposals in the package that had been backed by the Energy Council meeting in June 2007. It settled the principle of more power to and the harmonization of duties for national regulators so that they are able to issue binding decisions on companies and impose penalties on those that fail to comply with EU regulation. National regulators would have authority over their own budgets and strict rules for management appointments for true independence of industry interests and government intervention.

The creation of a new European Agency for the Cooperation of Energy Regulators (ACER) was agreed with the tasks to oversee and improve cross-border regulatory cooperation for gas and electricity transmission between Member States. The agency would not have any direct regulatory authority at the national or European level, but it would have the power to intervene in the event that national regulators fail to cooperate effectively. ACER will inter alia submit to the Commission nonbinding framework guidelines on cross-border flows of electricity and gas, which will serve as a basis for the network codes adopted by the Commission. ACER will also complement at the European level the regulatory tasks vested with the national regulators by adopting individual regulatory decisions in a number of specific cross-border situations as well as decisions on technical issues when so provided for in the package.

Cooperation between national TSOs for gas and electricity, formerly taking place on a voluntary basis, was formalized through the establishment of a European Network for TSOs (ENTSOs). The main tasks given the ENTSO-E and ENTSO-G (electricity and gas, respectively) were to harmonize codes for access to and use of pipelines and grids, and coordinate and ensure proper network planning and investments in order to prevent blackouts.

The third-country reciprocity did not prevail in its proposed form. It only requires companies from non-EU countries to demonstrate compliance with the same unbundling requirements as EU companies before they are certified to operate in the common market and does not demand changes of market rules in the investor's home market country, as initially proposed (Grätz 2009, 78). To be sure, the new regulation says that Member States must refuse certification if it is deemed to "put at risk the security of energy supply of the Member State and the Community."

Why Was Ownership Unbundling Proposed and Not Accepted?

The Proposal: Looking first at the question why the Commission proposed ownership unbundling, we find this measure to be the logical endpoint of the vision the Commission has pursued since the internal energy market was proposed in the late 1980s: to create a truly independent grid accessible for transport of energy by all parties without discrimination. Separation of ownership of grids and commercial activities would simply provide the best guarantee for such independence. The Commission had been an active promoter of this idea since the start (Lyons 1992). It had long opted for MOU but failed to propose this when the first two packages were up for discussion due to major opposition by the Member State governments.

There is clear evidence that the decision to finally table it as a proposal in 2007 reflected Commission confidence that it had surely gained clout vis-à-vis Member State governments reluctant to hand over powers to the EU in energy market affairs. An important part of this new clout was the new and greater role played by DG-COMP in applying its powers under general EU treaty rules. This new role is well illustrated when seen through the lens of history. Back in the late 1980s, when the Commission formulated its first ideas about the internal energy market, it acknowledged that the national vertically integrated gas and electricity utilities represented a challenge to real market opening and, as noted above, mooted various decision procedures for dealing with this challenge, but DG-COMP thus found itself constrained from playing an active role in EU internal energy market policies.

The Commission nevertheless continued to threaten Member-State governments with EC Treaty competition rules unless implementation was forthcoming, as in 2001, to press acceptance of a second liberalization package (CEC 2002). By then, moreover, several Member States backed the idea of MOU. Six member countries had by then voluntarily implemented ownership unbundling in their national electricity sectors and two in their national gas sectors (CEC 2003). Fronting the pro-group, the UK had implemented ownership unbundling back in the 1980s. British politicians, championing neoliberal thinking in Europe, had a central role when the Commission drafted its first internal market directives (Lyons 1992). The Scandinavian countries and the Netherlands were also among the early reformers. In addition, most European Parliamentarians now supported radical market opening, with strong Parliamentary voices calling for MOU (Eikeland 2008). Fronting the antigroup were France and Germany, which even argued against "legal unbundling" (Council of the European Union 2002).

Energy consumers continued to voice dissatisfaction, complaining of discrimination in access to grids from the vertically integrated energy groups and the resultant higher tariff levels. The new Commission appointed in 2005 under the presidency of José Manuel Barroso therefore took a new line in internal energy market policies. As part of his overall plan to revitalize the Lisbon agenda, Barroso promised a more proactive role for DG-COMP in the screening of industrial sectors for barriers to competition (CEC 2005). The internal energy market was chosen as a pilot case, with DG-COMP and the Directorate-General for Transport and Energy (DG-TREN) jointly launching a major inquiry into competitive conditions in European electricity and gas markets.

This joint project ushered in a new era of close cooperation between the two directorates in internal energy market policies. When the first results of the energy sector inquiry came in, DG-COMP was convinced that a new liberalization package was needed. DG-TREN was not fully convinced, but the preliminary report of early 2006 tipped the scales, leading the two DGs and commissioners Neelie Kroes and Andris Piebalgs to agree on the need for a new, more radical energy liberalization package.[8]

In January 2007, the Commission adopted the strategic energy review proposed a year ahead and endorsed by the Council (CEC 2006a). This put gas and electricity market liberalization on top of the list of further action needed to achieve community energy policy objectives. The Commission also proposed a third legislative package that put MOU at the top of priorities. The European Spring Council 2007 agreed on the need for new legislation but the Energy Council in June warned the Commission not to propose ownership unbundling

(EurActiv 2007). The Commission did not give in to these warnings, however, and presented its proposal with MOU included. Interviewees in Brussels give DG-COMP much credit for this decision.

The proposal was coauthored by DG-COMP and DG-TREN—an unusual procedure in the Commission, which was normally bound by the high-level agreement that DGs should not interfere in each other's policy domains.[9] The alternative ISO model was secured as a fallback position, clearly more in line with the incremental consensus-seeking procedure preferred by DG-TREN. The new extended role of DG-COMP became evident also in the toning down of "regionalization" as an option for step-wise full internal market integration—a strategy promoted by the electricity supply industry and supported by DG-TREN back in 2003. DG-COMP feared such a procedure could increase the chances of regional cartelization.[10]

The extended role of DG-COMP in internal energy market policies was further demonstrated in its initiation of investigations and court-filing against major companies suspected of breaching community competition rules such as: allegedly using long-term contracts to abuse their dominant position (Distrigaz, EDF, and Suez-Electrabel) and manipulating wholesale and balancing markets. DG-COMP proceeded to prepare cases for the ECJ, the most highly profiled one being against the company German Energy On (E.On).

DG-COMP presented these companies with deals that would reduce fines for infringement of EU competition rules in return for the sell-off of their network businesses, in turn weakening their incentives to lobby Member-State governments and providing leeway for other national forces to convince the governments to alter their stances. The Commission knew that energy-intensive industry associations in Member States supported ownership unbundling. For example, the German Steel Industry Association, in a policy statement to Germany's EU presidency in 2007, made it clear that "If, as a result of the current regulations on grids, the intended market inputs fail to materialize in the medium term, an ownership unbundling of grids must be considered as a further step, as this is the only way to ensure that the structure of grid access is really free of discrimination for all potential grid users" (*Wirtschaftsvereinigung Stahl* 2006). Supporters of MOU also included the Federation of German Consumer Organizations, which refuted arguments from the government that it would run contrary to constitutional guarantees for property (*Europe Energy*, 2007). In addition, BNE, the German association for new energy suppliers, opted for strict unbundling to prevent market-dominant companies from exploiting their position, and their EU-level federation European

Renewable Energy Council (EREC) took a clear pro-MOU position (Eikeland 2008).

Interviews show that central officers within DG-TREN and DG-COMP expected companies to eventually sell off their grids even without regulatory demands in place. This was based on perceptions of the future electricity grid coming to resemble the Internet, with many small agents dispatching renewable energy to fulfill the new EU climate goals, dramatically changing the current business of serving a few central producers and making specialized grid operators better commercially prepared.[11] The tendencies toward stricter national rules on ownership conduct and national regulators squeezing grid tariffs were other factors reducing the commercial rationale of owning electricity grids. The Commission expected companies to sell off their grids voluntarily, and that this in the next round could change the political dynamics at the national level, leading Member-State governments to shift their position on MOU.

Hindsight proved the Commission right in assuming that major companies would eventually strike deals that included ownership unbundling, to avoid fines for infringing EU competition regulations. On February 28, 2008, the German energy giant E.On confirmed such a deal (*Economist* 2008),[12] but this did not change the anti-MOU position of the German government.

The Commission added the third-country reciprocity clause to the proposal as a carrot intended to appease Member States reluctant to accept MOU for fear that Russian Gazprom might seize the opportunity to buy networks on sale and gain a firmer grip on the European gas market. The last-minute "third-country clause" was particularly important in getting new eastern Member-State governments to accept MOU. With many of these states eager to connect to the EU and the NATO umbrella after leaving the much hated planned economy and Soviet sphere of interest, the Commission obviously hoped for their support in its strategy to combine market forces internally with a united voice in talks with Russia. They proved split on the issue, however. Planning economy structures are still evident in many of their energy sectors, and some of these states remain hesitant about yielding to a new international structure that might limit their own national sovereignty.

To sum up, we see clear evidence during the Barroso presidency of a shift in the will and power of the Commission to push market integration a major step forward. This will was shared also by the other major EU supranational institution, the European Parliament. On July 10, 2007, the Parliament Plenary Session backed the Commission's

January 2007 proposal, including ownership unbundling. The vote was based on a report prepared by the Committee on Industry, Research, and Energy (ITRE) representative Mr. Alejo Vidal-Quadras, Spanish MEP and leader of the EPP-ED group (Group of the European People's Party—Christian Democrats—and European Democrats in the European Parliament), lashing out against efforts by certain governments, such as France and Germany, to create "national energy champions" as a form of protectionism.[13] The report went far in its critique of national energy industry structures, portraying France's public companies European Development Fund (EDF) and Italy's Ente Nazionale per l'Energia eLettrica (Enel) as noncompatible with free competition, suspecting them of subjecting the functioning of the internal market to national political considerations. The Commission therefore had strong reason to expect continued support from the Parliament when tabling its proposal. In fact, the Parliament majority was supportive also of the second liberalization package adopted in 2003, a change from the 1990s when the Parliament was less enthusiastic about radical market opening when discussing the first energy market package.

The Final Outcome: The new will and power of the supranational institutions were not sufficient, however, for the proposal of MOU to prevail. Opposition from the Member-State governments was too strong. Germany and France headed a group of Member States that tabled the alternative ITO-model, only a slightly revised version of the existing unbundling model. The group included the ministers from Austria, Greece, and Luxembourg as well as those of the new EU members the Czech Republic, the Baltic states, Slovakia, and Hungary, all hosting vertically integrated energy groups and lagging behind in implementing previously adopted internal market policies (Eikeland 2008). In 2007, the countries that had voluntarily implemented MOU had increased to 13 for the electricity sector and 10 for the gas sector (CEC 2008), but this was still short of a majority vote in the Council.

To gain a deeper understanding of the differences in the dispute, we need to look into deeper perceptions concerning a free market's ability to deliver on PSOs such as security of supply and environmental protection. We see clearly that the skeptics of full MOU argued that dismantling their strong national champions would weaken their power in negotiations with major foreign upstream companies, thus reducing national security of supply (Eikeland 2008, 2011). Those in favor, backed by the Commission, argued that MOU would guarantee the independence of TSOs, as well as bolstering crucial trade and investments in new infrastructure, beneficial for security of supply (Eikeland 2008).

These differences were not new in Europe. Back in the 1990s, the first energy liberalization package was adopted only after the Council had insisted on the inclusion of a provision in the directives that gave Member States the right to derogations if opting to instruct their national industries to take on PSOs. Article 3 of the 1996 EU Electricity Directive defined public services as related to *"security, including security of supply, regularity, quality and price of supplies and environmental protection"*. Also, the French Government's insistence on including the option to allow a central agency to be responsible for the purchasing of the country's electricity, the so-called "single buyer" model, was justified by the need for governments to retain powers to induce PSOs on their national firms.

When climate change rose higher on the agenda in the late 1990s with calls for an increased share of CO_2-neutral renewable energy sources in the EU energy mix, conflicting views surfaced again. Some Member States, notably the UK, argued strongly for market-based policy instruments, which they viewed as compatible with trade and competition in the internal energy market. Other countries, notably Germany, argued that allowing the market to choose between renewables would not stimulate the broad technological change viewed as necessary for long-term combat of climate change. The competitive market would be too shortsighted, the German government argued, picking only the least cost technologies that were not in need of much development support in the first place. Instead, Germany, which had already introduced a feed-in tariff system in 1990, giving renewable energy investors fixed prices independent of the market tariff, took the lead and convinced a majority of Member States to clamp down efforts by the Commission to make mandatory a system of renewable electricity certificates as part of the new directive on the promotion of renewables in electricity production, adopted by the Council in 2001.

From 2000 onward, energy security gained new topicality in EU energy policy, due in part to fresh energy growth figures showing an increase in import dependencies[14] and other figures showing an aggravation of the situation after the 2000 Nice Summit opened the EU up to new applicant countries from Eastern Europe in 2004. The years 2002 and 2003 added to the concerns, as massive blackouts caused havoc in California, Italy, Sweden, and Denmark. Voices were once again being raised questioning whether liberalized energy systems would bring about more vulnerability and short-term risks of supply distortions than under the former centrally planned systems. A sudden and persisting growth in oil prices also fanned security of supply concerns. From 1999 to 2000, crude oil prices (the Brent Blend average prices) jumped from $17.88 per barrel to $28.39 per barrel, reflecting a series of geopolitical events: unrest in the Middle East and the rapid rise in oil demand in China and other South Asian countries. By 2007, the average price had reached $72 per barrel.[15] Oil prices continued to escalate in 2008, reaching peaks above $140 per barrel.

Early 2006, the security of supply concerns were evoked after Russia shut down its gas deliveries to Ukraine, which within the EU was taken as a sign of Russia's readiness to use its gas resources as a card in seeking geopolitical influence. Since vital gas infrastructure connecting Russia and the EU passed over Ukrainian territory, EU countries also felt a reduction in the volumes supplied in early January 2006. Thus a new sense of vulnerability now dispersed among European Member-State governments, which lifted long-term energy supply to the top of priorities for policy development with a call for the Commission to develop a strategic energy review for Europe.

The security of supply issue consolidated the split already existing between the Member States on the extent and pace that should be taken in internal energy market reforms, illustrated well also by the split in the European Parliament during the debate on ownership unbundling in July 2007. This debate showed a division along national lines rather than political party lines. Germany, France, and several new Member States formed an alliance against Commission demands for dismantling their national vertically integrated companies, arguing that this would reduce the companies' clout in negotiations with major foreign upstream companies. On the other side, the UK, the Netherlands, and the Scandinavian countries headed the alliance that backed the Commission proposal of further liberalization as necessary for increasing the security of supply. Full ownership unbundling would guarantee the independency of TSOs and bolster trade and investments in new infrastructure, pivotal to security of supply, according to these Member States.

A deeper understanding of the differences comes when looking at the strategies pursued by the governments of Germany and like-minded allies for securing their supplies from Russia. The German government has in combination with a bilateral diplomacy vis-à-vis Russia accepted Gazprom acquisitions of shares in national gas infrastructure in return for German acquisitions in Russia, based on the philosophy that cross–ownership will give joint commercial interests in ensuring stability in supply.

The challenge for the Commission has not lessened lately, with Gazprom increasing its influence in several member countries. Illustrating this point, Gazprom in January 2008 signed a deal with Austria's state-dominated company OMV to turn the Baumgarten gas transmission centre near Vienna into a joint venture, robbing the Commission–supported Nabucco pipeline project of its planned outlet for supply from non-Russian sources (*Eurasia Daily Monitor* 2008).

Evaluation of Progress in Completing the EU Internal Energy Market

Looking at the 20-year history of internal energy market policies in Europe, we see considerable progress in institutional reforms paving the way for a free and fair energy market to evolve. However, the institutional reforms have still been insufficient, partly because of implementation failure and partly because the reforms adopted have not yet gone far enough.

As noted, the reforms carried out in 2003 (the second package) forced the Member States to ensure that all consumers would be eligible for switching suppliers by 2007. This reform also mandated grid companies to transparently inform market agents about terms of access to grids. Still, this reform did not solve fully the important organizational issue of how to ensure that grids were run independently of particular supply interests. It mandated an organizational split of grid and supply operations (legal unbundling) but not a fullfledged split of ownership. This latter solution was at the core when the Commission tabled its proposal for a third policy package in 2007. But after intense deliberations, MOU did not come through in the final decision in July 2009.

Looking beyond the institutional design to what the Member States have actually carried out in terms of policy implementation, the conclusion is strengthened that EU internal energy market policy so far can be denoted as only partially successful. The Commission has documented this well in its annual benchmarking reports submitted to the Council and Parliament since 2001. In its 2009 benchmarking report on implementation of the internal energy market rules, the Commission gave a mixed picture, stating that Member States still lagged behind in implementation. Günther Oettinger, European

Commissioner responsible for energy, said at the launch of the report: "The full and correct implementation of the energy rules has still not been achieved. This situation needs to change and the Commission will use all means available to make this happen. What is at stake is our ability to reach the goals set in the Europe 2020 Strategy through a secure, competitive and sustainable supply of energy to our economy and our society" (CEC 2010c).

As noted already in the first Commission benchmarking report from 2001,[16] asymmetrical implementation of the directives between the Member States had created different market conditions across Member States in Europe, affecting both energy consumers and energy companies. The 2003 benchmarking report added attention to yet another problem for free and fair competition: the *high degree of market concentration* found in the gas and electricity industries in many Member States. This problem was increasing because of the wave of mergers and acquisitions seen between companies in the gas and electricity industries, creating fewer and larger vertically integrated energy groups. Fears were voiced that companies operating in countries shielded from competitive pressure used their monopoly revenue to buy up companies in countries correctly abolishing monopoly conditions, which were less able to fatten up on monopoly rents.

In June 2009, the Commission initiated infringement procedures against 25 Member States for incorrectly implementing internal electricity market provisions and against 21 Member States for deficiencies in transposition of the gas market rules. The key violations identified were lack of transparency, insufficient efforts by TSOs to make interconnection capacity available, absence of regional cooperation, lack of enforcement by national regulators, and lack of dispute settlement procedures (CEC 2010a, 2). The benchmarking report for 2009 shows that most Member States have finally transposed the legal provision guaranteeing all consumers the right to shift suppliers in the national electricity and gas markets, with a few still lagging behind, however. Nevertheless, the report shows that the actual rate of shifts is rather small in many countries. Of those actually making these data available to the Commission, most members recorded no or close to no switching in 2008 in the retail electricity and gas markets (CEC 2010b, 7–8). This indicates that competition is still not very intensive in the retail markets. And to be sure, EU legal unbundling requirements are still applicable only for the major TSOs and not the many distribution companies operating in Europe. The 2009 Benchmarking Report shows that few of the electricity distribution system operators in Europe were ownership unbundled and that only around 42 percent even had legal unbundling (CEC 2010b, 36). This indicates a clear lack of independence prevailing in European grid operations. Moreover, the benchmarking report shows that the market dominance problem continues in many Member States, with 15 Member States stated to have very highly or highly concentrated electricity market conditions, and the situation is no better for the gas market (CEC 2010b, 12–16). On top of this, lack of infrastructure capacity across the borders and, hence, lack of cross-border trade accentuates the asymmetrical situation across Europe, with some companies operating in home-markets shielded from and others quite exposed to competitive pressure.

The Road Ahead—Prospects for Free and Fair Competition in the European Energy Market

While failing to achieve full ownership unbundling as a guarantee of grid independence, and given the many problems with asymmetrical implementation still making the internal energy market characterized by deficiencies to free and fair competition, the Commission still records an increasing number of allies that share the idea that free market conditions should be realized in an all-European market. The growing number of Member States that have actually carried out voluntary ownership unbundling in the electricity and gas markets illustrates such a will. There is thus much to indicate that the Commission will perceive further proposals in the field as highly legitimate, and not stop with the results achieved through the adoption of the third policy package.

Next, the third policy package provides for new soft-law measures to create a level internal energy market. Alongside application of EU treaty rules and the specific framework directives targeting deregulation of the electricity and gas industry, soft law constitutes the third pillar of EU internal energy market policy, starting out with the establishment of the Florence and Madrid Forums in the late 1990s. This pillar emerged in response to needs for deepening implementation of legislation adopted through the traditional community method. In particular, the Commission acknowledged different harmonization needs (the need to establish common codes of conduct) for TSOs concerning operation of and investments in cross-border transmission infrastructure to enable free trade in energy across the community. More specifically, the Commission acknowledged that there would be no well-functioning trade in electricity without harmonization of such factors as:

- transmission tariff structures;
- modes by which capacity is allocated when networks are congested, which is the normal situation since cross-border capacity is poorly developed (congestion management);
- modes by which TSOs are compensated for use of their networks in transition of power from one country to another (inter-TSO transit compensation);
- transparency for market agents concerning availability of capacity on interconnectors and tariffs for using them; and
- planning of investments in new interconnector capacity.

The Commission-established Florence Forum created a meeting place and a *process* whereby private industry agents (consumers, producers, and TSOs), national regulators, and EU institutions committed to work for *voluntary* joint solutions. European TSOs established the all-European organization ETSO in response, to coordinate internal discussions.

In 2003, soft law efforts were to a far greater extent codified with regulations adopted under the second internal energy market package. These regulations vested more control with the Member-State governments, notably the European group of national regulators, CEER, and proposed the new organization European Regulators' Group for Energy and Gas (ERGEG) (as CEER's extented arm functioning as the formal advisory group of CEER to the Commission) in leading further work on the development of guidelines for how such common codes of conduct should look. The new regulation meant that if agreement was reached through comitology, codes of conduct related to cross-border trade would be adopted by the Commission and included in the annex to the regulation and function as community hard law. Proceeding from pure voluntarism to community regulation (comitology) reflected the view that the former voluntarism had not created the results hoped for.

In the following years, national regulators (CEER, ERGEG) and the industry itself (ETSO) proceeded with efforts at detailing and negotiating guidelines and codes of conduct, now with a *regional* focus, expecting that splitting up negotiations in smaller groups could bring the process more effectively forward. By 2007, the Commission still voiced great dissatisfaction with the existing leadership of ERGEG. As part of the third internal energy market legislation package, institutional change has been initiated with greater formalization of TSO cooperation in new EU-level bodies responsible for developing codes of conduct (ENTSO-E for electricity and ENTSO-G for natural gas) as well as a new EU-level regulatory body, ACER.

To be sure, the Commission has great hope that these bottom-up processes will produce results that will eventually increase transparency and harmonization of grid operation codes across Europe and manage to create agreement on investments in new infrastructure seen as pivotal not only for cross-border trade to increase competition in the internal energy market but also more security of supply and better conditions for independent producers of climate-friendly renewable energy. As such, the ambitious climate and renewable energy goals agreed upon by EU Member State leaders in 2007 are currently an important driver of continued internal energy market efforts to open up existing networks and invest in new energy infrastructure across the Member States.

Notes

1. In 1996, the Dutch appeal court, taking the Court of Justice ruling as its base, found that the public service obligations presented by the generators were not sufficient grounds for imposing an import monopoly, and thus the generators had acted contrary to the Treaty's provisions (Lyons 1998, 34).
2. Article 25 (1) of the Electricity Directive and Article 27 of the Gas Directive (European Parliament and the Council 1996; 1998).
3. COM (1998) 167 final. March 16, 1998.
4. COM (97) 599 *Energy for the future—renewable sources of energy*. White Paper.
5. Ibid., 9.
6. Interview with a senior Commission official, February 2008.
7. EurActiv. 2007. *EU states reject breaking up energy firms*. June 7.
8. Interview with Lars Kjølbye, Head of Unit Antitrust—Energy & Environment, DG-COMP, European Commission, Brussels, February 2008.
9. Interview with Matti Supponen, Electricity & Gas Unit, DG-TREN, European Commission, Brussels, February 2008.
10. Interview with Lars Kjølbye, Head of Unit Antitrust—Energy & Environment, DG-COMP, the European Commission, Brussels, February, 2008.
11. Information received in interview with Lars Kjølbye, Head of Unit Antitrust—Energy & Environment, DG-COMP, the European Commission, Brussels, February 2008.

12. In late July 2008, Vattenfall Europe AG, the German subsidiary of the Swedish Vattenfall, followed suit, announcing that it would sell off its high-voltage grid (EurActiv, 2008).
13. EurActiv. 2007. *MEPs call for dismantling of energy giants* July 11.
14. CEC (2000b). The Green Paper presented risks of short- and long-term supply distortions, based on the trends of EU's ever-widening dependence on energy imports, expected to rise from 50 percent of its energy requirements to 70 percent the next 20 to 30 years if no countermeasures were taken. Energy imports represented in 2000 6 percent of total imports, whereas 45 percent of oil imports came from the Middle East and 40 percent of natural gas came from Russia.
15. *BP Statistical Review of World Energy 2007.*
16. SEC (2001). 1957. December 3, 2001.

Works Cited

Andersen, S. S. 2000. *EU Energy Policy: Interest Interaction and Supranational Authority.* ARENA Working Papers WP 00/5.
BP Statistical Review of World Energy. 2007.
CEC. 1988. *The Internal Market for Energy.* May 2. COM 88(238) final.
CEC. 1999. *Report to the Council and the European Parliament on harmonisation Requirements: Directive 98/30/EC Concerning Common Rules for the Internal Market for Natural Gas.* Brussels. November 23, 1999. COM (612).
CEC. 2000a. *Second report to the Council and the European Parliament on Harmonisation Requirements, Directive 96/92/EC Concerning Common Rules for the Internal Market in Electricity* (recent progress with building the internal electricity market). Brussels. 16.5 COM (297).
CEC. 2000b. *Towards a European Strategy for the Security of Energy Supply.* COM (769).
CEC. 2001. *Summary of the implementation of the Electricity and Gas Directives* (first benchmarking report). December 3. SEC (2001) 1957.
CEC. 2002. *XXXIST Report on Competition Policy 200* final. SEC (2002) 462.
CEC. 2003. *Second Benchmarking Report on the Implementation of the Internal Electricity and Gas Market.* Commission staff working paper. Brussels. April 7. SEC (2003) 448.
CEC. 2005. *Working Together for Growth and Jobs, A New Start for the Lisbon Strategy.* Brussels. February 2. COM (24) final.
CEC. 2006a. *A European Strategy for Sustainable, Competitive and Secure Energy.* Brussels. March 8. COM (105) final. Green Paper. SEC (2006) 317.
CEC. 2006b. *Inquiry Pursuant to Article 17 of Regulation (EC) No 1/2003 into the European Gas and Electricity Sectors* (Final Report). Brussels. January 10. COM (851) final. SEC (2006) 1724.

CEC. 2007a. *DG Competition Report on Energy Sector I Inquiry.* Brussels. January 10, 2007. SEC (2006) 1724.
CEC. 2007b. Communication from the Commission to the European Council and the European Parliament. *An Energy Policy for Europe.* Brussels. COM (1) final. SEC (2007) 12.
CEC. 2008. *Progress in Creating the Internal Gas and Electricity Market.* Brussels, April 15. COM (192) final. SEC (2008) 460 (the 2007 Benchmarking Report).
CEC. 2010a. *Report on Progress in Creating the Internal Electricity and Gas Market.* Brussels. March 11, 2010. COM (84) final.
CEC. 2010b. *Technical Annex to the Report on Progress in Creating the Internal Electricity and Gas Market.* Brussels March 11, 2010. Com (2010) final. SEC (2010) 251.
CEC. 2010c. *Benchmarking Report: Correct Implementation of EU Energy Law and Infrastructure Investment Top Priority.* Press release. IP/10/264. March 11, 2010.
Council of the European Union. 2002. Preparation of the Transport, Telecommunications, Energy Council on 3 & 4 October, Internal Market in Electricity and Gas, Amended Proposal for a Directive of the EP and of the Council Amending Directives 96/92/EC (Electricity) and 98/30/EC (Gas) Concerning Common Rules for the Internal Market in Electricity and Natural Gas. 11986/02. Brussels. September 19.
Economist. 2008. *Neelie's Deal—Why E.On Made an Unexpected U-turn.* March 6.
Domanico, Fabio. 2007. Concentration in the European Electricity Industry: The Internal Market as Solution? *Energy Policy*, 35 (10), pp. 5064–5076.
Eikeland, P. O. 2004. *The Long and Winding Road to the Internal Energy Market—Consistencies and Inconsistencies in EU Policy.* FNI report 8/2004. Lysaker. FNI 2004.
Eikeland, P. O. 2008. *EU Internal Energy Market Policy—New Dynamics in the Brussels Policy Game?* FNI report 14/2008. Lysaker: Fridtjof Nansen Institute.
Eikeland, Per Ove. 2011. The Third Internal Energy Market Package: New Power Relations Among Member States, EU Institutions and Non-State Actors? *Journal of Common Market Studies*, 49 (2), pp. 243–263.
Eising, R. 2002. Policy Learning in Embedded Negotiations: Explaining EU Electricity Liberalization *International Organization.* 56 (1): 85–120.
EurActiv. 2007. *EU States Reject Breaking Up Energy Firms.* June 7.
EurActiv. 2008. *Vattenfall Power Grid Sale Buoys EU.* July 29.
Eurasia Daily Monitor. 2008. OMV joins with Gazprom to undercut Nabucco. 5(17).
Europe Energy. 2007. Ownership Unbundling: German Consumers Refute Constitutional Objections. September.

European Parliament and the Council. 1996. *Directive 96/92/EC of the European Parliament and of the Council of 19 December 1996 Concerning Common Rules for the Internal Market in Electricity* (Official Journal L 027, January 30, 1997).

European Parliament and the Council. 1998. *Directive 98/30/EC of the European Parliament and of the Council of 22 June 1998 Concerning Common Rules for the Internal Market in Natural Gas* (Official Journal L 204, July 21, 1998).

European Parliament and the Council. 2003a. *Directive 2003/54/EC of the European Parliament and of the Council of 26 June 2003 Concerning Common Rules for the Internal Market in Electricity and Repealing Directive 96/92/EC.*

European Parliament and the Council. 2003b. *Directive 2003/55/EC of the European Parliament and of the Council of 26 June 2003 Concerning Common Rules for the Internal Market in Natural Gas and Repealing Directive 98/30/EC* (Official Journal L 176, July 15, 2003).

European Parliament and the Council. 2003c. *Regulation (EC) No 1228/2003 of the European Parliament and of the Council of 26 June 2003 on Conditions for Access to the Network for Cross-Border Exchanges in Electricity* (text with relevance).

Grätz, J. (2009). Energy Relations with Russia and Gas Market Liberalization. *International Politics and Society*. Bonn, Germany: Verlag J. H. W. Dietz Nachfolger GmbH: 66–803.

Lyons, P. K. 1992. *EC Energy Policy—A Detailed Guide to the Community's Impact on the Energy Sector*. London: Financial Times Business Information.

Lyons, P. K. 1998. *EU Energy Policies towards the 21st Century*. Elstead (UK): EC Inform. Available at archive website uk.geocities.com/ec_inform/.

Stern, J. 1990. *European Gas Markets—Challenges and Opportunities*. London: Royal Institute of International Affairs.

Stern, J. 1998. *Competition and Liberalization in European Gas Markets—A Diversity of Models*. London: Royal Institute of International Affairs.

Wirtschaftsvereinigung Stahl. 2006. *Policy statements by the steel industry in Germany for Germany's Presidency of the EU Council of Ministers during the first half of 2007*. Düsseldorf. October 2006. Available at http://www.stahlonline.de/medien_lounge/Hintergrundmaterial/ForderungenEURatspraesidentschaftENGL.pdf.

Chapter Two

Foreign Policy and Energy Security: Markets, Pipelines, and Politics

Richard Youngs

Few policy areas have witnessed such intense activity and rapid evolution in recent years as that of energy security. With its dependence on external oil and gas supplies inexorably rising, the European Union (EU) has set out to become a lead player on energy questions. This applies especially to the foreign policy dimensions of energy security. There has been much policy activity during the last five years that would seem to suggest an incremental Europeanization of key dimensions of energy security.

In formal terms, the EU has staked out an approach to energy security that is based heavily on liberal internationalist norms. Its stated cornerstones are interdependence, market integration within and beyond Europe, and a convergence of governance standards. Time and time again EU documents, European ministers and policymakers reject realist geopolitics as a basis for energy security. The EU also lays claim to a "rules-based governance" approach to energy security. Integral to the liberal approach is the conviction that more open and accountable governance in producer states is a necessary part of Europe's own energy security interests. In practice, however, energy security is an area where geopolitical realism has made one of its most spectacular comebacks. In their foreign policy strategies, Member-State governments seek the influence that flows from Europe-wide market rules while simultaneously pursuing short-term gain from highly geopolitical behavior.

The shift back to geopolitical realism militates against the centralization of EU external energy policy. This does not negate EU unity quite as much as is sometimes assumed. But it is certainly the case that today the dynamics of bilateralism and EU coordination exist uneasily together. Sometimes, support for common, supranationalized EU rules is seen by Member States as the best form of geopolitics. At least as often, however, such rules are discarded as unduly constraining. A crucial question is whether Member States can continue to benefit from the advantages of both EU commonality and national maneuverability over the long term. Are these two perfectly proper elements of a balanced external energy policy or mutually incompatible dynamics that betray the EU's inability to cohere its strategic thinking?

New Institutionalized Commitments

At one level, it is remarkable how many formal EU energy security initiatives have been established in the last decade. An impressive range of new commitments has been enumerated, establishing the foundations for significant Europeanization of the external dimensions of energy policy. This is illustrative of the value, in formal terms at least, that Member States have attached to developing such centralized commitments as a means of pursuing their own energy interests.

A quick run through some of these initiatives suffices to demonstrate how dense the network of external EU commitments now is. An EU-Russia energy dialogue commenced in 2000. November 2004 saw the launch of a Black Sea and Caspian Sea cooperation initiative, aimed at the progressive integration of this region into the European energy market. In October 2005, the Energy Community of South East Europe (ECSEE) Treaty was signed, with the aim of incorporating Balkan states into the European regional market for gas and petroleum products; this initiative extends the EU energy acquis to the Balkans and coordinates infrastructure linkages, with World Bank financial support (Grant 2006). A Memorandum of Understanding on energy cooperation was signed with Ukraine in December 2005, reflecting Kiev's aspiration to join the Energy Community of South East Europe Treaty. Similar bilateral energy partnerships were signed in 2006 with Azerbaijan and Kazakhstan.

Subregional energy dialogues were developed with the Maghreb and Mashreq from the late 1990s under the Euro-Mediterranean Partnership (EMP). The European Neighbourhood Policy (ENP) also contains an energy component. A notably reinforced program of such energy cooperation began under the rubric of Algeria's EMP association agreement. Outside the scope of formal EU frameworks, after 2003, efforts were made to initiate energy dialogue with Libya. In December 2004, bilateral political dialogue between the EU and the

Organization of Petroleum Exporting Countries (OPEC) was formally established and developed from 2005.

If policy-makers recognized that such initiatives had developed in a fragmented fashion, deliberation then (apparently) moved to a more overarching strategic level. Discussion was pushed in particular by the United Kingdom (UK) presidency in the second half of 2005. The October 2005 EU summit at Hampton Court agreed to a formal commitment to move toward the definition of a common European energy policy. A first set of proposals was set out in the European Commission's (hereafter: the Commission) March 2006 Green Paper. This paper started from the premise that "acting together, [the EU] has the weight to protect and assert its interests" (Commission of the European Communities 2006a). The paper identified a number of practical, technical priorities in relation to the internal dimensions of energy policy. The most significant new departure was, however, at the international and strategic level. The Commission argued that the EU needed a "coherent external energy policy," agreement on which would represent "a break from the past"—a past characterized by a conspicuous lack of unity and coordination. The paper proposed a Strategic EU Energy Review, with regular follow-up of political discussions; a network of "energy correspondents" to facilitate coordination between Member States; "a better integration of energy objectives into broader relations with third countries"; coordinated response mechanisms in relation to crises in energy supplies; and the development of interconnecting energy systems between different geographical areas, as a means of transcending the so far partial technical cooperation pursued separately with individual partner states (Commission of the European Communities 2006b).

Responding to the Green Paper, Member-State representatives in the European Council accepted that "foreign and development policy aspects are gaining increasing importance to promote energy policy objectives with other countries." They backed the Commission's calls for better coordination, and more specifically for a comprehensive Strategic Energy Review, "addressing in particular the aims and actions needed for an external energy policy over the medium- to long-term" (Council of the European Union 2006). In a follow-up note to the Council, the Commission stated that energy security policy "must also be consistent with the EU's broader foreign policy objectives such as conflict prevention and resolution, nonproliferation and promoting human rights" (Commission of the European Communities 2006a). Such linkages were pushed inter alia by the Benelux states (Belgium, the Netherlands, and Luxembourg), which urged the Political and

Security Committee to drop its reluctance to engage in energy matters and argued that European leverage would be strengthened by "embedding energy in a wider range of subjects" (Benelux Position Paper 2007).

The then external relations commissioner Benita Ferrero-Waldner revealed that the aim to bolster the foreign policy dimensions of energy policy was the key driving force behind the ENP. She admitted that the Russia-Ukraine gas dispute at the beginning of 2006 was "a wake up call, reminding us that energy security needs to be even higher on our political agenda" (Ferrero-Waldner 2006). Indeed, some analysts saw energy security concerns as the only factor linking the diverse regions included within the ENP and as the main issue according the latter some logical rationale (Danreuther 2006). At the first high-level ENP conference held on September 3, 2007, Commissioner Ferrero-Waldner listed energy as a top priority and floated the idea of a new "neighbourhood energy agreement" (Ferrero-Waldner 2007).

Further initiatives commenced to deepen energy cooperation with Turkey, in recognition of the latter's importance as a transit route into the EU and Ankara's influence in the wider Black Sea and Caspian regions. By 2007, energy was a prominent issue in nearly all external political dialogues, where it had been barely mentioned five years previously—this, according to one official, requiring Member States to look at energy from a common European perspective and not merely through the lens of their national policies. Twenty-two million euros from one of the Commission's post-2007 external relations budgets—the development cooperation instrument (DCI)—was allocated to energy projects, representing 7 percent of funding. Eurobarometer polls suggested a clear majority of the European population wished to see a more common EU energy policy (although in a number of Central and Eastern European states and in Finland the balance of opinion was against such deeper cooperation) (European Commission Eurobarometer Unit 2007).

Rhetorical commitments incrementally intensified. At the end of 2006, Commission president José Manuel Barroso declared that energy had been "until recently a forgotten subject in the European agenda. Now it is back at the heart of European integration, where it began with the creation of the Coal and Steel Community. And where it belongs." He was confident that by this stage a "quick revolution" had taken place, with Member States dropping their nationally centered approaches and genuinely agreeing on the desirability of a common European energy strategy (Barroso 2006). He committed the EU to making energy a priority topic in all summits with third countries.

During his stint as external relations commissioner, which ended in 2004, Chris Patten had engaged little with energy issues; for his successor, Ferrero-Waldner, energy became a staple part of diplomatic activity. The deputy director general for energy at the Commission railed that "those who try to hide the fact that energy has moved into the realm of foreign policy are trying to forget reality...Why can't Europe bring energy politics into the core of external policies?" (Barabaso 2007).

A number of institutional innovations reflected the new priority attached to energy issues. The network of "Energy correspondents" was launched in May 2007, linking together the key personnel covering energy issues in Member States and the Brussels institutions. This was conceived as the core of "an energy crisis management system" (*PlattsEU Energy* 2006). An energy unit was created within the Commission's external relations department, with instructions from commissioners that energy be woven into policies in each geographical area: this unit was charged with ensuring that henceforth geographical departments assessed and justified policies in terms of how these contributed toward energy security. A number of Member States advocated moving all decisions on energy security to qualified majority voting (QMV)—they contrasted the stagnation of unanimity-bound foreign policy making with the qualified majority voting that had, they argued, ensured more productive debate in the area of climate change.

On January 10, 2007, the Commission published its eagerly awaited Strategic Energy Review. This reiterated the main principles and objectives that had taken shape during 2006: the need for greater "capability to react in times of external energy security pressure"; the importance of international partnerships based on "shared rules or principles derived from EU [internal] energy policy"; the desirability of "comprehensive partnerships based on mutual interest, transparency, predictability and reciprocity"; the need for some form of energy supply solidarity mechanism, especially for states dependent on a single gas supplier; the intention to make available increased funding for energy projects through the EU's new financial instruments; the need to promote "transparent legal frameworks" in producer states; and the idea of European coordinators to represent EU interests in key international energy projects (Commission of the European Communities 2007).

The March 2007 EU summit agreed on an energy action plan for 2007–2009. This reiterated a series of core principles, based on the need for diversification; crisis response mechanisms; transparency both between Member States and within producer states' governance structures; and an assessment of current patterns of energy imports into different Member States (Commission of the European Communities 2007). The June 2007 summit, at which the new Lisbon Treaty was hammered out between European leaders, included a number of developments pertinent to energy. A new legal base was introduced in the Treaty for EU legislation in the field of energy, along with provisions for qualified majority voting in some areas of energy policy. Poland insisted on a new energy solidarity clause, this representing one of its threats to veto a new Treaty mandate—although the reference to energy policy needing to be in accordance with "a spirit of solidarity between Member States" was less committal and specific than Poland had wanted. Some of the more general reforms agreed also had relevance for energy security. The powers of the high representative to speak on behalf of the EU were enhanced, fusing powers hitherto falling to a number of different commissioners. Some Member-State representatives reported that they supported this revision thinking in particular of energy policy. In mid-2008, preparations began for a new strategic review that would consider the need for additional energy security policy instruments.

Under the Lisbon Treaty a new energy department has been created, combining energy and foreign policy diplomats—a move that offers the possibility of a more security-informed energy strategy. However, the Treaty also provides for separate energy and climate change commissioners, with the new high representative for foreign and security policy seemingly marginal to both these issues. At the time of writing, it is clear that the Lisbon Treaty reinforces a formal European energy security mandate but it remains to be seen exactly how this will be developed in terms of institutional innovation. DG Energy now leads on the external dimensions of energy policy rather than the new External Action Service. Some Brussels insiders ponder in private whether this once again militates against a systemic linkage between energy and the Common Foreign and Security Policy.

Part of the explanation for this incipient Europeanization is to be found in external factors. Indeed, it is not difficult to intuit the geopolitical concerns driving all this new activity. The Commission's 2005 paper famously suggested that the EU's import dependency for oil was set to increase from 52 percent in 2003 to 95 percent in 2030, and for gas from 36 to 84 percent over the same period, and that in absolute terms EU import requirements would double by 2030 (Commission of the European Communities 2006c) The International Energy Agency (IEA) estimated that $200 billion worth of investment per year—equivalent to 2 percent of global gross domestic product—would be needed in increases to production capacity to meet energy requirements by 2030. It was also calculated that by 2012 the EU would face a 30 percent shortfall in its gas import requirements. While reserves are set to decrease, demand for oil and gas is predicted to rise exponentially. It is estimated that in 2035 global energy consumption will be double that of 2005, with fast-developing economies such as those of China and India hungry for ever-increasing supplies of oil and gas. Record high oil prices during the mid-2000s, Russia's periodic interruptions of gas supplies to Ukraine, and terrorists' threats to target energy pipelines have all additionally helped propel energy to the top of the foreign policy agenda.

The Liberal Model of Energy Security

Adding to concerns over rising dependency is an internal dynamic that accords more to institutionalist, spillover-type explanations. If Europeanization has advanced in the energy sphere, this can only be understood in the context of the interstice between internal and external policies.

A liberalized internal energy market is routinely presented as Europe's best foreign policy tool. The internal market fosters a more efficient and flexible distribution of energy supplies within Europe. And it also shapes the external dimension of energy security. Internal market rules help break up powerful non-European energy multinationals. State-backed oil and gas giants from non-European countries are less able to play divide-and-rule politics with Member States, as supplies flow without restriction across European borders. Moreover, the internal market serves as the model for regulatory rules and standards to be extended to oil- and gas-producing states in other regions. The single European energy market also acts as a more powerful incentive for producer states to sign up to the principles of energy interdependence. It is the EU's best negotiating tool to win concessions from producers.

The Commission has pushed to deepen internal market liberalization by requiring companies to separate out (or "unbundle") the generation of power from control over its distribution. The Commission has presented this as key not only to internal efficiency but also to external security. To the extent that large third-country companies, such as Russian giant Gazprom, would also be required to "unbundle" within the European market, this would protect EU consumers from these firms gaining a dominant position. Breaking apart national energy champions within Europe would make it harder for large non-European firms, like Gazprom, to negotiate their way into dominant positions simply through a small number of bilateral deals. Internal EU competition laws condition foreign policy positions. For example, they have required non-EU oil-producing countries to drop "destination clauses," through which they traditionally prevented a buyer passing on surplus supplies to other states. Removing such provisions undermines the exclusivity of bilateral contracts. Supplies are better able to flow to where they are needed within the European Union, and national EU governments gain leverage over producer states. Europeanized internal rules are what provide foreign policy influence and unity.

European policy-makers have readily acknowledged that completing the internal market in energy is necessary for external influence and unity. The rules and regulations of the internal market are defined as the key foundation to the EU's international projection in energy matters. New EU energy partnerships around the world offer cooperatively to draw producer states into a European market–governance area. Integration and partnership are said to reign rather than zero-sum geopolitics. Most recently, new energy cooperation clauses have been inserted into the EU's eastern partnership. The EU has also supported and sought to harness the Energy Charter Treaty as a pivot of rules-based multilateralism in energy.

Among Member States, British energy policy has been the most market oriented. Having already liberalized its own markets, the UK has the most to gain from ensuring that market reform is implemented in other EU states and beyond Europe. One diplomat defines the aim of external UK energy security as, "To take the politics out of energy." Officials insist that liberalization has increased long-term investment to increase production capacity, rebutting fears that investors need long-term contracts protected from market instability. The UK is forceful in urging the EU to push for more competitive international oil and gas markets. It insists that offering Gazprom downstream access into the EU market is the best way of pushing this supposed bogeyman of international energy into making long-term investments to increase production capacity. While the UK is the most pro-market of Member States, others have adopted similar rhetoric. Spain has largely privatized its energy sector and invested heavily in liquified natural gases (LNGs) as a way of injecting greater fluidity into gas supplies. Even French policy-makers recognize that energy security should be predicated on a "logic of market integration" (Lamy 2007).

Geopolitics Return

Part of the story of external energy policy is indeed liberal internationalist. But another part is decidedly geopolitical. And it is this part that is in the ascendant. Significantly, so far this trend has fractured EU unity rather than act as a prompt to deeper coordination. Geopolitics have been as much about zero-sum competition between different Member States as between producer states and the EU as a whole.

Producer states' more assertive emphasis on short-term national interests has led EU governments to question market-based approaches. The "economization" of international energy has been arrested. The fear is prevalent that the internal market is already too open to third-country producers to give the EU sufficient leverage to negotiate reciprocal liberalization for their investments in producer states. Even in relation to oil supplies, which are more market-based than gas trading, the reliance on bilateral, highly politicized energy deals is on the rise. Many Member States have not definitively given up on the market but they are "hedging" bilateral energy deals in case things become more acutely geopolitical in the future (Linde 2007). European policy may not be as geopolitical as United States (US) energy security strategy—which most analysts judged to have become increasingly militarized during the Bush administration—but it does exhibit more of a geostrategic flavor than hitherto.

The internal market is still not integrated enough—even at the level of basic infrastructural links within Europe itself—either to serve as a common regulatory-governance magnet for producer states or to absorb external shocks. Member States have rejected proposals, for example, for common strategic storage facilities managed by an EU-level agency. A September 2008 IEA report expressed concerns over the EU's failure to implement commitments to market liberalization (Platts EU Energy Review 2008). Another independent review carried out for the European Parliament highlighted the extent to which bilateral agreements are distorting efficiency and leading the EU into the uncertainties of prisoners' dilemma diplomatic brinkmanship (Keppler 2007). In summer 2009 the Commission opened infringement procedures against a total of 25 Member States related to energy market protectionism (EurActiv 2009a).

Most notably, the principle of "unbundling" has been blocked by a coalition of market-skeptical Member States, led by France and Germany. The European Parliament's two-year battle to retain full unbundling came to an end in March 2009, when it assented to a diluted package of reforms. Member States are now able to choose one of three options: the full unbundling of ownership, the independent operating of the energy distribution system, or the independent operating of transmission (with parent companies in charge of supervision). Several have already unbundled ownership unilaterally, but the majority look set to rein back market principles.

This dilution of market principles has important external dimensions. Much revolves around the more technical detail of energy questions; but from this detail emerge crucial questions of high politics. The proposal for an EU-level clause providing for reciprocal market access between the EU and producer states has in essence been dropped. Each European government will have the freedom to decide whether or not big energy contracts are to be based on producer states providing reciprocal access to their markets. Now all deals involving non-European companies have to be approved by national regulators. One regulator alone can block a deal with pan-European coverage, rather than there being a one-stop EU-level mechanism to approve market opening deals. Member States have ensured that they will not be required to abide by an approach based on market interdependence rather than geopolitical trade-off. The new European Agency for the Cooperation of Energy Regulators is limited to overseeing loose coordination between national regulators and is bereft of powers to force liberalization on reluctant Member States.

Russia had made the fair point that the proposed "reciprocity clause"—or what the press dubbed the "Gazprom clause"—would have imposed on Russian suppliers a degree of liberalization and market discipline to which the EU was unwilling to subject its own energy companies. Russia argued that this clause was legally incompatible with the EU-Russia partnership and cooperation agreement provisions on nondiscrimination. While the UK expressed concerns that the principle of reciprocity was being used to legitimize protectionism, its own reaction to Gazprom's interest in Centrica (British Gas) was defensive. Vladimir Putin threatened to drop the Nord Stream pipeline project if the EU did not give Russia a guaranteed level of demand for future years. Faced with a choice of either extending to itself the market openness it would have Gazprom abide by or retracting from liberal principles externally as well as internally, the EU chose the latter option. The EU has abandoned the liberal argument that the best defense against Gazprom and other third-country energy giants is full liberalization and unbundling, which would prevent these companies buying up distribution networks and establishing a dominant market position.

The increasingly preferential protection accorded to national energy champions represents a dramatic return to "economic nationalism" within Europe (Vos 2006). When President Nicolas Sarkozy pushed through a merger between Suez Gulf Power Company (Suez) and Gaz de France (GDF) unashamedly creating a new powerful "national champion" in 2007, French Europe minister Jean-Pierre Jouyet stated that such preferential strategic measures represented the "vision of what could be the energy policy for Europe."[1] Italy has pumped increasing amounts of financial sweeteners into Ente Nazionale Idrocarburi (Eni) to subsidize international deals whose financial viability is dubious.

With governments backing their respective national champions in signing bilateral contracts, EU competition law has not been invoked against such deals. The Commission's competition directorate has been reluctant to get drawn into the external politics of energy, and no Member State has pushed this in the European Court of Justice. When the Commission took its antimonopoly action against Microsoft, energy experts noted the political significance of the fact that similar action against Gazprom had not been contemplated. The Commission says it has no locus over the political conditions included in long-term bilateral contracts, as long as they do not include destination restrictions—that is, as long as German Energy On (E.On), for example, can sell Russian gas to the wider European market and other suppliers. In practice even this basic transferability of energy is absent, with the European market carved up into fiefdoms served by separate contracts with Gazprom and other external suppliers.

External energy supply is now driven by the need for a diversification of supplies. Producer states complain that the EU preaches mutually beneficial, market-based solutions but then urges policies that reduce political dependence on these "partners" (Stern 2002). With oil supplies supposedly fungible and governed by markets that should clear and self-correct at any given price, diversification is a clearly geopolitical design. The tilt toward geopolitics is further driven by the increasing importance of gas supplies—which are shaped by political deals over fixed supply routes rather than, as in the case of oil, supplied onto an open international market. While much European rhetoric insists that energy supply is a matter for private companies rather than government command, the EU increasingly seeks to direct producer governments to increase production and export capacity.

European energy companies commonly criticize governments and the Commission for being insufficiently pro-market and for increasingly intervening in a political fashion. But their own behavior in practice prioritizes alliance building and the protection of existing dominant market positions. Energy officials in the Commission note that network industries are the most resistant of all sectors to liberalization. European energy companies have fought hard to gain support from their respective national governments to secure long-term preferential deals with individual third-country producers on a bilateral basis.

The debate now is not so much about reverting from political deals to market principles, but whether the EU can substitute the current plethora of contracts signed by individual companies for overarching, umbrella deals to buy certain quantities for Europe as a whole. Such deals have notably been concluded with Turkmenistan and Iraq. In addition, the Caspian Development Corporation (CDC) has been created to undertake common, bulk purchasing of Central Asian and Caspian supplies. However, these common accords remain the exception rather than the rule, and those that have been signed do little to remove doubts about whether commonly contracted supplies will actually reach European markets.

Many officials suggest that the tougher international energy panorama requires the EU to drop the pretence that energy policies are to be based on liberal interdependence. Officials increasingly lament that it is "unrealistic" to expect key producer states to sign up to a model based on the extension of the EU's own internal market. They point to a whole range of disquieting trends. Azerbaijan responded to the 2008 Georgia conflict by diverting additional supplies to Russia and eastward, nervous about relying so much on the Baku-Tbilisi-Ceyhan (BTC) pipeline to the west. Gazprom has proposed to buy all Libya's oil and gas exports. In most Member States foreign ministries have fought to gain a say over energy policy, to politicize what they tend to see as the overly technocratic approach followed by energy and trade departments. One report concludes that decision-making on energy security has already moved in significant measure into the hands of national security strategists (Austin and Bochkarev 2007).

One senior official acknowledges that the host of supposedly rules-based Memorandums of Understanding that the EU has signed with third countries have produced nothing more than "empty talks." Diplomats prefer to define the EU model as one of "regulated liberalization"; a "third way...between markets and geopolitics," predicated upon "political dialogue and cooperation." One of the EU's particularly senior producer-state interlocutors observes that the EU is "egotistically geopolitical" but seeks to mask this with rules-based discourse.

These trends are evident in all main producer regions. The reach of EU internal market norms remains especially limited in the Gulf. Here Member-State governments have rather sought energy cooperation on the back of traditional geopolitical forms of engagement, such as security cooperation and arms sales. In North Africa the EU has offered increasing amounts of technical cooperation to boost energy links and regulatory harmonization in the energy sector, based on the existing market-oriented acquis of the EMP. The EU talks of creating a Mediterranean Energy Ring. However, with North African producers resistant to the market-governance model, in countries like Algeria bilateral political agreements and deals have increased in number. An interesting aside to the sagas of "pipeline politics" is that public funding for LNG facilities has not been readily forthcoming. LNGs may be more market-susceptible, but policy-makers fret that they are geopolitically more vulnerable to attack.

It is, of course, in relation to Russia that Europe's geopolitical stance has emerged most clearly. The well-known differences between Member States are not over the need for a more geopolitical approach toward Russia on energy issues. Rather, they are over what such a political approach should consist of: confrontation or uncritical engagement (Youngs 2009). Most states, and particularly Germany, have sought to engage more in pursuit of long-term bilateral contracts. A majority of Member States have now signed bilateral deals of some kind with Russian energy companies. Several new Member States, of course, argue for a tougher stance. Polish politicians admonish Member States for their increasingly furtive energy deals with Russia. Lithuanian president Valdas Adamkus insists that the EU must respond in kind to Russia's securitization of energy and drop the "mantra" that the market by itself will provide for Europe's energy security (*Eurasia Daily Monitor* 2007). A low-level Energy Dialogue with Russia has existed since 2000, aimed at extending market rules, deepening regulatory convergence and improving the governance of foreign investment. But progress at this level has been stymied by high-politics tensions. Increasing Russian heavy-handedness has led to some notable measures, such as the EU's focus now on extending its Energy Community Treaty from the Balkans to Ukraine, Turkey, and Moldova. In the wake of the Russia-Ukraine gas dispute of January 2009 the EU has increased subsidies available to large energy companies to build interconnectors between different

European countries—which some have criticized as another step away from a free market model (Platts EU Energy Review 2009a). Council officials acknowledge that since the Georgia conflict and the 2009 Russia-Ukraine dispute the "market purists" are in full retreat. The prospect of Russian control over key pipelines passing through Georgia has further politicized energy calculations.

In September 2008 the Commission and the African Union formally established a new energy partnership. This could attract up to 1 billion euros for energy infrastructure projects in sub-Saharan Africa, including help for the Trans-Saharan gas pipeline. Energy Commissioner Andris Piebalgs noted that these new steps in Africa represented an overtly political reaction to a new Gazprom partnership with Nigeria as well as to the Georgian conflict (*Financial Times* 2008). In Africa the EU talks the same talk of extending internal market rules. Economic Partnership Agreements are formally to involve liberalizing energy markets. But this approach in practice has little resonance. Most energy experts see the Trans-Saharan pipeline as a purely geopolitical venture whose economic fundamentals do not make sense. Diplomatic deals are increasingly pursued by France and others with Angola. Several European states help the US navy in patrolling the Gulf of Guinea. Responding to China's presence in Africa is seen as requiring a more geopolitical approach and presence.

Pipeline Politics

The geopolitical dimension is indeed starkly manifest in the thickening intricacies of "pipeline diplomacy." There is now a great deal of new activity relating to the development of additional pipeline capacity from the Caspian Basin and Central Asia into Europe. European governments' preferences remain balanced between support for routes involving Russia and those designed to exclude Russia, especially the Nabucco pipeline set to run through Turkey into southeastern Europe. Prompted by many Member States, the Commission says it is now more willing than before to back big (Russia-bypassing) infrastructure projects and take a more geopolitical view on these—including not only Nabucco but also the more speculative White Stream pipeline planned to run directly from the Caucasus across Ukraine. It is perceived that without backing, the long-planned Nabucco pipeline may not get off the ground. Unlike most pipeline projects that are constructed by upstream producers to get their gas to export markets, Nabucco is being led by a consortium of consumer-state companies without firm guarantees yet of supplies to fill the pipeline. It is a clearly political rather than purely commercial undertaking.

However, it is doubtful that this represents the beginning of any deep Europeanization of pipeline geopolitics. Major differences remain between Member States on this issue. Germany remains unenthused over European backing for the Nabucco pipeline, in preference to its cooperation with Russia on the Nord Stream line. Hungary, Italy, Bulgaria, and Greece have all backed the Russian-sponsored South Stream project, support that some experts see as fatally undermining Nabucco. The Hungarian opposition has pressed for Hungary to pull out of South Stream. In July 2009, the new Bulgarian government announced plans to switch from South Stream to Nabucco. Conversely Silvio Berlusconi has led Italy into a position even more supportive of the Russian-led project. The summer of 2009 witnessed further spats and divisions. The Lithuanian government reprimanded Andris Piebalgs for his support of Nord Stream. The French energy giant GDF Suez then negotiated its way into the Nord Stream consortium, after being denied a role in Nabucco by the latter's Turkish partner (EurActiv 2009b).

With Nabucco's costs now estimated at 8 billion euros, industry experts judge that it would need Iranian gas to make it viable. Many policy-makers and experts opine that Nabucco still needs the involvement of at least one European oil major to be workable. The Kazakh government rails that the EU has been offering small-scale technical cooperation for a generation, but has built nothing; the Chinese arrived recently in Kazakhstan and very quickly set to work building a pipeline eastward. While Germany seeks partnership with Russia on energy, the Czechs retort that "you need two for a partnership" and that the EU and Russia will increasingly be rivals for finite resources.

The Russian invasion of Georgia in the summer of 2008 led some European governments to conclude that Nabucco needs stronger political backing. Others have reached the opposite conclusion, that solutions must be sought through and collaboratively with Russia. European policies consequently exhibit an inchoate mix of the two stances. The European Council in March 2009 asked for "concrete action" to develop access to Caspian supplies. The Commission allocated 200 million euros of funding for Nabucco and supported creation of the CDC (Platts EU Energy Review 2009b). What Nabucco needs even more than public money is governments' backing to unlock political blockages. Some Member States are beginning to agitate for such involvement. However, Caspian states want a broader strategic partnership, and not be treated merely as gas suppliers. Even after two European companies, Austrian mineral oil authority (OMV) and Hungarian Oil and Gas Public Limited Company (MOL), signed contracts in Kurdistan in May 2009 to feed Iraqi oil into Nabucco, coleader of South Stream Eni opined that Nabucco would still not fly (*Financial Times* 2009). Also, when the EU presented its "southern corridor" initiative in May 2009, offering Central Asian suppliers guaranteed levels of long-term demand, Kazakhstan, Uzbekistan, and Turkmenistan walked away, complaining that Europe had placed insufficient incentives on the table. In July 2009 Nabucco's five transit states finally signed the necessary intergovernmental accords to give the project legal grounding. But producer states declined European pressure to accompany the signing ceremony with firm promises of supplies into Nabucco. Even after this agreement, the lack of funding rendered the project doubtful (Denison 2009), and key transit state, Turkey, also gave its backing to the South Stream project only a month later.

Institutionalized Rules Versus Political Maneuverability

So, what can we conclude from these policy trends in terms of the reach of Europeanization? The question pertinent to this volume is what all these evolving features of policy mean for the extent of commonality in European external energy policies. Analysts of European foreign policy routinely point to a range of factors seen to be pushing in the direction of deeper EU unity: the ongoing processes of "socialization" within the Common Foreign and Security Policy (CFSP); the emergence of a "network" of common security perspectives within Europe; the influence of convergent "transborder" linkages between functionaries, including in the energy sphere. However, the evolution of external dimensions of energy security suggests that such dynamics of convergence remain weaker in this sphere than analysts have detected in other areas of the CFSP agenda. Common European approaches have certainly created the frameworks for potential socialization. But, in practice governments' pursuit of energy security tells a more varied story.

It is commonly claimed that the gradual deepening of the internal market will drive convergence in the external dimensions of energy security policy. The evidence suggests that this has occurred only to a limited extent. Some Member States have resisted even the most basic principles of transparency and information sharing with their EU partners. Such divergence exists not only at the political level but also among diplomats and technical experts—if a transborder epistemic community exists in the energy sphere it is no more than incipient and still often diluted by the disparate winds of fierce national competition.

What has determined this outcome? France's external energy dependency is relatively low, undercutting its commitment to foreign policy unity. Germany has been even more the "spoiler" through its Russia policy and increasingly its bilateral efforts in Central Asia. Italy gives increasingly explicit political backing to national, bilateral energy deals. Conversely, the traditionally skeptical UK has become more supportive of EU cooperation, as its own energy dependency is set to increase fast. The Netherlands—the EU's remaining significant gas producer—advocates a balance between unity and retaining scope for bilateral policies. Objective energy dependencies and mixes still engender very different energy narratives between Member States.

At a more fine-toothed level, the balance between convergence and divergence itself differs across regions. Russia provides the most conspicuous examples of disunity. Member-State governments have backed their respective national energy champions in signing long-term bilateral contracts with Gazprom—and have indeed been minded to argue that such deals represent a success for energy security. Even in the case of Russia, however, the pull of EU cooperation is not entirely absent, and unity has tightened to some degree as Russia has adopted increasingly heavy-handed tactics in the wielding of its new energy-based international power. Differences over Russia additionally engender contrasting views among Member States on how assertive the EU should be in prioritizing Central Asia within its energy security strategy. This is witnessed at a very general level–in differences over how far the EU should challenge Russian primacy in Central Asia—and in relation to more specific policy decisions—such as whether to offer Kazakhstan a place in the ENP or whether sanctions should have been retained against Uzbekistan. At the other end of the spectrum to Russia, energy strategy in sub-Saharan Africa has been least subject to high political tensions between Member States, as the EU has sought to take the first steps toward regaining its lost influence on the continent.

Policy in the Middle East and North Africa has benefited from more institutionalized long-term partnerships that the EU has sought to use as a base from which to deepen energy cooperation. While this undoubtedly renders common EU-level initiatives of great significance, even under the rubric of the EMP—the most strongly institutionalized

EU framework embracing oil- and gas-producer states—competitive dynamics are at least as evident as collusion. Member States increasingly undercut each other in an effort to gain access to Algerian energy supplies, this compounded by the latter's rejection of the ENP action plan offered to it. Spain and Italy in particular have justified such bilateralism by expressing frustration at the lack of north European backing for deeper EU-level engagement in North Africa. Outside the scope of the EMP, Libya has attracted even more of an open rivalry between Member States keen to gain early preference with the internationally rehabilitated Colonel Gaddafi—even as they talk of enticing Libya into the EMP and/or the Neighborhood Policy (at least until the recent conflict broke out).

In the Gulf, the weight of national diplomacy is even more pronounced in relation to the impact of common EU forums and initiatives. This is due to a combination of factors: the determination of the larger Member States to safeguard their national deals and channels of access; the relative disinterest in the region of most other Member States; the tendency of Gulf Cooperation Council states themselves still to prioritize their links with national capitals rather than conceive the EU as primary interlocutor; and the limited purchase in the area of traditional EU economic, developmental, and regulatory policy instruments. EU unity is notable in relation to Iran's nuclear program, but differences predominate over the prospect of energy cooperation with the Islamic Republic. Here Italy has been increasingly the most forward-leaning state in seeking to deepen energy ties on a bilateral basis with Teheran. A limited degree of Europeanization has taken shape in policy toward Iraq but—even aside from the original differences over the 2003 invasion—the nature of this country's security situation and political challenges continue to engender contrasting views among Member States. These militate against the possibility of establishing the foundations for a common energy strategy toward Baghdad.

In sum, the long-term vision based on a commitment to promoting market-governance reform in the management of energy resources is giving way to crisis-mode geopolitics. Pipeline brinkmanship and a "race to contract" are displacing cosmopolitan holism. As one EU policy-maker acknowledged: "There will only be a common energy policy when there is a crisis big enough to create it." At present, Member States appear content to continue with a nominal commitment to market-based energy policy and to the better governance of energy sectors, while also adopting bilateral strategies that pull in the opposite direction on both of these questions.

Note

1. Quoted in *Financial Times*, September 4, 2007.

Works Cited

Austin, G. and D. Bochkarev. 2007. Energy Sovereignty and Security: Restoring Confidence in a Cooperation International System. In *Energy and Conflict Prevention*. Ed. G. Austin and M. Schellekens-Gaiffe. Brussels: Madariaga European Foundation. 2007: 36.
Barabaso, F. 2007. Cited in *PlattsEU Energy*, March 23, 2007.
Barroso, J. M. 2006. Opening Speech at the External Energy Policy Conference. Brussels. November 20, 2006.
Benelux Position Paper. 2007. *External Energy Policy for Europe*. February 2007. mimeo.
Commission of the European Communities. 2006a. *An External Policy to Serve Europe's Energy Interests*. Paper from the Commission/SG/HR for the European Council. Brussels: European Commission.
Commission of the European Communities. 2006b. *Green Paper: A European Strategy for Sustainable, Competitive and Secure Energy*, COM(2006) 105. Brussels: European Commission. March 8, 2006: 4.
Commission of the European Communities. 2006c. *Green Paper: A European Strategy for Sustainable, Competitive and Secure Energy*. COM(2006) 105. Brussels: European Commission. March 8, 2006: 19, 24.
Commission of the European Communities. 2007. *An Energy Policy for Europe*. COM(2007) 1. Brussels. European Commission. January 10, 2007: 18–19.
Council of the European Union. 2006. *Presidency Conclusions 23–24 March 2006*(7775/1/06 REV 1). Brussels: European Council. May 18, 2006: 16.
Council of the European Union. 2007. *Presidency Conclusions, March 8/9 2007, European Council Action Plan (2007–2009): Energy Policy for Europe*. Brussels: European Council. May 2, 2007.
Danreuther, R. 2006. Developing the Alternative to Enlargement: The European Neighbourhood Policy. *European Foreign Affairs Review*. 11(2): 183–201.
Denison, M. 2009. *The EU and Central Asia: Commercialising the Energy Relationship*. EUCAM Working Paper 2. Madrid. FRIDE: 6.
EurActiv. 2009a. June 26, 2009.
EurActiv. 2009b. September 2, 2009 and July 30, 2009.
Eurasia Daily Monitor. May 14, 2007.
European Commission Eurobarometer Unit. 2007. *Eurobarometer Survey*. Brussels: European Commission.

Ferrero-Waldner, B. 2006. The European Neighbourhood Policy: The EU's Newest Foreign Policy Instrument. *European Foreign Affairs Review.* 11(2): 139–142.

Ferrero-Waldner, B. 2007. Opening Speech at the European Neighbourhood Policy Conference. Brussels, September 3, 2007. Available at http://europa.eu/rapid/pressReleasesAction.do?reference=SPEECH/07/500.

Financial Times. September 17, 2008.

Financial Times. May 18, 2009.

Grant, C. 2006. *Europe's Blurred Boundaries: Rethinking Enlargement and Neighbourhood Policy.* London. Centre for European Reform: 65.

Keppler, J. H. 2007. International Relations and Security of Energy Supply: Risks to Continuity and Geopolitcal Risks. *European Parliament Policy Department.* February, 2007: 7–8.

Lamy, J. 2007. Que Signifie Relancer la Politique Énergétique Européenne?. *Revue du marchécomún et de l'Unioneuropéenne 506.* March, 2007: 141–145.

Linde, C. 2007. *External Energy Policy: Old Fears and New Dilemmas in a Larger Union.* In Fragmented Power: Europe and the Global Economy. Ed. A. Sapir. Bruegel, Brussels, 2007: 276, 280, 295.

PlattsEU Energy. October 20, 2006.

Platts EU Energy Review. 2008. 191. September 19, 2008: 12.

Platts EU Energy Review. 2009a. 206. April 24, 2009: 10.

Platts EU Energy Review. 2009b. 202. February 27, 2009: 1.

Stern, J. 2002. *Security of European Natural Gas Supplies: The Impact of Import Dependence and Liberalization.* RIIA Working Paper. London: Royal Institute of International Affairs. July 2002: 4.

Youngs, R. 2009. *Energy Security: Europe's New Foreign Policy Priority.* London.

Vos, S. 2006. Europe's Infant Energy Strategy Looks Muddled and Unclear. In *Europe's World.* 4, Autumn 2006: 133–137.

Chapter Three

Common Rules without Strategy: EU Energy Policy and Russia

Jonas Grätz

The European Union's (EU's) energy policy toward Russia—or, to put it more precisely—the absence of a coherent policy, is a hotly debated topic in academic and policy circles. The overall message is clear and has been reiterated for many years: As long as the EU does not act in a (vertically) coherent way it cannot be externally effective. But coherence would require that Member States limit their individual sovereignty over decisions for the sake of a greater autonomy at the community level. This has proven to be especially problematic with regard to energy policy, which may be regarded as a domain of "high politics" in external relations and is subject to politicized debates internally as well. Historically, energy policy has been regarded as a national prerogative, strongly linked with national security and public service. Also, a common external policy needs an agreement on what it is about: Should energy policy toward Russia concentrate mainly on maintaining energy security or should it be seen as the core of the overall foreign policy toward Russia? As energy is an important aspect both for the EU and Russia, a conflation between external energy policy and foreign policy in general can easily occur. This makes it even harder to arrive at a common position, as there are far more possible objectives in general foreign policy than in energy policy. In addition, foreign energy policy does not only involve state actors, but also big economic actors that control the economic processes underlying energy policy.

This chapter evaluates the EU's external energy policy toward Russia according to the general criteria of energy security policy. After giving an overview over the challenges Russia poses to EU energy security, the chapter will examine the policy measures the EU has taken vis-à-vis Russia. When evaluating the success of the actions taken, special emphasis will be on the goals of the various actors in the EU. The account of the EU's energy policy toward Russia focuses on the following three levels: External initiatives, aimed at enhancing energy security via a reduction of risks effected by Russian detrimental behavior; external initiatives, aimed at increasing resilience by diversifying energy supply routes; and internal initiatives in the gas market, which have direct effects on Russia. Specific attention will be given to the natural gas sector, as it has been in the focus of the EU-Russia energy relationship. This is due to its high capital intensity and the rigid grid-bound transportation needs, which bind suppliers and consumers closely together in a long-term relationship. This necessitates a much higher degree of coordination than the oil or coal markets. In addition, Russia's reserves of natural gas are much bigger than its oil reserves.

The Russian Challenge to EU Energy Security

Declining indigenous production of the EU and substantial Russian gas reserves result in a mutual interest of the EU in Russian gas supplies and of Russia in the EU gas market. However, notwithstanding this mutual interest, the goals of the actors diverge substantially. With some simplification, the challenge to the EU is most often described as being the result of a Russian worldview and corresponding priorities that fundamentally differ from those of the EU (Finon and Locatelli 2008, 424). Whereas the EU adheres to a "markets and institutions" approach envisaging strong and binding rules allowing markets to allocate value, Russia pursues a realist "regions and empires" strategy, focused on establishing the state as the prime decision-maker, presiding over the economy. This goes along with a fuzzy boundary between economic and political goals.[1]

Thus, current Russian energy policy is based on the conception of oil and gas resources as strategic goods, requiring the reliance on direct influence of state actors rather than on market forces to regulate their extraction and distribution. Increasing state influence and regulation of the sector by manipulation of laws is partly a consciously planned policy in order to be able to use oil and gas corporations, especially the gas monopoly Gazprom, as domestic and foreign policy tools in the absence of other attractive instruments (ideological, institutional etc.) and partly the result of spontaneous processes of property redistribution to the bureaucracy and security services (Easter 2008; Treisman 2007; Zudin 2006).

In this context, several challenges have been discussed:

- Some have argued that the renationalization of the oil and gas sector and the resulting deinstitutionalization of the sector led to underinvestment in exploration and production in Russia. This was seen as a possible threat to future gas export possibilities.[2] However, substantial room remains for reducing gas demand inside Russia, which is Gazprom's biggest market from a volume, but not from a revenue perspective. Meanwhile, more than 60 percent of Gazprom's revenues are generated on the EU market (Grätz 2009, 67). Thus, because of the attractiveness of the EU market for Gazprom, a supply shortfall is not very likely. Rather, it makes sense for Gazprom to foster the perception of resource scarcity by upholding information scarcity on investments, in order to obtain more price-setting power by simultaneously driving a strategy of high market penetration (Christie 2009, 10).
- Gazprom drives an expansion strategy to the EU's downstream markets striving to enlarge its market share and profits. As the highest profits can be obtained by rising barriers toward possible competitors, Gazprom has a vested interest in segmenting Member States' markets (Noel 2008). Thus, Gazprom tries to use the opportunities of gas market liberalization in order to monopolize markets and thereby to undercut the EU's liberalization and market homogenization agenda. What is more, in an effort to monopolize the EU market, it tries to obstruct the EU's diversification strategies by launching competing pipeline projects and co-opting potential independent suppliers from Central Asia (Milov 2008, 6; Götz 2008). As this increases Gazprom's market power it endangers energy security by hampering supplier diversification and imposing artificially high prices on consumers.
- This economic strategy goes along with a strategy to harvest the political gains that go along with economic dependence (Liuhto 2010). In the "near abroad," Gazprom traditionally used the dependence of Central Asian countries on export routes through Russia, relieving it from the pressure to invest in drilling and exploration at home and achieving the additional goal of binding these states to Russia politically (Christophe 1998; Westphal 2003; Vahtra 2005). As a new development, Gazprom and state-owned Transneft' were used as foreign policy tools against "unfriendly" neighbors such as Ukraine, Georgia, or Lithuania (Milov 2008, 7f; Finon and Locatelli 2008). Thus, Russia aims

at reaping the "double dividend" of revenue flows and political influence generated by market power (Christie 2009, 12).

External Initiatives toward Russia

The EU's external energy policy toward Russia can be traced back to the beginning of the 1990s. Since the last days of the Soviet Union, the European Commission's (hereafter: the Commission) approach was not to limit dependence on Russian energy imports per se, but to use structural power by involvement of capital from the EU in Russia's energy sector and, most important, by protecting these investments not on the basis of personal deals but on the basis of institutionalized rules agreed at the international level. Such an international regime would have limited the potential of political actors to interfere with commercial transactions in an unforeseeable way and thus would have limited the security of supply risk of arbitrary behavior by Russia. As these efforts failed, the Commission consistently tried to develop new formats for promoting its vision. But Member States were not helpful in the Commission's efforts, as they established their own bilateral cooperation schemes and could deliver on Russian demands far more effectively.

The Energy Charter Treaty

The first major tool was the Energy Charter, which evolved into a multilateral treaty. The Charter process was started in June 1990 by Dutch prime minister Ruud Lubbers, who surprised other heads of state when he distributed his proposal at the European Council summit in Dublin. The basic idea was to export European rules to Eastern Europe and the Soviet space in order not only to solve the problem of property rights protection, but also to spur the transition to a market economy and to stabilize the European neighborhood macroeconomically (Balmaceda 2002: 22; Kemner 1996: 210; Konoplyanik 1992). This idea was then packed with symbolic meaning by comparing the plan to the European Coal and Steel Community that started the EU integration process back in 1952. So, not only were energy policy goals strived for but also wider goals of foreign policy, such as the stabilization and ultimately the integration of Russia into a European rules-based order. Institutionally, the plan not only foresaw the guarantee of property rights for investors, but it should also be able to regulate transportation, market access, and constant access to all hydrocarbon reserves.[3]

The plan reflected several structural conditions present at that time. First of these is the decrepit situation of the Soviet energy sector and the Soviet economy in general that was in desperate need of capital injections; second, low energy prices with oil hovering between $15–20 per barrel, resulting in low investment levels; third, the need of Western and Eastern Europe for energy imports and possible vulnerabilities arising from excessive reliance on oil imports from the Middle East; and finally the capital and technological resources Western Europe had to offer. At the same time, a historical situation was seen to be present which could result in an integration process between the Soviet space and Europe on the EU's own terms.

The proposal met the approval of the other heads of state and the European Council mandated the Commission to elaborate on the basic principles of an Energy Charter. The Commission started to work immediately and won the approval of Soviet diplomats already in the beginning of July, who claimed that it was in accord with the Soviet "vision of the solution to Europe's energy problems."[4] Momentum was added due to the unraveling Gulf War and plunging Soviet oil production. The Commission was especially interested in the proposal, as it fit in perfectly with its internal goals of energy market liberalization that were worked upon at the same time (Matláry, 1997). More specifically, the Energy Charter could be used to support competition on the production level that was sought after as a useful complement for the liberalized internal market (EC - COM(91) 548 final: 25). The proposal crafted by the Commission contained much more liberal provisions than the original Lubbers proposal—for example it postulated the free access to known and future energy resources and to their extraction, as well as a free energy market (EC-COM(91) 36 final: 9). The Council granted negotiation rights to the Commission in April 1991.[5] Notwithstanding the August coup and the breakup process of the Soviet Union, the political declaration initiating the Energy Charter process was signed on schedule in December 1991 with both the Soviet Union and the Soviet Republic as signatories.[6] The Charter contained the political commitment to work on a binding multilateral treaty that would regulate energy investments, transport, trade, and innovation. It was opened to all interested parties; the signatories included Japan and the United States. The treaty would contain a basic agreement and several issue-specific protocols.

The negotiations that followed proved to be much more difficult, as negotiated provisions were to be made binding. The basic principle of the Energy Charter Treaty (ECT) is the extension of GATT principles to energy trade and investment, specifically most-favored-nation treatment and national treatment.[7] But the negotiation process of the ECT was delayed substantially not because of the resistance from Russia but because of the disunity on approaches to regulatory policy in the EU and the Organisation for Economic Co-operation and Development (OECD) camp in general. As the Charter foresaw a far-reaching liberalization of transport networks, some Member States feared losing their grip over the energy sector. As a result, the proposal for mandatory third-party access (TPA) to export and transit pipelines put forward by the Commission and supported by the United Kingdom (UK), was dismissed by France and other Member States. This resulted in a watering down of the provision, which now provides only for negotiable access.[8] The same disagreements came to the forefront regarding foreign direct investment, where notably France and Norway resisted the mandatory national treatment principle of foreign investors, which as a result was made nonbinding (Doré 1996, 142; Liesen 2004, 52). These disagreements revealed the lack of consensus on gas and electricity market liberalization in the EU and substantially delayed the negotiation process.[9]

Further delays occurred because of a lack of competence on the side of diplomats and experts from the former Council for Mutual Economic Assistance (Comecon) states, which had to familiarize themselves with capitalist treaty provisions. But in contrast to the internal divisions of the OECD camp, these delays did not reflect a disagreement with ECT principles on the Russian side. The only caveat from the Russian side was a temporary exemption from certain rules for transition countries, to allow for relevant laws to be adopted. The Russian negotiating team was reform-oriented and favored a quick negotiation process, as the energy sector was still weakly organized and domestic opposition to the treaty had not yet been voiced (Doré 1996, 147; Wälde 1996, 316). In this context, the Russian side, aware of possible future difficulties, wanted to use its "window of opportunity" of a certain autonomy vis-à-vis certain domestic pressure groups to agree on an international accord that would then limit the influence of these groups. But the negotiations stalled again in 1993, this time due to opposition voiced by the United States, who found that provisions on investment were lagging behind other bilateral treaties it had concluded with different producer countries.[10] This led to a delay of one year, with the basic ECT being signed in December 1994, without the United States. At that time, one of the Russian negotiators already spoke of possible resistance in the Duma and oil-extracting Russian republics.[11] As a result, a crucial window of opportunity may have been missed by the West in drawing out negotiations on the treaty. Thus, the EU itself established disincentives for Russia to ratify the treaty by its disunity and its incoherent approach to the ECT. This is not to claim that Russia would definitely have ratified the treaty if Member States had acted in a coherent way. But this is a recurrent problem, which will be explained later in the chapter.

While the ECT was still promoted by the Russian government in the 1990s, it was more and more seen as an infringement on sovereignty, especially in the Duma, which at that time still constituted a force of its own. Leftist factions viewed the ECT as a threat to the Russian national interest because it would spur energy exports, would represent a "sell-out of the homeland," and weaken the position of domestic capital.[12] They were reportedly supported by Gazprom who feared obligations to open up its pipeline network to third parties and to grant transit rights to Central Asian countries, which would have weakened its power (Balmaceda 2002, 23). So, ratification was stalled in the Duma committees from 1996 to 1998, and an attempt at ratification failed in 1998. As time went by, it became increasingly obvious that Russia would not ratify the treaty. In the meantime, as it had signed the treaty, Russia was obliged to apply the ECT provisionally, as foreseen in Article 45. This gave some investment protection to corporations of Member States and led to an arbitration case by YUKOS (Yuganskneftegas Kuibyshevnefte OrgSintez) shareholders. But in August 2009, Prime Minister Vladimir Putin signed a decree to withdraw Russia's signature from the treaty.

The EU-Russia Energy Dialogue

As the failure of the ECT became more and more evident, the president of the Commission, Romano Prodi, launched the bilateral "Energy Dialogue" with Russia in 2000 to at least communicate with Russia about planned steps in energy market liberalization and to promote energy market harmonization. The Energy Dialogue was established in October 2000 on a bilateral basis. The Dialogue was based on the Partnership and Cooperation Agreement signed between Russia and the EU in 1994. Both the Commission and the Kremlin appointed "single interlocutors," who are responsible for the process of cooperation. Apart from normal intergovernmental negotiations the interlocutors organized some "round tables," where all relevant stakeholders from European and Russian energy business met with government officials to discuss their positions and to agree on issues of common interest (EC-COM (2004) 777 final). At the outset, four issue areas were identified: the implications of the internal energy market for the EU-Russia relationship, the sustainable use of energy, security of supply and the harmonization of markets. The policy content stayed the same: "establish predictable trade rules, improve networks and encourage investments by promoting a more stable and transparent legal framework."[13]

In the beginning, the Commission tried to use the Energy Dialogue to promote the ratification of the ECT. But this was fruitless, as energy prices had recovered, alleviating Russia's need for FDI. The central Russian political elite now strived for achieving as much control as possible over the energy sector. The central task for them was now to curb the autonomy of private capital and the regions. New foreign investors would only be detrimental to this process.

In connection with the first issue area the Commission also wanted to tackle the problem of long-term delivery contracts for gas, including destination clauses.[14] But attempts were not too successful. No overall agreement prohibiting destination clauses has been reached, only a renegotiation of contracts to eliminate such clauses on a case-by-case basis could be agreed upon.

Since the mid-2000s, the Energy Dialogue has been used by the EU mainly as a device to keep some contact to the Russian side and to try to exchange information on energy issues. But even these attempts are often jeopardized by the Russian side: Some of the subgroups do not meet due to a lack of interest by Russia, which often refuses to appoint representatives or agree on schedules. Recently, progress has been reported mainly on the energy efficiency topic, most likely due to the reason that an amount of 5 million euro in EU funds was allocated to promote energy efficiency in Russia in 2009 (EC 2010b, 22f).

Observers of the Energy Dialogue point to the fact, that Russia was able to "monopolize" the dialogue several times for its own purposes, playing on its bargaining power as a major energy supplier (Westphal 2005, 18). This is not only due to structural issues such as growing energy demand, tighter markets, and high prices that were present from 2002 until 2008, which resulted in a "new energy paradigm," as some argued (Helm 2007; Spanjer 2007). These structural conditions cannot fully explain the lack of attention given by Russia to the EU level—especially not after the abrupt drop in energy prices in mid-2008. What is more, the EU does not possess the necessary institutional and structural features to act coherently in the energy sphere, as Member States followed their own interests and cooperation projects with regard to Russia (Barysch 2004, 53f; Westphal 2008). As a result, Russia was not interested in the EU level, but oriented its efforts toward Member States. A sufficient explanation must therefore be sought from a more detailed examination of the Member State's strategies toward Russia.

The Member State Agenda: Fostering National Champions

The Western European gas industry traditionally operated on the basis of national or regional distribution monopolies, which negotiated with the suppliers, mainly Algeria, the Netherlands, Norway, and Russia (Finon 2004, 185; Wybrew-Bond 1999). The monopolies could keep the balance between supply and demand via their function as "gatekeepers." They were controlling market access and concluded accompanying long-term, take-or-pay contracts based on rigid oil product-based pricing formulae. Competition only took place between fuels and to a very limited extent between gas producers when new contracts were negotiated. The pricing formula ensured the "competitive" pricing of gas in every market situation and for every consumer group and thus guaranteed margins for distributors. For suppliers, this arrangement meant that gas could only be sold at the border to the monopolies, a condition they were willing to tolerate as it guaranteed them substantial long-term stability of demand (IEA 1998, 32; Stern 1998).

Privatization and liberalization of the EU's gas market, which began in the early 1990s, began to threaten this order and at the same time opened up new possibilities for the national monopolies and suppliers. The easier entry of competitors was threatening their position at the same time as they could become competitors in other markets as well. Therefore, they tried to keep their traditional position in their home market to the largest extent possible, at the same time trying to penetrate other markets. Substantial vertical and horizontal integration took place (Finon and Midttun 2004), supported by national politics, in order to form "national champions," which would be able to compete on a European scale without falling prey to a hostile takeover. The companies argued that big national champions were needed in order to counterbalance the power of suppliers (Bergmann 2005, 3). Thus, as liberalization moved on, incumbents and national politicians formed an alliance to protect their vested interests—the former fearing a deterioration of their position and the latter a loss of control over energy policy. This led to a joint "beggar-thy-neighbor" strategy of Member States and market incumbents, which were on the one side eager to exploit the new possibilities opened up by liberalization in other markets, whereas they strived to limit competition in their own market as far as possible.

This strategy of strengthening national capital was also played out in external relations. While claiming to enhance the EU's security of supply, especially German and Italian politicians would offer their national incumbents concrete support in gaining access to Russian upstream assets by providing and sustaining an undisturbed political environment, as well as facilitating asset swaps and granting exemptions from national regulations.

At least in Germany, this policy was pursued with a general frame of reference that went beyond energy security goals: A general policy of integration very much in line with the initial motivations of the Energy Charter process was pursued, but this time in absence of the common framework the Charter wanted to provide. This policy was justified within a renewed "Ostpolitik" framework, claiming that integration of Russian and German-cum-European capital would eventually contribute to political rapprochement, peace, and integration (Rahr 2007; Steinmeier 2007; Whist 2009, 179). Former German chancellor Gerhard Schröder, who is now working for Russia's Gazprom, has added geopolitical reasoning to this German strategy and "uploads" it to the EU: he claims that the EU needs to pursue integration with Russia in order to compete economically, politically, and culturally against the United States and rising Asian powers such as China (Schröder 2006; 2010). The policy that follows from this agenda is opposed to a policy that would result by focusing on energy security, where reduction of dependence on a particular supplier and not its increase would be in order. Needless to say, this foreign policy orientation did not reflect the goals of central Eastern European nations, which adopted an Atlantic orientation and wanted to integrate with the West, but not with Russia.

The German example shows that a policy that is problematic from an energy security viewpoint was deliberately taken out of this policy domain and justified with the wider rationale of contributing to economic and eventually political integration. However, even if the goal of political integration between Russia and Germany (or, for that case, the EU) is accepted as a legitimate and achievable goal, it is difficult to comprehend how integration of energy sectors could contribute to political integration, as the Russian energy sector is marked by deep politicization and subjected to strategic goals of the Russian political elite (Liuhto 2010). These bilateral deals that are pursued by Member States were to the detriment of the EU's policy of promoting a common framework. These deals rendered it very cheap for the Russian side not to respond to demands made by the EU. On the contrary, "gatekeepers" to the Russian market such as Gazprom could gain high yields from their control of the rules and resources. They could use this control, as well as the readiness of European companies to compete with each other, for advancing their own projects through asset swaps.

In addition, the national strategies contributed to suboptimal outcomes for the internal energy policy from a community point of view. For example, transit avoidance pipelines such as Nord Stream are not only more costly than onshore pipelines but also bypass several EU member countries that could have benefited from the additional supplies. Other cases in point are exemptions from EU competition regulations, granted for new projects by national authorities in order to make investments more profitable.[15]

Facilitating Dependence Reduction: Promoting Supplier Diversification

Apart from trying to limit the risks of dependence on Russia by promoting common rules, the Commission tried to promote alternative supply projects, such as LNG regasification terminals and import pipelines. Here, the Commission mainly proposed to act as a coordinator and facilitator of projects already proposed by the industry. It started in 1996, when the Council adopted two decisions on trans-European energy networks of "common interest," later termed TEN-E projects (EC-96/391/EC,1996; EC-1254/96/EC 1996). Priority was given to electricity, specifically to interconnections in the internal market, and on connecting isolated energy networks to the EU-wide grid. Besides, it included also gas interconnection and supply projects. With these decisions the Commission got awarded relatively wide-ranging competencies: Apart from the task to facilitate cooperation between Member States, it could also decide on granting financial assistance to the designated projects. Nevertheless, all measures had to be agreed upon in regulatory comitology procedure by a qualified majority of the committee's Member State representatives. The Commission acted swiftly, first, by granting funds for feasibility studies for several projects and then even by co-financing the capital costs of two electricity undersea cables in 1998, linking Sweden and Poland as well as Norway and the Netherlands (ECEnergy 1998). It also proposed to broaden the list of projects several times and obtained the approval from the EP and the Council. However, except for granting priority status to some LNG terminals, no efforts were made to diversify away from traditional gas suppliers.

In the early 2000s, external gas infrastructure was given specific attention, in line with rising energy prices and the first Commission Green Paper on the security of energy supply. The Green Paper explicitly mentioned new supply routes from the Caspian Sea basin and southern Mediterranean as remedies for insecurities associated with growing import dependency (EC - COM (2000) 769 final: 73). In 2002, the Commission proposed to create a new category for dedicated "Priority Projects," which should form a special subset of "common interest" projects. Such projects should be "very important" for realizing competition in the internal market or the strengthening of security of supply (EC - COM (2001) 775 final: 42). They should be entitled to receive as much as 20 percent of estimated total investment costs from the community budget (EC - COM (2001) 775 final: 23). The Commission also identified three "priority axes," including two pipelines from Algeria, one northern corridor from Russia to the U.K., now being realized with the Nord Stream and BBL pipelines, and one southern corridor from the Caspian Basin via Turkey and Greece to the Central European grid, now known as the partly competing Nabucco, Interconnection Turkey Greece Italy (ITGI) and Trans-Adriatic Pipeline (TAP) projects. These proposals were adopted in mid-2003 with no major changes (EC - 1229/2003/EC 2003). From now on, the bulk of the community funding was allocated to gas projects, predominantly in the Mediterranean region, where gas markets were still in their infancy. The Nabucco project and associated pipelines received the largest portion of financial support, amounting to 11.4 million euro (EC - COM(2006) 443 final: 31).

Already at the end of 2003, the Commission submitted a new proposal on improving the gas network development together with other proposals aimed at improving network access and energy efficiency. This was mainly in order to broaden the scope of priorities of network development toward meeting the needs of accession countries (EC - COM(2003) 743 final). In addition, the Commission proposed to add a third category of projects that would receive highest priority. This was due to the fact that the Commission was dissatisfied with the lengthy authorization procedures new projects encountered in many Member States. For these "projects of European interest" the Commission proposed to appoint a coordinator in consultation with Member States in case of difficulties. In case of severe delays the Commission also foresaw the right to withdraw the attribute "European interest" from the concerned project. The new category was deleted entirely in the Council's first reading and substantially watered down after its reinsertion by the Commission. Neither did the Commission receive the right to appoint a coordinator on its own, nor to withdraw the attribute "European interest" from the project in the decision adopted in 2006. The list of projects of European interest was mainly composed of those projects that were termed "priority projects" before (EC - 1364/2006/EC). In 2007, four project coordinators have been appointed by the Commission, three of them for electricity projects internal to the EU and one for the coordination of gas supplies from the Caspian basin (Nabucco). The coordinators have produced reports and recommendations to the Commission based on their findings and seem to act mainly as an additional external source of information for the Commission.[16]

The budget allocated to TEN-E energy projects has been minimal—about 20 million euros annually. Thus, the EU could only contribute small amounts to each of the projects. This situation has changed in 2009, when the Council approved a "European Economic Recovery Package" as an extraordinary measure to smoothen the impact of the 2008 economic crisis (EC - COM(2010a) 203 final). Consequently, 1,39 billion euros were granted to gas pipeline projects, in order to avoid bottlenecks when demand would pick up in line with an anticipated economic recovery and to avoid a drain in skills in the construction sector. Under the package, 200 million euros were approved to the Nabucco project and a further 100 million euros to the ITGI pipeline (EC 2010a). These projects would eventually contribute to diversification away from traditional European suppliers.

In sum, the success of the EU's policy on diversification in the gas sector is not overwhelming, despite considerable Commission activity in providing assistance. As many factors and players are involved it is hard to judge the impact precisely. However, no clear interrelationship between funds granted and progress of a "priority project" seems to exist. This is especially true for the northern European region, where out of six priority projects four received EU funding, three of which were postponed indefinitely (Skanled, Baltic Pipe,and Yamal II). In contrast, the Nord Stream pipeline, which received no EU funding but is backed by Gazprom as a powerful supplier and by distribution companies, began construction work in 2010. In the Mediterranean, more projects that received EU funding have been completed or made steps forward, but others like the Greenstream pipeline from Libya to Italy have been completed without such funding (EC - COM(2010b) 203 final).

Three conclusions can be drawn from the EU's attempts at supplier diversification: First of all, the EU does not pay sufficient attention to the interests of the various players involved when selecting strategic projects. It is implicitly assumed that the actors involved would act in the interest of the common market and help to further the EU goals of security of supply, sustainability, and competitiveness. As a result, possible pitfalls and drawbacks of certain projects are not properly analyzed, at least not in public. A proper analysis of the actors involved in pipeline projects and their strategies would also help to focus EU funding on projects that would not go ahead otherwise. This leads to the second conclusion: The EU is good at throwing money at many different "priority" projects, but not at making strategic decisions on which projects to support. As a result, the EU has assigned the status of "European interest" to projects that are competing for the same supplies and markets and not diversifying suppliers, as exemplified by the Nord Stream and Yamal II projects. This is again due to a lack of common vision of Member States: They tend to advocate projects that can be promoted as being favorable from a European viewpoint but at the same time maximize their own benefit or the benefit of their "national champion." In order to bring the majority behind the list of European priority projects, more and more projects have to be added to the list. The Commission's effort to design additional subcategories for "top-priority" projects in order to concentrate efforts did not work out, as Member States then strived for to get their respective projects onto this list. But this is not an appropriate approach for decision-making on capital-intensive supply lines with significant long-term implications for energy security. Third, in line with the disregard for different actor interests pointed out above, regulatory issues are de-emphasized. This leads to the implicit assumption that pipeline infrastructure would always fulfill a public goods function, that is that it could be used to the benefit of the EU's economy. This would be the case if the pipeline were governed according to rules mandating TPA, which ensure equal access of all prospective customers. But this may not be the case. Indeed, most new infrastructure projects do not fall under EU or ECT jurisdiction or are exempted from TPA rules despite EU funding. In addition, it makes a substantial difference if an infrastructure is governed by effective rules mandating TPA and thus stressing the public goods function of infrastructure, or if it is regarded to be a private investment undertaken by incumbents. The latter version of investment may lead to substantial limitations regarding the usage of the asset, which in that case tends to be used for furthering the interests of market incumbents and suppliers. Thus, more attention has to be paid to the issue of pipeline governance *before* assigning priority status to a gas supply project.

Aggregating Market Power: The Internal Market

The internal market for energy is the most important field for community action but not the most visible in external relations, although it has an important impact on the relationship toward suppliers. The Commission's approach to energy policy has widened over time—it began with gas and electricity market liberalization as a measure to enhance economic competitiveness and was extended in line with climate policies to overall demand management measures such as energy efficiency and the promotion of renewables. This section only concern with market liberalization policy and accompanying measures as they have the most direct impact on the relationship with Russia.

Implications for Suppliers and Consumers

The Commission has pursued gas market liberalization since the late 1980s, according to the principle of "completion of the internal market" agreed upon in the Single European Act (EC - COM(91) 548 final). The overall goal of the liberalization was to facilitate competition in the grid-bound internal energy market, in order to reduce energy prices and to increase energy security by easing investments in interconnections between Member States. This, in turn, would increase global competitiveness of the EU's internal market. The attention thus shifted from supply security and the public service character of the energy industry to their overall contribution to economic competitiveness in a globalized world. Due to space constraints, readers unfamiliar with the EU's policies on energy market liberalization should refer to the detailed analysis on energy market liberalization by Per Ove Eikeland in chapter 1 of this volume.

The most important implication of the liberal model for gas supply security is that it erodes the gatekeeper function of the big national energy transport companies. Therefore, it needs two preconditions to function for the benefit of consumers: (1) Sufficient supplies are, or can be made, available (liquidity); and (2) some diversity of suppliers (no monopoly).

This implies that liberalization policies contain some new opportunities for suppliers with high market power. As the pricing principle is changed from long-term indexation with oil products to a supply-demand based pricing model, suppliers may be encouraged to foster the perception of scarcity in order to push up gas prices, Thus, traditional long-term contracts may be a useful tool for consumers also in a liberalized market, if liquidity is lacking (Finon 2008). In addition, the erosion of the gatekeeper function of utilities and ensuing competition induces powerful suppliers to play importers off against each other. Suppliers may now engage in strategic bargaining with different companies supplying to the same market, which may result in substantial concessions of the latter. Also, the possibilities for downstream expansion of suppliers increase. This may have negative externalities for the EU's energy security, if suppliers with high market power acquire downstream assets in order to segment markets and influence demand. These problems have to be addressed by liberalization policies.

As a result, the core debate with regard to liberalization centered on the problem of market power and ensuing market distortions. The question was, whether the power of national incumbents should be curtailed by the state (the EU) in order to reduce their market power or instead be tolerated, enabling the companies to ensure national security of supply by aggregating demand and buffering markets from direct producer influence, while surcharging consumers for this service. Whereas the former results in greater control by state and the EU's institutions and passes on some of the risks to them, the latter leaves more control and risks to "national champions," implying a lower burden for state actors, better realization of national goals and less transfer of authority to the EU level. On the downside, of course, unchecked market power sustains fragmentation of markets, higher prices, and leads to substantial political control by corporations (Finon and Glachant 2004, 269f).

Safeguards Toward New Threats

As a safeguard toward the first problem of increased domination by a consolidated supplier as a possible ironic outcome of market liberalization, the Commission foresaw a "reciprocity clause" directed toward investors from third countries. The clause foresaw that unless a bilateral agreement between the EU and the investor country on mutual market access and third party access to pipelines in the investor's country of origin concluded, they would be completely banned from controlling transmission assets in the EU (van Hoorn 2009, 57). In effect, the Commission proposed to use the attractiveness of the EU's market for achieving a favorable outcome in third countries by altering the rules for market entry. If applied, two outcomes could have been possible: (1) a suboptimal outcome, where Gazprom would refrain from further investments in transmission assets in the EU and sell gas at the border; (2) a preferred outcome where Russia would alter the rules for access to upstream assets and pipeline infrastructure and would then invest into the EU's gas sector. This is tantamount to a ratification of the ECT and would also have contributed to supplier diversity and market liquidity. A third outcome that was widely discussed (van Hoorn 2009) but is unlikely due to the attractiveness of the EU's market, is the cessation of supplies by Gazprom to the EU.

But the clause met the fierce resistance by some Member States. As a result to resistance led by Germany, where Gazprom already possesses significant infrastructure assets and which regards the presence of Russian capital as a sign of "integration," the clause was completely scrapped during the Energy Council in October 2008. The underlying fear was that incumbents could no longer engage in asset swaps with Gazprom, which would further curtail their ability to bargain with suppliers. Now, investors from third countries face the same restrictions on vertical integration as domestic companies. Hence, Gazprom will have to prove the compliance of its subsidiaries with the unbundling regulations to the national regulator from 2011 onward (van Hoorn 2009, 58). In addition, the risk for security of supply of the EU has to be considered before the regulator approves an investment and the Commission has to be consulted prior to granting the approval. However, the Commission's opinion is nonbinding. In countries that opted for full ownership unbundling, subsidiaries of Gazprom or other corporations, representing the interests of Gazprom, cannot acquire transmission operators. But inherent problems with the approval procedure for foreign investors exist: The gathering of information about foreign investors by the regulatory body is difficult and the quality of information provided by the investor is likely to be low, as the body does not possess the intelligence or effective instruments to prove their accuracy. Office raids, which as an ultimate threat may back up demands of disclosure by the regulator, can be carried out only with great difficulty. This problem is severe especially in case of Gazprom's investments, who are often carried out by letterbox- and offshore-companies (Globalwitness 2009; Smith 2008). Ultimately, the momentum of a better exploitation of market power is lost, as Gazprom will have ample possibility to agree with Member States and national regulators on conditions for market entry on a bilateral basis. This way, the opportunity to reaggregate the EU's market power as a logical consequence of the liberalization process has been missed. This reflects the conflict between the models of integration based on corporate power and integration based on common rules outlined above. Here, corporate power has been privileged over regulatory coherence. This may move the liberalized gas market into an oligopolistic direction.

For the second complex of problems induced by liberalization—a weakened bargaining position of the EU's market players toward an oligopoly of suppliers, as well as demand uncertainty—no legislative solution has been proposed at all. When regional monopolies were intact, importers often negotiated as a consortium with suppliers, enabling the former to achieve favorable conditions and a balance between supply and demand. This is no longer possible in a competitive market. Some governments and researchers therefore suggested to re-monopolize demand by forming a "gas purchasing group" that would act as an interface between supply and demand and thereby aggregate demand toward suppliers (Andoura et al. 2010; Christie 2010). It could begin with European companies forming national, regional or EU-wide purchasing groups for gas that would negotiate with suppliers. Another possibility would be to establish an EU-wide purchasing agency. This public entity would negotiate all contracts for imported gas with the producers and could then sell the contracted volumes to buyers in the EU (De Jong 2008, 17). This would indeed be a logical development in view of demand insecurities and increased market power of suppliers, but it has not been scrutinized as to how such a mechanism could be put to work in a liberalized market.

The forming of gas purchasing groups implies a return to the earlier practice of purchasing consortia and would only be possible if substantial distortions to competition exist, under which the participating companies would not be able to sell in each other's markets. Otherwise, no incentives to cooperate exist. It would also mean that some market players would have to give up their special relationship to specific suppliers, guaranteeing them lower gas prices than competitors. This would be rather difficult to achieve, given the experience of substantial resistance even to more modest proposals (Finon and Locatelli 2008, 438). The establishment of a public purchasing agency would be a more reliable variant. However, it would have to temporarily take over the volume risk, as it would have to guarantee the purchasing of contracted volumes toward producers until gas volumes have been sold off internally. In any case, some solution toward demand aggregation has to be found if the power of suppliers should again pick up due to increased gas scarcity and/or supplier coordination.

In sum, the EU could not use gas market liberalization to play out the substantial power of a big market toward suppliers so far. The different goals of Member States have prevented such a solution. Instead of regulatory integration, utilities are integrating European markets on a corporate basis. This is also a form of market integration which could eventually lead to a more European orientation of Member State interests (De Jong 2008, 17). It is more compatible to the Russian institutional setup and does not necessitate adaptations on the Russian side. At the same time, it is not the form of integration envisioned by the Commission, as it serves to aggregate market power, which may be detrimental to energy security by distorting the market. At the same time, a possible transformative impact on Russian institutions is lost. In order to reduce the mismatch between corporate power and EU market liberalization rules, the EU should apply competition regulation in a proper way, as well as elaborate on new legislative proposals to alleviate the new risks induced by market liberalization.

Conclusions

As has been argued, the EU's external energy policy toward Russia as well as internal measures with external implications failed to a great extent. In energy policy terms, whereas the Commission promoted an external and internal liberalization policy that aims to redistribute power away from corporate actors toward regulatory agencies and from the national to the EU level, big continental Member States backed their incumbents, which were seen as the most appropriate tool to ensure national energy security. This was mirrored in external relations, where deals were made between incumbents and suppliers that traditionally had established tense relations. The deals were backed and facilitated by national foreign policies. There was thus no need for Russia to attach importance to the European level, as a positive payoff to current policies was provided by Member State initiatives, whereas the EU's policy would have involved costly changes to existing institutions and behavioral scripts in Russia. Here, the EU's problem arose from the refusal of Member States to confer the necessary decision-making authority to the EU level and to change their internal economic rules.

The difficulty to arrive at a common energy policy toward Russia was exacerbated by the fundamentally differing perceptions and accompanying goals of policies toward Russia, held by the Member States. Thus, whereas the Commission together with smaller and new Member States from central eastern Europe advocated an external energy policy concentrating on safeguarding security of supply, older Member States such as Germany discounted supply security and infused energy policy with the greater vision of binding Russia closer to Germany and/or the EU by integrating energy sectors. As a result, a common energy policy was complicated by the disagreement about what this policy should be about: energy policy or "integration" by default in order to reach wider goals. This problem has to be solved in order to make sure that "integration" policies toward Russia pursued by particular Member States rely on an internal consensus and do not contribute to a disintegration of the "ever closer Union."

Notes

1. In this context, it has been argued that the EU approach of market liberalization is deficient in a world of increasing resource scarcity and high commodity prices, giving rise to a "new energy paradigm," see Helm (2007); Spanjer (2009). However, market developments are not so unidirectional and clear to allow such a wide-ranging conclusion. See: Paillard (2007: 12ff); Peters (2003: 22ff); Riley (2006); Milov (2008); Noel (2008: 5f).
2. See: Paillard (2007: 12ff); Peters (2003: 22ff); Riley (2006); Milov (2008); Noel (2008: 5f).
3. See: Dutch Prime Minister suggests first step toward Soviet integration. *The Guardian,* June 26, 1990: 9.
4. Brussels and Moscow agree energy plan. *Financial Times,* July 6, 1990, International : 3.
5. See: *Energy Charter Progress Delayed despite Strong Soviet Support.* In European Energy Report, May 1991, S1.
6. See Soviet Republics Sign International Energy Exchange Accord, *Associated Press,* December 17, 1991. Eventually, this was the first official recognition of Soviet Republics as separate entities and three days later the Soviet Union was dissolved.

7. See Art. 29 II a) ECT.
8. Vgl. Final Charter Treaty text sent out to all participants. *EC Energy Monthly*, September 1994: 1. Matláry (1997, 48).
9. When agreement could be finally reached in 1994 the United States did not sign the treaty, as it did not encompass the liberal rules once envisaged. On the negotiation process in general see Dor (1996); Matláry (1997); *Energy Charter Progress Delayed despite Strong Soviet Support*. In European Energy Report, May 1991, S1.
10. EC and US clash over Charter. *EC Energy Monthly*. December 1993: 9.
11. See: Mixed reception awaits Energy Charter in Russia, East European Energy Report, 25. November 1994: 5.
12. See: U energetičeskoj chartii v Rossii malo storonnikov. *Segodnja*. No. 31, 18.2.1997; Ėnergetičeskaja chartija pod perekrestnym ognem. *Segodnja*. No. 123, 18.6.1997; Zyplakov (1998).
13. COM/2004/777 final: 9.
14. Destination clauses prohibit the reselling of energy resources to other states than the contracting partner and are therefore in conflict with the internal energy market of the EU.
15. A good case in point are the Ostsee Pipeline Anschluss-Leitung (Opal) and Norddeutsche Erdgas Leitung (NEL) pipelines built by German Gazprom/Wintershall joint venture Wingas, which shall be connected to the Nord Stream pipeline in order to transport gas to Southern and Western Europe: Wingas applied for an exemption from competition rules for the new pipelines. See: OPAL NEL TRANSPORT GmbH beantragt Ausnahme von Regulierung, WINGAS PM, 28.07.2008, http://www.wingas.de; Opal will allein glänzen, in: Der Spiegel, 45/2008. November 3, 2008: 80.
16. See: Energy infrastructure—European Coordinators. http://ec.europa.eu/energy/infrastructure/tent_e/coordinators_en.htm (accessed May 18, 2010).

Works Cited

Andoura, S., L. Hancher, and M. Woude. 2010. *Towards a European Energy Community: A Policy Proposal*. Paris.

Balmaceda, M. 2002. *EU Energy Policy and Future European Energy Markets: Consequences for the Central and East European States*. Mannheim.

Barysch, K. 2004. *The EU and Russia. Strategic Partners or Squabbling Neighbours?*. Centre for European Reform. London.

Bergmann, B. 2005. Vorwort des Vorstandsvorsitzenden. E.on Ruhrgas Jahresbericht 2005. Essen.

Christie, E. 2009. European Security of Gas Supply—A New Way Forward. In *EU-Russia Gas Connection: Pipes, Politics and Problems*. Ed. K.

Liuhto. Publications of Pan-European Institute 8/2009 Turku School of Economics. Turku, 3–22.

Christie, E. 2010. *Natural Gas Demand in the European Union and in Russia.* Available at http://publications.wiiw.ac.at/modPubl/download.php?publ=WS20100503_3 (accessed May 19, 2010).

Christophe, B. 1998. Von der Politisierung der Ökonomie zur Ökonomisierung der Politik: Staat, Markt und Außenpolitik in Rußland. In *Zeitschrift für Internationale Beziehungen.* 5(2): 201–240.

De Jong, J. 2008. *The Third EU Energy Market Package: Are We Singing the Right Song?.* CIEP briefing papers. February 2008. Available at http://www.clingendael.nl/publications/2008/20080200_ciep_briefingpaper_jong.pdf (accessed May 20, 2010).

Doré, J. 1996. Negotiating the Energy Charter Treaty. In *The Energy Charter Treaty: An East-West Gateway for Investment & Trade.* Ed. T. W. Wälde. London: 137–155.

Easter, G. 2008. The Russian State in the Time of Putin. *Post Soviet Affairs* 24(3): 199–230.

EC 2010a. *Commission of the European Communities: Economic Recovery: Second Batch of 4-Billion-Euro Package Goes to 43 Pipeline and Electricity Projects.* Available at Http://europa.eu/rapid/pressReleases Action.do?reference=IP/10/231&format=HTML&aged=0&language=EN&guiLanguage=en (accessed May 18, 2010).

EC 2010b. *Commission of the European Communities: EU-Russia Common Spaces Progress Report 2009.* Available at http://ec.europa.eu/external_relations/russia/docs/commonspaces_prog_report_2009_en.pdf (accessed May 11, 2010).

EC. COM (2000) 769 final. *Commission of the European Communities: Green Paper— Towards a European Strategy for the Security of Energy Supply.* November 11, 2000.

EC. COM (2001) 775 final. *Commission of the European Communities: Report on the implementation of the guidelines for Trans-European Energy Networks in the period 1996–2001.* December 20, 2001.

EC. COM (2003) 743 final. *Commission of the European Communities: Communication to the European Parliament and the Council: Energy Infrastructure and Security of Supply.* December 10, 2003.

EC. COM (2004) 777 final. *Commission of the European Communities: The Energy Dialogue between the European Union and the Russian Federation between 2000 and 2004.* December 13, 2004.

EC. COM (2006) 443 final. *Commission of the European Communities: Annex to the Report from the Commission to the European Parliament, the Council, the Economic and Social Committee and the Committee of the Regions on the Implementation of the Guidelines for Trans-European Energy Networks in the Period 2002 –2004.* August 7, 2006.

EC. COM (2010a) 203 final.*Commission of the European Communities: Report on the Implementation of the Trans-European Energy Networks in the Period 2007–2009.* May 4, 2010.

EC. COM (2010b) 203 final. *Commission of the European Communities: Annex to the Report on the Implementation of the Trans-European Energy Networks in the Period 2007–2009.* May 4, 2010.

EC. COM 91(36) final. *Commission of the European Communities: European Energy Charter.* February 14, 1991.

EC. COM 91(548) final. *Commission of the European Communities: Proposal for a Council Directive Concerning Common Rules for the Internal Market in Natural Gas.*

EC. 96/391/EC. *Council of the European Union: Decision of 28 March 1996 Laying Down a Series of Measures Aimed at Creating a more Favourable Context for the Development of Trans-European Networks in the Energy Sector.*

EC. 1229/2003/EC. *Council of the European Union and European Parliament: Decision Laying Down a Series of Guidelines for Trans-European Energy Networks and Repealing Decision No 1254/96/EC.*

EC. 1254/96/EC. *Council of the European Union and European Parliament: Decision Laying Down a Series of Guidelines for Trans-European Energy Networks.*

EC. 1364/2006/EC.*Council of the European Union and European Parliament: Decision Laying Down Guidelines for Trans-European Energy Networks and Repealing Decision 96(391) EC and Decision No 1229/2003/EC.*

ECEnergy 1998. European Commission: Two Power-Tens Co-Financed. In *EC Energy Monthly* (December 1, 1998). Seite 12.

Finon, D. 2004. European Gas Markets: Nascent Competition and Integration in a Diversity of Models. In *Reshaping European Gas and Electricity Industries: Regulation, Markets and Business Strategies.* Ed. D. Finon, and A. Midttun. Elsevier. Amsterdam: 183–235.

Finon, D. 2008.*Why Would Oil-Indexation In Gas Contracts Survive In Europe?.* Available at http://www.energypolicyblog.com/2008/06/29/why-would-oil-indexation-in-gas-contracts-survive-in-europe/ (accessed April 28, 2010).

Finon, D. and J. Glachant. 2004. Competition and Market Integration in Europe: Towards a Multienergy and Multidomestic Oligopoly. In *Reshaping European Gas and Electricity Industries: Regulation, Markets and Business Strategies.* Ed. D. Finon, and A. Midttun. Elsevier. Amsterdam: 237–272.

Finon, D. and C. Locatelli. 2008. Russian and European Gas Interdependence: Could Contractual Trade Channel Geopolitics? *Energy Policy* 36(1): 423–442.

Finon, D. and A. Midttun. 2004. Reshaping European Energy Industry: Patterns and Challenges. In *Reshaping European Gas and Electricity Industries: Regulation, Markets and Business Strategies.* Ed. D. Finon, and A. Midttun. Elsevier. Amsterdam: 357–387.

Globalwitness. 2009. *More Funny Business in Europe's Gas Trade.* Global Witness Briefing. Available at http://www.globalwitness.org

/media_library_get.php/889/1244496335/gw_emfesz_may09. (accessed June 13, 2009).

Götz, R. 2008. A Pipeline Race between the EU and Russia? In *Pipelines, Politics and Power: the Future of EU-Russia Energy Relations*. Ed. Barysch and Katinka. London. Centre for European Reform: 93–101. Available at http://www.cer.org.uk/pdf/rp_851.pdf (accessed October 8, 2008).

Grätz, J. 2009. Energy Relations with Russia and Gas Market Liberalization. *Internationale Politik und Gesellschaft*. 3(2009): 66–80.

Helm, D. 2007. The New Energy Paradigm. In *The New Energy Paradigm*. Ed. D. Helm. Oxford: 9–35.

IEA. 1998. *Natural Gas Pricing in Competitive Markets*. International Energy Agency. Paris.

Kemner, M. 1996. *The Strengths and Weaknesses of the Energy Charter Treaty*. Konstanz.

Konoplyanik, A. 1992. Lubbers Plan: Soviet Energy as a Standpoint for Improving Economic Reforms in the USSR. *The Energy Journal* 281–294.

Liesen, R. 2004. Der Vertrag über die Energiecharta vom 17. Dezember 1994. Ursprung, Voraussetzungen, Inhalt, Bedeutung, Bochum, Univ. Diss.

Liuhto, K. 2010. *Energy in Russia's Foreign Policy*. Electronic Publications of Pan-European Institute. 10(2010). Turku.

Matláry, J. H. 1997. *Energy Policy in the European Union*. Basingstoke. Hampshire u.a.

Milov, V. 2008. *Russia and the West: The Energy Factor*. CSIS/IFRI. July 2008. Washington, DC and Paris. Available at http://www.ifri.org.

Noel, P. 2008. *Beyond Dependence: How to Deal With Russian Gas*. ECFR Policy Brief. November 9, 2008. London.

Paillard, C. A. 2007. *Gazprom, the Fastest Way to Energy Suicide*. Russie Nei Visions. No. 17. ifri Russia/NIS Center. Paris.

Peters, S. 2003. *Building Up the Potential for Future Resource Conflicts: The Shortcomings of Western Response Strategies to New Energy Vulnerabilities*. EUI Working Papers 2003/09. Available at http://www.iue.it/RSCAS/WP-Texts/03_09.pdf (accessed February 6, 2007).

Rahr, A. 2007. Der "Kalte Krieg" ist Geschichte. *Internationale Politik*. March 2007: 12–19.

Riley, A. 2006. *The Coming of the Russian Gas Deficit: Consequences and Solutions*. CEPS Policy in Brief, No. 116. October. 2006. Brussels.

Schröder, G. 2006. "Der deutsche Zeigefinger sollte nicht so groß sein," Interview mit Gerhard Schröder. *Süddeutsche Zeitung*. October 10, 2006.

Schröder, G. 2010. Interview with Gerhard Schröder. April 9, 2010. Available at http://www.m4-tv.com/en/video/?id=799 (accessed May 12, 2010).

Smith, K C. 2008. *Russia and European Energy Security. Divide and Dominat*.,October 2008. CSIS. Washington, DC.

Spanjer, A. 2007. Russian Gas Price Reform and the EU-Russia Gas Relationship: Incentives, Consequences and European Security of Supply. *Energy Policy.* 35(5): 2889–2898.
Spanjer, A. 2009. Regulatory Intervention or Dynamic European Gas Market—Neoclassical Economics or Transaction Cost Economics. *Energy Policy.* 37: 3250–3258.
Steinmeier, F. W. 2007. Verflechtung und Integration. *Internationale Politik.* March 2007: 6–11.
Stern, J. 1998. *Competition and Liberalization in European Gas Markets: A Diversity of Models.* London.
Treisman, D. 2007. Putin's Silovarchs. *Orbis* 51(1): 141–153.
Vahtra, P. 2005. Russian Investments in the CIS—Scope, Motivations and Leverage. *Electronic Publications of Pan-European Institute* 9/2005. Available at http://www.tukkk.fi/pei/verkkojulkaisut/Vahtra_92005.pdf (accessed November 0, 2007).
van Hoorn, V. 2009. "Unbundling," "Reciprocity" and the European Internal Energy Market: WTO Consistency and Broader Implications for Europe. *European Environmental law Review.* 18(1): 51–76.
Wälde, T. W. 1996. International Investment under the 1994 Energy Charter Treaty. In *The Energy Charter Treaty. An East-West Gateway for Investment & Trade.* Ed. T. W. Wälde. London u.a: 251–316.
Westphal, K. 2003. Russische Konzerne im postsowjetischen Raum: Transnationalisierungsprozesse zwischen (Re-)Integration und Expansion. In *Rußland und der postsowjetische Raum.* Ed O. Aleksandrova, R. Götz, and U. Halbach. Baden-Baden: 122–146.
Westphal, K. 2005. The EU-Russian Relationship and the Energy Factor: A European View. In *A Focus on EU-Russian Relations.* Ed. K. Westphal. M: 1–33.
Westphal, K. 2008. Germany and the EU-Russia Energy Dialogue. In *The EU-Russian Energy Dialogue. Europe's Future Energy Security.* Ed. P. Aalto. Aldershot u. a: 93–118.
Whist, B. S. 2009. Nord Stream—A Solution or Challenge for the EU? In *EU-Russia Gas Connection: Pipes, Politics and Problems.* Ed. K. Liuhto. Publications of Pan-European Institute 8/2009. Turku School of Economics. Turku: 166–203.
Wybrew-Bond I. 1999. Setting the Scene. In *Gas to Europe. The Strategies of Four Major Suppliers.* Ed. R. Mabro. and B. L. Wybrew. Oxford University Press: 5–32.
Zudin, A. I. 2006. Gosudarstvo i biznes v Rossii: ėvoljucija modeli vzaimootnošenij (Staat und Wirtschaft). In *Russland: Evolution von Modellen ihrer wechselseitigen Beziehungen. Neprikosnovennyj Zapas* 6: 200–212.
Zyplakov, S. 1998. Vzaimoponimanie partnerov—zalog investicij. In *Neftegazovaja Vertikal.* March 3, 1998.

Chapter Four

EU Emissions Trading: Achievements and Challenges

Jørgen Wettestad

The European Union Emissions Trading Scheme (EU ETS) is based on an EU Directive that was adopted in 2003 and started functioning in 2005 (Skjærseth and Wettestad 2008).[1] It caps industrial emissions and allows trade of emission rights (hereafter: "allowances").[2] EU officials refer to the ETS as both the "cornerstone" and the "flagship" of EU climate policy.[3] As it represents something completely new for the EU, analysts have called the ETS the "new grand experiment" (Kruger and Pizer 2004).

The ETS has now been functioning for five years. To what extent is a big celebration warranted? According to EU environment commissioner Stavros Dimas, "the EU has a well-functioning trading system, with a robust cap, a clear price signal and a liquid market, which is helping us to cut emissions cost-effectively" (EurActiv 2009b). Point Carbon reports a relatively thriving market, apparently only moderately affected by the current financial crisis, and see the ETS as a substantial driver for emissions reductions (Point Carbon 2009a). However, some highly critical reports can certainly be noted. For instance, climate-policy analyst Dieter Helm has claimed that the EU has "landed itself with a complex and relatively inefficient tradable permits system" (Helm 2009, 11). Furthermore, the British environmental organization Sandbag has warned that the ETS at present is "a blunt tool" (Sandbag 2009).

This chapter seeks to take stock of the main achievements so far, in terms of institution building and ultimate effects on corporate practices. As further elaborated in the section "Achievements So Far: Mostly Mixed?" there are both strengths and weaknesses to be noted. In the section "Explaining Mixed Achievements: 'Grand Experiment'—And Grand Uncertainty?" some key explanations are discussed, organized according to the main actors and institutions involved: nonstate actors (industry and environmental organizations), Member States, EU institutions, and global actors and institutions. This leads up to an analysis in the section "A More Optimal ETS? Changes for the 2013–2020 Phase" of the considerable changes in the ETS for the post-2012 phase that were adopted in December 2008. The concluding section, "Conclusion: Beware of Hasty and Bombastic Judgements," sums up the main findings and discusses some key uncertainties ahead for this intriguing and important political experiment. As I think the literature on international regime effectiveness can provide useful analytical tools and insights (see, for example, Miles et al. 2002; Young and Levy eds. 1999), this chapter should also be seen as a first and probing effort to draw upon some of these insights and apply them to the study of ETS achievements.

The first ETS Directive was adopted in mid-2003 (Directive 2003/87). It established a three-year pilot phase (2005–2007) to precede the main commitment period of the Kyoto Protocol (2008–2012). It covers around 50 percent of EU GHG emissions, and some 10,000 installations are included in the system. The ETS was initially established as a system in which Member States would have considerable power and flexibility, so the initial ETS is generally characterized as a decentralized system. Key decisions about the amount (the "cap") and allocation of allowances were in the hands of the Member States, who drew up National Allocation Plans (NAPs). The overall cap on emissions then became the aggregate of national caps. As we shall see, the European Commission (hereafter: the Commission) was a core actor in the establishment of the system, but was allocated more of a backseat watchdog role in the subsequent national allocation processes and first phase of implementation. Allowances were mainly handed out free of charge,[4] and the system was rather narrow in scope. It targeted first and foremost the power sector and some selected energy-intensive industries (such as refineries, cement, steel, and pulp and paper), with an initial regulatory focus on CO_2 emissions. Although power producers and consumers were differently positioned in the energy systems and national economies, the 2003 Directive provided no signals to Member States about distributing allowances differently between sectors. As to the links between the ETS and global climate institutions, a specific Linking Directive was adopted in 2004.[5] A central element in this later Directive was the opening up for the possibility to import credits from third countries through the Kyoto Protocol flexible mechanism, Clean Development Mechanism (CDM) credits from 2005, and Joint Implementation (JI) credits from 2008.

The link was initially based on a loose "less external credits than domestic abatement" rule, but was tightened in 2006.
How then has this system worked so far?

Achievements So Far: Mostly Mixed?

As discussed and clarified by the Norwegian regime theory scholar Arild Underdal (see, for example, Underdal 2002), there are at least two principal dimensions in assessing the effectiveness of international collaborative efforts and policy instruments:

- *"The distance to the collectfive optimum"*: the contribution that the institution/instrument makes to solving the problem at hand. As this optimum is extremely hard to pinpoint, a simple proxy can be the attainment of official goals.
- *"The relative improvement,"*: pertaining to the extent to which the institution/instrument has improved matters compared to a situation with no collaborative effort at all.

It would seem that how we assess the results of the ETS depends at least in part on which of these rather different (and certainly both analytically challenging) assessment lenses we emphasize. Furthermore, it should be noted that the ETS is the first large-scale, multinational system of its kind in the world. No wonder that it has been hailed as the "new grand experiment." Not many years have passed, and the implementation of this unprecedented, complex transnational system is in many ways still in its infancy. Here we might recall that, according to conventional wisdom in implementation theory, in order to fully assess the implementation success of policies, considerable time should have passed—eight to ten years or so (see, for example, Cerych and Sabatier 1986, 6). Let us first sum up some elements of the ETS that have been seen as quite successful, before turning to some important criticisms.

Important Institution Building—And "Cognitive" Effects?

As noted and claimed by several scholars, in terms of fundamental institution building, the ETS has made considerable progress (see Asselt 2009, for a good summary).[6]

First, an unprecedented transnational marketplace has been established. EU emissions trading started officially on January 1, 2005. As of winter 2010, and even after the worldwide financial crisis really started to bite, allowance trading in the EU has clearly taken hold. In 2008, the EU ETS accounted for two-thirds of total global carbon market volume and three-quarters of the value (Point Carbon 2009a, 3, 5). As to allowance prices, as further discussed below, some volatility has indeed been experienced. But in recent years, allowances for phase two of the ETS have stayed within a band between 10 euros and 20 euros.[7]

Second, the infrastructure necessary for a properly functioning market has been established, including the assignment of competent authorities, national registries and the Community Independent Transaction Log (CITL). Most registries were operating in 2007, but faced scheduled and unscheduled downtime (EEA 2008,10). Reporting systems were established, and the reporting practices of the Member States have been improving steadily (EEA 2008). Some governments have also started gaining experience with auctioning allowances (Asselt 2009, 38).

Third, related to these ETS institutional achievements but certainly a different, "cognitive," type of achievement, it has been argued the perceptions and mindsets of corporate leaders as to the climate-change issue have started to change. In an interesting interview in June 2009, chief ETS architect and Commission official Jos Delbeke stated that the most successful element of the ETS is the way it has "forced company boardroom activity to consider climate change...Attitudes toward CO_2 and the climate have changed since there has been a price on carbon" (Point Carbon 2009b). In a somewhat similar vein, analyst Frank Convery has stated that "carbon emissions trading in Europe has finally lifted environment from the boiler room to the boardroom, and from ministries of environment to ministries of finance. For chief executives of many corporations, the environment has become an omnipresent, if not always welcome, guest at their strategic tables" (Convery 2009,121). Furthermore, according to reports from the Carbon Disclosure Project, governance of climate change at board level has increased over time (Carbon Disclosure Project 2009, 11).

...But Also Institutional Weaknesses and Limited Behavioral Bite?[8]

This section first sums up and discusses some main criticisms of the ETS, related to allocations and price fluctuations; some "internal anomalies" (windfall profits); and some possible "external anomalies" ("carbon leakage"). The extent of behavioral bite so far is then discussed, with regard to effects on abatement and shifts in technology utilization and/or innovation attributable to the ETS.

Generous Allocations and Price Fluctuations: Already in 2004/2005, preliminary assessments of the first National Allocation Plans (NAPs) indicated very moderate levels of ambition on the part of Member-State governments (see Ecofys 2004; Zetterberg et al. 2004).[9] Nevertheless, allowances prices climbed to a surprisingly high level throughout 2005, peaking around 30 euros in April 2006. But suspicions of generous governmental handouts of allowances were further confirmed when the first verified emissions data were published in May 2006, showing that 4 percent more allowances had been handed out than actual emissions. This led to an immediate halving of the allowance price and a subsequent further drop, to almost zero. Trading actors saw the pilot phase of the ETS as clearly over-supplied; as there was no possibility to bank allowances for use in later phases, prices plummeted.

Although Member States in 2006 started out the allocation of allowances for phase two of the ETS (2008–2012) in the same generous manner, as further described in the section "Explaining Mixed Achievements: "Grand Experiment"—And Grand Uncertainty?" the Commission acted tougher as a watchdog and managed to turn a prospective 5 percent surplus to an anticipated 5 percent deficit (Carbon Trust 2007, 6). However, not least due to the global economic recession, updated estimates indicate that phase two will be some 300 million tons long (i.e. more emissions than allowances), not short (e.g. Carbon Trust 2009, 02). As surplus allowances from the second phase are bankable for use in phase three (2013–2020), a phase two surplus has the potential to dampen phase three allowance prices and incentive effects. As of May 2010, ETS allowances are traded for around 16 euros.

Internal Anomalies: Windfall Profits: The dominant initial method of allocating allowances, by handing them out for free, led to more than just over-generous allocations. It has also had the effect of giving power producers considerable "windfall profits." Energy-intensive industries first warned that power producers might reap huge windfall profits in 2004 (Wettestad 2009b). These profits would emanate from the fact that electricity prices would increase related to the introduction of the ETS. Power producers would then gain huge profits, as they received allowances for free and would have no initial expenses due to the introduction of emissions trading.

From late 2005 on, these warnings became increasingly substantiated. For instance, a British 2006 report indicated a yearly profit increase of at least GBP 800 million for six large United Kingdom (UK) electricity generators related to the introduction of the ETS. Subsequently, several studies substantiated the reaping of considerable windfall profits (see e.g. Sijm et al. 2006). In a 2008 report, Point Carbon estimated ETS phase two windfall profits at between 23 euros billion and 71 billion in five central ETS countries (Point Carbon 2008).[10] Over time, it has also become increasingly clear that generous and continued handing out of free allowances means windfall profits among energy-intensive industries as well, and possibly also airlines from 2012 on (see ENDS Europe 2009b; 2009c, Sandbag 2010).

External anomalies: carbon leakage?: "Carbon leakage" basically refers to the process whereby a carbon-producing firm in Europe reduces output which is then replaced by a producer operating from a noncarbon-constrained jurisdiction (see Convery 2009, 127).[11] Early studies of the ETS and carbon leakage possibilities, focused on the UK, indicated that only a few industries were at any serious risk (Carbon Trust 2004). Of the five sectors studied (electricity, cement, paper, steel, and aluminum), except for steel, global concerns would kick in only in a long-term scenario with considerably higher allowance prices (ibid.).

Political attention to this possible external anomaly increased in the EU from 2006 on. The issue was given considerable attention in both the High Level Group on Competitiveness, Energy and the Environment, and in the European Climate Change Programme's ETS review stakeholder meetings in 2007 (Wettestad 2009b). But consultant and research reports have consistently presented a far more sober and less alarmist picture of this phenomenon than the industries themselves (which is of course not that surprising) (e.g., European Commission, 2006). One of the most recent reports is a German Marshall Fund study published in 2009 (Grubb et al. 2009). A central conclusion is here that "for most manufacturing sectors, cost differentials due to labor and other inputs far outweigh those induced by international differences in the cost of carbon" (p. 4; see also Wråke 2009, 26).

Low effects on company practices?: But what about the real "proof of the pudding"—the actual effects on companies' abatement efforts, and how they utilize and invest in greener technologies? Is today's situation of relatively floundering market activity bringing about more abatement, new technologies and environmental improvement, which remain the ultimate goals of the ETS venture? Given the institutional weaknesses indicated above, and the limited time that has elapsed, expectations should be moderate in terms of finding significant effects on company practices.

It is important to emphasize that our knowledge is so far quite limited, although some scattered indications and data are available. Let us start with some survey data. In the Point Carbon annual surveys, the number of respondents stating that "the EU ETS has already caused emissions reductions in my company" has remained quite stable, with around 45 percent supporting this statement in 2007, 2008, and 2009. Around 30 percent reported no ETS-related reductions in 2008 and 2009 (Point Carbon 2009a, 8). A German survey, combining German company respondents and international experts, comes up with more modest results (KFW/ZEW 2009). Among the conclusions we may note: "while the majority of firms have implemented CO_2 reduction measures, price signals for CO_2 seem to have had only minor influence on investment strategies so far. Only 6 percent indicated that the reduction of CO_2 has been the main reason for the realization of a measure" (ibid., 56, 57).

Denny Ellerman and Barbara Buchner have analyzed 2005 and 2006 emissions data that the EU Member States reported to the Community Independent Transaction Log (Ellerman and Buchner 2007; 2008). Does the reported figure of 4 percent lower emissions than allocated allowances mean simple "over-allocation"—or can this be interpreted as a sign that real abatement has taken place, hence providing support to the more optimistic Point Carbon survey data? After carrying out a counterfactual analysis, attempting to take into account the development of such control factors as economic growth, carbon intensity and energy prices, they tentatively conclude that the ETS *has* led to some modest reductions, between 50 and 100 million tons in each of these years (Ellerman and Buchner 2008, 286). Total ETS emissions in 2006 were slightly over 2 billion tons of CO_2. With regard to the sectoral picture, analysts agree that most effects have taken place among power producers (e.g. Grubb et al., 2009).

Kettner et al. (2008) have carried out a complementary analysis of the CITL data and the extent to which sectors and countries have been "short" (with more emissions than allowances) or "long" (the opposite). On the whole, they question the ETS abatement effect: "Given the rather low carbon prices, it is also extremely unlikely that industries with a heavy CO_2 cost component, such as cement and lime, have reduced their production levels because of the stringency of allowances." But in a few installations, the option for a fuel shift may have been used (Kettner et al. 2008, 59).

However, that behavioral effects so far have been moderate does not necessarily mean that there has been no effect on corporate strategies and investment plans (note the "cognitive effects" mentioned above), so that more and deeper behavioral effects may be seen in the years ahead. For instance the study conducted by Martin Cames on ETS effects in the German electricity industry concludes that expected carbon prices *are* taken into consideration in the companies' investment decisions and "play an important role when it comes to the question of which technology or fuel should be applied." Clean coal and particularly, carbon capture and storage (CCS) are the most relevant technologies (Cames 2008; 174-175). In December 2009, the consultancy firm New Energy Finance published a survey covering 13 large EU power companies.[12] All these companies responded that they factored a carbon price into their investment decisions. However, the consultancy firm noted that "the carbon price (current and projected) is not sufficient *in isolation* to justify an immediate wholesale shift to lower CO_2 emitting technologies" (New Energy Finance 2009, emphasis added).

The reported increasing effect on investment decisions is certainly an interesting element. However, there is a clear need for further counterfactual analyses here. For instance, CCS policy has experienced a significant development of its own (see, for example, Claes and Frisvold 2009), which makes it more difficult to single out and measure the specific ETS policy signals.

Summing Up: Mixed Performance So Far

Reports like those recently published by Sandbag (2009) and Helm (2009) are important reminders that the ETS design has so far been clearly sub-optimal. Allowance allocations have been generous, resulting in a surplus that again has led to volatile and, over time, seriously decreasing allowance prices in the pilot phase. More scarcity has been created in the current second phase, but considerable uncertainty remains. The handing out of allowances for free has meant significant windfall profits for power producers, and eventually also other industries. Lack of similar regulation of industries elsewhere in the world has led to unrest in EU industries about carbon leakage. Thus it is hardly surprising to find that the available evidence, although limited, indicates that fluctuations and reductions in EU emissions can only to a very limited extent be attributed to the ETS. However, all actors interested in the ETS should bear in mind that its overall score in terms of "relative improvement" is most likely better—although acknowledging also here the substantial analytical challenges involved in carrying out a satisfactory counterfactual assessment. After the "grand failure" of the 1990s to adopt an effective, EU-wide climate-policy instrument—a carbon tax (see, for example, Skjærseth 1994; Wettestad 2001)—the EU has now succeeded in putting into place a cornerstone climate-policy instrument. Important institution building has taken place, both at the EU level and in all its Member States. Market activity has become quite substantial, also in a global perspective, and the ETS seems to have survived the financial crisis fairly well. It can be argued that the ETS has been an important factor in making corporate leaders more aware of the climate change issue and to some extent also more positive to climate-policy regulation and making new, "greener" investments.

Furthermore, as will be further substantiated in the section "A More Optimal ETS? Changes for the 2013–2020 Phase," the ETS has also developed and improved considerably over time. Not least, significant further harmonization of the ETS post-2012 means that the EU will, at least from that point in time, have a quite well-developed common policy in this area. This gives greater support to claims that the ETS is now really starting to influence corporate investment decisions. Although it may be more daring to declare grand successes or failures, for the overall achievement score it is tempting to echo Cerych and Sabatier's title from 1986: "great expectations and mixed performance."

Explaining Mixed Achievements: "Grand Experiment"—And Grand Uncertainty?

In the following, I identify and discuss some key explanatory factors. For analytical purposes, these are organized according to main actors and institutions, at various societal levels. The resultant perspectives are fundamentally grounded in and related to important on-going debates about the main and "real" driving forces in EU policy-making.[13] However, a debate about the relative explanatory power of these perspectives is not the main point in this paper. The perspectives are here used simply as complementary heuristic lenses, helping to organize and make sense of a complex web of relevant evidence.

Nonstate Actors: Cautious Industry; Skeptical Greens

Industry: a Cautious and Differing Embracement: How did industry feel about emissions trading back in 1997/1998, when the idea of an ETS was taking shape? A few industrial front-runners, mainly big oil companies such as BP and Shell, saw this almost untried instrument as promising and set about establishing internal pilot emissions trading schemes (see Victor and House 2006). Overall, the mood can be characterized as cautiously positive.[14] Industry wanted to avoid the detested carbon tax option, but would also ideally have preferred softer voluntary agreements.

Already from 1999/2000, it became apparent that there were also clear sectoral differences within EU industry with regard to attitudes toward the emissions trading instrument. Power producers were quite open-minded and curious, and carried out several trading simulation exercises.[15] Energy-intensive industries, on the other hand, held far more mixed and generally cautious positions. They had difficulty seeing what was in it for them with this instrument. Most skeptical was the chemicals industry—which was, in the end, also left out of the system. However, EU industries were quite united in favoring getting allowances for free, and having a basically flexible and not overly harmonized system.

In the subsequent processes of producing the initial National Allocation Plans in 2004 (for the ETS pilot phase, 2005–2007), industrial actors tried to cope with considerable uncertainty about the *practical* workings of this new instrument by lobbying for a maximum amount of allowances. This is a classic example of perfectly understandable individual rationality leading to collective sub-optimal outcomes. In the NAP I process, there is evidence from both the UK and Germany about the success of industry in this regard. Member States needed a cooperative industry, and in a situation with high uncertainty, it was probably tempting to simply let industry have its way.

Political decision makers were more successful in withstanding industry pressure in NAP II (in distributing allowances for the 2008–12 phase). But industry has still managed to secure so much in terms of allowances that they may need to conduct very little actual abatement to comply with the caps set for this phase. In fact, due also to the financial crisis and lowered production (and hence less emissions), industry might even be able to bank (i.e., save) a considerable portion of allowances for the post-2012 phase, thereby seriously challenging the dynamic effect of the ETS also in this phase.

This said, there are still certain sectoral differences within this general picture. Generally, the power sector has experienced stricter allocations in phase two of the ETS, as is particularly clear in the case of the UK (*ENDS Daily* 2006). This unequal treatment seems to have been silently accepted by the power sector (and institutionalized in the revised ETS, as further described in the section "Conclusion: Beware of Hasty and Bombastic Judgements"). A main reason for this acceptance is probably the above-mentioned windfall profits earned by the power producers. Moreover, this difference in strictness of sectoral allocations can contribute to explain why most behavioral change and abatement seem to have taken place within this sector.

ENGOS: Skeptics Struggling to Embrace Trading: The Environmental Non-Governmental Organizations (ENGOs) initially opposed emissions trading for both substantive and normative reasons, arguing that trading pollution was ineffective as well as morally questionable. This resistance was gradually overcome by the belief that a cap-and-trade system in Europe, if appropriately designed, could guarantee a positive environmental outcome. Then, by around 2000, ENGOs had become more positive to the idea of emissions trading in Europe.[16] This can probably be explained by these actors starting to recognize the potential of this complex instrument.

Still, along the way, ENGOs have continued to function as an external critical watchdog—in the process, strengthening the hand of those inside actors pushing for the most environmental ambitious options, such as the European Parliament. With regard to focused issues, ENGOs have given particular attention to the link between the ETS and the Kyoto Protocol mechanisms and the possible "flooding" of the ETS with CDM credits—and the related detrimental effects for the carbon price and incentives for internal EU abatement (see Open Europe 2007; Sandbag 2009; WWF 2006).

However, the intrinsically complex and technical nature of emissions trading as an instrument is poorly suited to the spectacular stunts often favored by ENGOs (Pinkse and Kolk 2009; Voss 2007). Although ENGOs have become much more positive to emissions trading over time, it seems fair to say that they have struggled in seeking to learn to *love* the instrument. A more systematic comparison with other issue areas may reveal that ENGOs have been far more effective pushers for a further greening of policies in other issue areas than emissions trading. Recognizing this rather "tame watchdog" role helps us make sense of the moderate ETS achievements so far, although it is far from being among the most important factors.

Member States: Securing Control

The previous section "Achievements So Far: Mostly Mixed?" emphasized the new and untried character of the emissions trading instrument and the related cautiousness of nonstate actors. Very much the same goes for the EU Member States. When the Commission started to prepare the ground for an EU emissions trading system in 1998, only two Member States had begun to consider establishing domestic trading systems: Denmark and the UK. The latter, in several ways a key EU country, was generally open to market-based and flexible policy instruments in the 1990s. The UK was hence not opposed to the development of an EU-wide trading system, but it favored a flexible and decentralized ETS, in order to ensure compatibility with its domestic system.

But other important EU countries embraced trading much more reluctantly. Turning first to Germany, due to the size of its economy and the magnitude of the related emissions, the country was destined to be one of the really key ones in the ETS. Up to 1998/1999, climate policy in Germany mixed traditional regulation with voluntary agreements and eco-taxes, and there was no prior regulatory emphasis on flexibility instruments (Wurzel 2008, 13). Voluntary agreements sat well with German industry, which therefore saw little need to introduce new, different instruments. In the decision-making process that led up to the initial ET Directive, Germany emphasized exemptions and national flexibility.

In the first round of producing National Allocation Plans, assessments of ambitiousness (in aiming for emissions reductions) gave the German NAP a very average score.[17] When the first verified ETS emissions figures were put on the table in 2006, Germany's emissions proved to be 4.2 percent below its cap (hence possible "over-allocation"). Germany's uneasy relationship with the ETS was further witnessed in the second round of producing NAPs. In something which has been described as a catalytic event in the history of the ETS (see Carbon Trust 2007), in November 2006 the Commission cut the proposed German NAP by 7 percent. After some weeks when "Brussels stood still," Germany reluctantly accepted the Commission's cut.

Poland can certainly be added to the list of important EU countries that have embraced the ETS only quite cautiously. It was greatly delayed in producing an initial NAP, with both the government and observers blaming limited administrative capacity. But Poland's will to adopt ambitious ETS policies can also be questioned. As in several other Central and Eastern European Countries (CEECs), the Polish energy system is centered on coal power. A key priority for Poland has hence been to protect the future of this industry—and that includes securing a sufficient number of allowances to this industry. Poland has quarreled with the Commission over its suggested emission caps in both the first and second round of producing NAPs. In the second round in 2006, Poland's NAP was among those cut most severely by the Commission—by a full 27 percent! This brief overview has shown that central EU Member States have embraced emissions trading only cautiously, giving priority to national control over environmental ambitiousness, and, related to this, a decentralized and flexible ETS design. These priorities can shed considerable light on the sub-optimal working of the ETS so far.

EU Institutions: Only a Tiny Crew Manning the Flagship?

As further analyzed in Skjærseth and Wettestad (2008), from 1998 on, there was only a small group of dedicated emissions trading entrepreneurs in the Directorate-General for Environment (DG ENV). Their main professional background was economics. A key figure was Jos Delbeke, who had been closely involved in the futile efforts to get a carbon tax adopted, and was now definitely ready to work on something else that could be more successful. The task facing DG ENV was truly formidable. So it is highly understandable that information dissemination and knowledge improvement became a key strategy. This involved both getting reports from external consultants such as the British FIELD institute and the US Center for Clean Air Policy, and efforts to develop a trading-friendly "epistemic community" of nonstate actors and Member States through stakeholder meetings. The DG ENV entrepreneurs concluded that a centrally governed ETS would be the environmentally optimal design, but realized early on that this idea was at odds with the sentiments of important Member States and industries.

Within the Commission, in the process of preparing the initial ET (Emissions Trading) Directive proposal in 2001, DG ENV successfully fought back efforts from other DGs such as Enterprise to weaken the proposal further. In the subsequent EU processes, the clear impression is that the ETS remained something of a DG Environment "baby," and perhaps even more than that: a "Delbeke drive." Indeed, it is quite striking that the ETS became an EU cornerstone based on a very modest administrative foundation; *a flagship steered by a tiny (but dedicated) crew.*

But what about the European Parliament—could not the Parliament and particularly its comparatively large and influential Environment Committee (see for exampleWeale et al. 2000) have helped steer the ETS more smoothly through these rough waters? Here it should be kept in mind that the Parliament has been characterized as suffering from a "technological deficit" (e.g. Wurzel 2002, 71), and hence struggled in really getting a grip on the complex case of emissions trading. Among other things, this manifested itself in a problem of focusing on the truly key issues. Furthermore, in the decision-making process, the Parliament stood forward as the key proponent of a rather centrally governed ETS, but it failed to move the outcome very much in this direction. So, somewhat similar to the case of ENGOs, an actor that has otherwise often managed to push EU policies in greener directions achieved little in the case of the ETS.

From 2004 on, one of the central ETS tasks for the Commission was to act as a NAP watchdog.[18] With the substantial leeway granted to the Member States by the directive, this watchdog job proved to be a tall order indeed. As pointed out by Commission official Peter Vis, "the Commission's job was a difficult one.... Several plans were submitted to the Commission without elements that were nevertheless essential for the Commission's assessment... The assessment process of all national allocation plans [in the pilot phase] took 15 months in total, in contrast to the three months foreseen in the Directive" (Vis 2006, 202, 203).

But, particularly in the second NAP process, the Commission made important contributions to achieving a more environmentally ambitious outcome. Overall, the Commission managed to turn a proposed aggregate emissions *increase* of 5 percent from 2005 levels into a 5 percent *decrease* (Carbon Trust 2007, 6). One strength for the Commission in this work has been a substantial continuity of key personnel, with Jos Delbeke as the "ETS captain" on board all the way.

Global Actors and Institutions: Not Securing Comparable Efforts to the EU?

Turning first to the Kyoto Protocol itself, the adoption of this protocol and not least the flexibility mechanisms in December 1997 served as an important stimulant for the subsequent EU turn-about and development of an ETS. A very important "catalytic" event happened in May 2001: The USA, under President George W. Bush, decided to withdraw from the Kyoto Protocol. The immediate and short-term effect of this was in fact positive for the EU actors seeking to get an ETS established. As noted by Brussels insiders, "the huge luck the Commission had was Bush's withdrawal...It united the EU in an extraordinary way." On the other hand, as a more enduring, long-term cognitive effect, the lack of comparable climate-policy action in the United States—the key economic competitor to the EU—has acted to impede EU efforts. The US climate-policy impasse has functioned as a legitimating concern for actors within industry, Member States and EU institutions warning of the detrimental effects of a too strong and front-running EU system that imposes tougher carbon constraints than competitors.

From 2004 on and with the development of NAPs, institutional interaction with the Kyoto Protocol's flexibility mechanisms, in particular the Clean Development Mechanism (CDM), became more of a reality. The entry into force of the Kyoto Protocol in February 2005 further bolstered the linkage between the ETS and the protocol and its mechanisms. However, in the pilot phase, this link was of scant practical relevance. Very few states announced any intentions to use such external credits, and the subsequent abundance of ETS allowances and the delayed formal link between the EU and global registries made this aspect rather irrelevant.

It was first and foremost in connection with the processes of producing the NAPs for the second phase of the ETS (the 2008–2012 phase) that this issue became more important. Generally, Member States announced intentions to utilize substantial amounts of external credits. This led ENGOs and independent analysts to fire several warning shots about the possible damaging effects of an overly liberal inflow of external credits, with a related weakening of carbon prices and abatement incentive effects (see, for example,, Open Europe 2007; WWF 2006). To some extent, the Commission paid heed to these warnings. An *ad hoc* cap was introduced in the fall of 2006, and the Commission managed to cut the planned use of CDM and JI of key Member States considerably.[19] In total, the EU ETS installations are allowed to use 1400 Mt of CDM/JI credits for compliance in the 2008–2012 period.[20]

Although it is still quite early days in the Kyoto Protocol commitment phase, reported figures show that the external link (which finally became real and formal in October 2008) has not mattered that much in practice. Data from 2008 show that companies used around 6 percent of the total (European Commission 2009a). So there has certainly been no "external flooding of the ETS," and the specific links to the global flexibility mechanisms shed almost no light on the moderate results achieved so far.

A More Optimal ETS? Changes for the 2013–2020 Phase

The processes of revising the ETS for the period 2013–2020, which took place mainly in 2007 and 2008, must then be seen against the backdrop of this in many ways malfunctioning ETS up to that point. As described above, the "old ETS" had been decentralized, based on the handing out of free allowances, and with an initial loose link to the global CDM/JI mechanisms, with an ad hoc cap introduced in 2006.

Compared to this, the new ETS from 2013 onward, adopted by the European Council in December 2008, will be governed quite differently, in a far more centralized way (see Directive 2009/29).[21] There will be a common and tighter ETS cap, based on the ETS' contribution to achieving the overall ambition of a 20 percent cut in GHG emissions by 2020.

The cap is so far to achieve a 21 percent cut of ETS emissions by 2020, compared to a 2005 baseline. Further allocation specifications mean that the considerable flexibility enjoyed by Member States under the old ETS will disappear almost completely in the new ETS. Furthermore, much more allowances will be auctioned.

Most of the power sector's allowances will be auctioned, while initially only around 20 percent of the allowances of energy-intensive industries (but increasing over time). Industries identified as particularly vulnerable to global competition and hence "carbon leakage" will be guaranteed free allowances all the way to 2020. A preliminary list produced by national experts and presented by the Commission in September 2009 identifies 164 sectors deemed to be at risk as to carbon leakage, representing 77 percent of the total emissions of manufacturing industries under the ETS (EurActiv 2009c; European Commission, 2009b). With regard to external links to the Kyoto flexibility mechanisms, the *ad hoc* cap has now been strengthened and written into the formal ETS constitution. In addition, the sectoral scope has been broadened somewhat in terms of sectors and gases, and aviation will come into the ETS already from 2012.[22]

Although these changes mean that the Member States will lose earlier powers, it does not mean that all these powers are automatically transferred to the Commission. Some of these powers will be taken over by the Member States as a collective, as for instance the important, possible decision to tighten the ETS cap will ultimately have to be adopted by the Council and the Parliament. But the functions of the Commission as the general watchdog and overseer of the implementation of the ETS will be strengthened, for instance related to Member-States' use of increasing auctioning revenues. In this connection, it is interesting to note that the Commission sought also to centralize the auctioning process by establishing a single auctioning platform. But a coalition of key ETS Member States (i.e. Germany, Poland, Spain, and the UK) resisted this and the Commission backed down in the spring of 2010 (e.g. EurActiv 2010).

In order to understand these significant changes, in the same manner as the discussion carried out in the section "Explaining Mixed Achievements: "Grand Experiment"—And Grand Uncertainty?" a multilevel framework is useful. First, closer scrutiny reveals a significant shift in Member-State positions on what constitutes the best design of the ETS, and a related request for reform. As indicated, a likely central background factor is unsatisfactory experiences with the old ETS.

Second, putting on "EU-level" lenses, as has been indicated, the ideas of a centralized and harmonized ETS based on auctioning of allowances were initially launched and favored by both the Commission and the Parliament (and supported by ENGOs). Due to, among other things, the increased saliency of the climate-change issue in the EU from 2005 on, these positions could be put forward more forcefully in 2007 and 2008. In addition, the EU institutions, as arenas for initiating and negotiating the reform, changed significantly and affected the ETS outcome somewhat. As the ETS reform was a key element in a broader policy package initially launched by the Commission in January 2008, the reform was linked to new mandatory targets, EU energy policy and a package of binding climate instruments; among other things adding further weight to the Commission's quest for a more harmonized and effective design.

Third, putting on "international regime" lenses provides only limited additional explanatory value. The reform came not as a response to changes in the international climate regime, but partly as an effort to influence the international climate negotiations. In a way, the reform was to some extent a response to a *lack* of international change. The international regime context is thus relevant for understanding the outcomes, but in a different way than may be readily anticipated.

Conclusion: Beware of Hasty and Bombastic Judgments

EU emissions trading has celebrated its fifth birthday: has it been a success or failure so far? The verdict here depends partly upon the assessment lenses chosen: the distance travelled toward a truly "optimal" design—or the more counterfactual "relative improvement" made. When analysts such as the Carbon Trust call the global flexibility mechanisms, with the EU ETS as the cornerstone, a "remarkable success," they are probably implicitly adopting a "relative improvement" perspective (Carbon Trust 2009, 6). Without these mechanisms, with the ETS as the clear front-runner, the global political and institutional responses to climate change would probably have been quite meager indeed. But that does still not mean that the ETS has made a significant difference with regard to industrial practices so far.

Further, taking both assessment perspectives into consideration, ETS achievements stand out as mixed. There have been several institutional flaws, leading to among other things overgenerous allocations and windfall profits for power producers. The carbon price has been volatile, falling close to zero in the final half of the pilot phase. The scarce evidence of ultimate effects on company practices and emissions so far indicate quite moderate effects, although an increasing influence on investment decisions seems probable. But it is important to keep in mind that it is certainly early days in terms of expecting significant behavioral effects, and the recent strengthening of the ETS post-2012 will mean a substantially more optimal design for the future.

How then to explain such mixed results so far? Let us first sum up some of the main impediments, organized according to main actors and societal levels.

- Industry has only cautiously embraced the largely untried emissions trading instrument. Energy-intensive industries in particular have been quite lukewarm.
- ENGOs started out as rather fierce critics of the ETS. They have since moderated their stance, but have struggled to embrace this complex, "industry-friendly" and flexible instrument wholeheartedly, and function as a really hard-hitting external watchdog.

- Somewhat similar to industry, Member States have had a cautious attitude toward this new instrument, and have emphasized national control much more than environmental effectiveness. Certain key Member States like Germany have been particularly skeptical toward trading, due to the mismatch with their own preexisting climate-policy instruments.
- Although the entrepreneurial efforts by a dedicated group of DG Environment officials have been formidable, the Commission has struggled to keep abreast, due to the formidable regulatory challenges involved and a rather restricted mandate from the Member States.
- The long period of climate-policy inaction in the United States and a lax global climate regime have strengthened the arguments of those within the EU who resist a strong, ambitious front-running ETS.

The observations above also give some key clues to understanding the background for the achievements that *have* been made after all:

- *Some* key industries have been clear trading supporters and allies to the Commission all the way (the power producers).
- *Some* key Member States have been clear proponents of emissions trading (e.g., the UK).
- The entrepreneurial group in the Commission has been strong, with continuity in key personnel.
- Catalytic events in the global climate regime have helped Commission entrepreneurs at important crossroads—particularly the Bush/US exit from the Kyoto Protocol in 2001, and to some extent also the entry into force of the Protocol in 2005.

What about the prospects ahead? One important possible next step—particularly if and when anything substantial comes out of the negotiations on a new global climate regime, and if there is a related move of the EU from an overall 20 to 30 percent reduction target—would be to further tighten the ETS 2020 cap. The institutional machinery is in place (see Article 28 in Directive 2009/29). In spring 2010 it became increasingly probable that the EU would move to an overall 30 percent reduction target and a related deepening of the ETS cap from 21 percent to 34 percent (Point Carbon 2010). Several well-informed analysts predict an allowance price of around 40 euros as the most probable bet for 2020. This indicates a fundamental belief in real scarcity in the ETS post-2012. But few analysts had managed to foresee the "over-allocation" effects and ETS crisis in the spring of 2006, and there are definitely some uncertainties ahead.

First, there is uncertainty related to the effect of banking within the ETS. How much of the probable second phase surplus of allowances, including CDM surplus, will be carried over to the third phase? We should also note that the more long-term climate-policy success of the ETS is definitely not "controlled" by the ETS alone. There are several interaction effects. In the fall of 2009, increasing attention focused on the possibility of "hot air" surplus allowances in the Kyoto Protocol being carried over post-2012 and contributing to downward pressure also on ETS allowances prices (see, for example, Point Carbon 2009c). Another uncertainty is the interaction with other EU policies like energy efficiency and renewables. It has, for instance, been claimed that if energy efficiency really picks up speed, then there will be little need for an effective ETS in order to deliver the overall 20/30 percent EU emissions-cut targets (see, for example, *ENDS Europe* 2009a). To this, add how the financial crisis and the related drop in emissions have instructively demonstrated that factors totally unrelated to environmental policy affect emissions, the related need for allowances—and ultimately the carbon price and the related abatement incentive effects.[23]

Thus, even if the EU has already succeeded in seriously reducing the gap to the "optimal design" of an ETS from 2013 on, other factors may lead to a situation where the ETS will not manage a similar leap forward in terms of "relative improvement."

Notes

My thanks to Elin Lerum Boasson, Vicki Birchfield, John Duffield, Liv Arntzen Løchen, Stig Schjølset, Jon B.Skjærseth and participants at a workshop held in Atlanta in November 2009 for helpful comments to this draft manuscript. Many thanks to Susan Høivik for language polishing.

1. I.e., Directive 2003/87/EC.
2. Allowances are denominated in metric ton of carbon dioxide equivalent (CO_2 eq.). One ton CO_2 eq. is a unit of measurement reflecting the potency of greenhouse gases (GHGs).
3. See for instance European Commission (2008).
4. In the pilot phase, Member States were allowed to sell up to 5 percent of their allowances. This limit was increased to 10 percent in the 2008–2012 period.

5. I.e. Directive 2004/101/EC.
6. Here I concentrate on the "internal" effects and success of the ETS and do not discuss the possible front-runner inspirational influence the ETS may have had and has on efforts around the globe. For this, see e.g. Wettestad (2009a).
7. For instance, in March 2008, the price was 21 euros. One year later, it had sunk to 11.60 euros. However, by early September 2009, the price had climbed to 15.30 euros.
8. For a broad overview of weaknesses and criticisms of the ETS, see Asselt (2009). The Asselt report discusses among other things scope, cap setting, and allocation methods.
9. Ambitiousness is here understood as the setting of a cap on allowances reasonably below projected needs and hence contributing to overall market scarcity, relatively high and stable carbon prices, and related incentives for abatement.
10. These five countries were Germany, Italy, Poland, Spain and the UK.
11. For summaries of the carbon leakage issue, see EurActiv, January 27, 2009a (summary article) and Asselt, 2009, particularly pp. 62–69.
12. Among the companies included in the survey were E.On, RWE, Centrica, Scottish and Southern, Fortum, and EDF.
13. For a more comprehensive overview of these perspectives and debates, see for instance Skjærseth and Wettestad (2008), chapter two, and Boasson and Wettestad (2010).
14. For instance, the European industrial federation UNICE cautiously supported emissions trading in a 1998 position paper, stressing the need for a "well-designed" and "rigorous" system.
15. These were trading exercises organized by the power producers' federation EURELECTRIC: the GETS I exercise in 1999 and GETS II exercise in 2000. See Skjærseth and Wettestad (2008: 79–80).
16. Zapfel and Vainio (2002).
17. Ibid.
18. As to the concept of institutional interaction, see Oberthur and Gehring (eds., 2006).
19. For instance, both Poland's and Spain's proposed uses of external credits were halved by the Commission.
20. This is equal to about 10 percent of the total allocation for the period.
21. This section is a summary of several related analyses; see Wettestad (2009c) and Skjærseth and Wettestad (2010a and b).
22. The inclusion of aviation took place in a separate decision-making process.
23. Note here that there is also an interesting interaction effect the other way around: The extent to which a low carbon price will provide suboptimal incentives to the development of renewables and enhancing of energy efficiency.

Works Cited

Asselt, H. V. 2009. *Study on the Effectiveness of the EU ETS: The EU ETS in the European Climate Policy Mix: Past Present and Future.* Amsterdam: IVM. Report for the ADAM Project. July 8, 2009.

Boasson, E. L. and J. Wettestad. 2010. *Comparing EU Emissions Trading and Renewables Governance.* Paper Presented at the isa Convention. New Orleans. February 2010.

Cames, M. 2008. *Emissions Trading and Innovation in the German Electricity Industry.* Dissertation. Berlin: Øko-Institut. December 2008.

Carbon Disclosure Project. 2009. *Carbon Disclosure Project 2009.* Global 500 Report. Written for the cdp by Pricewaterhouse Coopers. June 2009.

Carbon Trust. 2004. *The European Emissions Trading Scheme: Implications for Industrial Competitiveness.* London: Carbon Trust.

Carbon Trust. 2007. *EU ETS Phase II Allocation: Implications and Lessons.* London: Carbon Trust. Publication CTC715. May 21, 2007.

Carbon Trust. 2009. *Global Carbon Mechanisms: Emerging Lessons and Implications.* London: Carbon Trust. March, 2009.

Cerych, L. and P. Sabatier. 1986. *Great Expectations and Mixed Performance: The Implementation of Higher Education Reforms in Europe.* Stoke-on-Trent: Trentham.

Claes, D. H. and P. Frisvold. 2009. CCS and the European Union: Magic Bullet or Pure Magic?. chapter 9 In *Caching The Carbon: The Politics and Policy of Carbon Capture and Storage.* Eds. J. Meadowcroft and O. Langhelle. Cheltenham: Edward Elgar. 211–235.

Convery, F. 2009. Reflections: The Emerging Literature on Emissions Trading in Europe. *Review of Environmental Economics and Policy.* 3(1). 2009: 121–137.

Ecofys. 2004. *Analysis of the National Allocation Plans for the EU Emissions Trading Scheme.* Ecofys. August, 2004.

EEA. 2008. *Application of the Emissions Trading Directive by EU Member States: Reporting year 2008.* EEA Technical Report no.13. 2008. Copenhagen: European Environment Agency.

Ellerman, A. D. and B. K. Buchner. 2007. The European Union Emissions Trading Scheme: Origins, Allocation, and Early Results. *Review of Environmental Economics.* 1(1). 2007: 66–87.

Ellerman, A. D. and B. K. Buchner. 2008. Over-Allocation or Abatement? A Preliminary Analysis of the EU ETS Based on the 2005–2006 Emissions Data. *Environmental Resource Economics.* 41. 2008: 267–287.

ENDS Daily. 2006. UK Publishes Second-phase Carbon Trading Plan. August 21, 2006.

ENDS Europe. 2009a. Tension between CO2 Trading and Efficiency Agendas. October 28, 2009.

ENDS Europe. 2009b. Carbon Leakage Plan "Could Generate Huge Profits." November 18, 2009.

ENDS Europe. 2009c. Airlines to Make Profit from EU ETS: UK report. December 4, 2009.
EurActiv. 2009a. *"Carbon Leakage": A Challenge for EU Industry*. January 27, 2009.
EurActiv. 2009b. *EU Defends Cap-and-Trade Scheme as 2008 Data Unveiled*. May 18, 2009.
EurActiv. 2009c. *EU Lists Industries Exempted from Carbon Trading*. September 21, 2009.
EurActiv. 2010. *EU backs down on single ETS auctioning platform*. April 8, 2010.
European Commission. 2006. *EU ETS Review: Report on International Competitiveness*. Report by McKinsey and Ecofys for the European Commission. December.
European Commission. 2008. *Questions and Answers on the Revised EU Emissions Trading System*. Memo/08/796. Brussels. December 17, 2008.
European Commission. 2009a. *Emissions Trading: EU ETS Emissions Fall 3% in 2008*. IP/09/794. Brussels. May 15, 2009.
European Commission. 2009b. *Emissions Trading: Member States Approve List of Sectors Deemed to be Exposed to Carbon Leakage*. Press Release. September 18, 2009.
Grubb, M., T. L. Brewer, M. Sato, R. Heilmayr and D. Fazekas. 2009. *Climate Policy and Industrial Competitiveness: Ten Insights from Europe on the EU Emissions Trading System*. Climate and Energy Paper Series 09. Report for the German Marshall Fund of the United States. Washington, DC.
Helm, D. 2009. *EU Climate-Change Policy: A Critique*. Smith School Working Paper Series. University of Oxford. September 2009.
Kettner, C., A. Koppl, S. P. Schleicher and G. Thenius. 2008. Stringency and Distribution in the EU Emissions Trading Scheme: First Evidence, *Climate Policy* 8. 2008: 41–61.
KFW/ZEW. 2009. *Leaving the Trial Phase Behind: Preferences & Strategies of German Companies under the EU ETS*. Frankfurt/Mannheim: KFW/ZEW.
Kruger, J. and W. A. Pizer. 2004. *The EU Emissions Trading Directive: Opportunities and Potential Pitfalls*. Report, Resources for the Future.
Miles, E. L., A. Underdal, S. Andresen, J. Wettestad, J. B. Skjærseth and E. M. Carlin. 2002. *Environmental Regime Effectiveness: Confronting Theory with Evidence*. Cambridge, MA: MIT Press.
New Energy Finance. 2009. Research Shows that Carbon Prices are Encouraging European Power Companies to build Cleaner Power Stations. Press Release. December 14, 2009.
Oberthur, S. and T. Gehring. 2006. *Institutional Interaction in Global Environmental Governance: Synergy and Conflict among International and EU Policies*. Cambridge, MA: MIT Press.
Open Europe. 2007. *Europe's Dirty S006 5cret: Why the EU Emissions Trading Scheme Isn't Working*. London, August 2007.

Pinkse, J. and A. Kolk. 2009. *International Business and Global Climate Change*. London: Routledge.
Point Carbon. 2008. *EU ETS Phase II: The Potential and Scale of Windfall Profits in the Power Sector*. A Report for wwf by Point Carbon Advisory Services. March 2008.
Point Carbon. 2009a. *Carbon 2009: Emission Trading Coming Home*. Point Carbon. Oslo. March 2009.
Point Carbon. 2009b. *Barcap Says EU ETS Long in Phase Two*. April 15, 2009.
Point Carbon. 2009c. *AAU Banking Will Erode Climate Efforts*. October 28, 2009.
Point Carbon. 2010. *Brussels sees ETS cap deepening to 34%*. April 29, 2010.
Sandbag. 2009. *ETS S.O.S: Why the Flagship "EU Emissions Trading Policy" Needs Rescuing*. London: Sandbag, July, 2009.
Sandbag. 2010. *The Carbon Rich List: The Companies Profiting from the EY Emissions Trading Scheme*. London: Sandbag. February, 2010.
Sijm, J., K. Neuhoff and Y. Chen. 2006. CO2 Pass-through and Windfall Profits in the Power Sector. *Climate Policy*. 6. 2006: 49–72.
Skjærseth, J. B. 1994. The Climate Policy of the EC: Too Hot to Handle? *Journal of Common Market Studies*. 32(1). March: 25–45.
Skjærseth, J. B. and J. Wettestad. 2008. *EU Emissions Trading: Initiation, Decision-making and Implementation*. Aldershot: Ashgate.
Skjærseth, J. B. and J. Wettestad. 2010a. The EU Emissions Trading System Directive Revised. Directive 2009/29/EC. Chapter in S. Oberthur and M. Pallemaerts. The New Climate Policies of the European Union: Internal Legislation and Climate Diplomacy. Brussels: ASP Editions.
Skjærseth, J. B. and J. Wettestad. 2010b. Fixing the EU Emissions Trading System? Understanding the Post-2012 Changes. *Global Environmental Politics*. 4(10).
Underdal, A. 2002. One Question, Two Answers. In E. L. Miles, A. Underdal, S. Andresen, J. Wettestad, J. B. Skjærseth and E. M. Carlin: Environmental Regime Effectiveness: Confronting Theory with Evidence. Cambridge, MA MIT Press: 3–45.
Victor, D. G. and J. C. House. 2006. BP's Emissions Trading System. *Energy Policy*. 34: 2100–2112.
Vis, P. 2006. The First Allocation Round: A Brief History. In *EU Energy Law, Volume IV EU Environmental Law, the EU Greenhouse Gas Emissions Trading Scheme*. Eds. J. Delbeke, O. Hartridge, J. Lefevere, D. Meadows, A. Runge-Metzner, Y. Slingenberg, M. Vainio, P. Vis and P. Zapfel. Brussels: Claeys&Casteels: 187–212.
Voss, J. P. 2007. Innovation Processes in Governance: The Development of "Emissions Trading" as a New Policy Instrument. *Science and Public Policy*. 34(5). June 2007: 329–343.

Weale, A., G. Pridham, M. Cini, D. Konstadakopulos, M. Porter and B. Flynn. 2000. *Environmental Governance in Europe.* Oxford: Oxford University Press.
Wettestad, J. 2001. The Ambiguous Prospects for EU Climate Policy: A Summary of Options. *Energy and Environment.* 12(2/3): 139–167.
Wettestad, J. 2009a. Interaction between EU Carbon Trading and the International Climate Regime: Synergies and Learning. *International Environmental Agreements.* 9: 393–408.
Wettestad, J. 2009b. EU Energy-Intensive Industries and Emission Trading: Losers Becoming Winners? *Environmental Policy and Governance.* 19(5): 309–320.
Wettestad, J. 2009c. *European Climate Policy: Towards Centralised Governance?* Review of Policy Research. 26(3): 311–329.
Wråke, M. 2009. *Emissions Trading: The Ugly Duckling in European Climate Policy?* IVL, Report B1856. Stockholm. July 2009.
WWF. 2006. Use of CDM/JI Project Credits by Participants in Phase II of the EU Emissions Trading Scheme: A WWF Summary of the Ecofys UK report. November 2006.
Wurzel, R. K. W. 2002. *Environmental Policy-Making in Britain, Germany and the European Union.* Manchester: Manchester University Press.
Wurzel, R. K. W.2008. The Politics of Emissions Trading in Britain and Germany. report for the Anglo-German Foundation for the Study of Industrial Society. October 2008.
Young, O. R. and M. A. Levy. 1999. *The Effectiveness of International Environmental Regimes: Causal Connections and Behavioral Mechanisms.* Cambridge, MA: MIT Press.
Zapfel, P. and M. Vainio. 2002. *Pathways to European Greenhouse Gas Emissions Trading History and Misconceptions.* FEEM Note 85. 2002. October 2002.
Zetterberg, L, K. Nilsson, A. S. Kumlin and L. Birgersdotter. 2004. *Analysis of National Allocation Plans for the EU ETS.* IVL. Gothenburg, August 2004.

Chapter Five

EU Renewable Electricity Policy: Mixed Emotions toward Harmonization

Måns Nilsson

The promotion of renewable sources of energy (RES) has, like energy policy overall, traditionally been a Member-State concern in the European Union (EU). At the national level it has a relatively long history: many Member States have supported the introduction of RES through various instruments and measures ever since the 1970s. In those early years, climate change and the environment were not among the primary drivers of policy. Instead, national governments were primarily responding to the global energy crisis and looked for a replacement for oil. In other words, renewable energy policy was primarily a response to concerns over energy supply security. Environmental concerns were slowly rising on the agenda during the 1970s but they remained secondary until the late 1980s, when the growing environmental awareness in society paved the way for green parties and policies across Europe.

Thus, the drivers behind RES policy have shifted, but, in any case, the result has been that a plethora of national governance approaches have flourished. Different Member States have developed different approaches to governing RES and also different technological niches. For instance, when it comes to renewable electricity promotion, Denmark became a forerunner in wind energy with its programs for supporting wind power industry, and is now home to the world's largest wind industry, VESTAS (West-Jutlandish steel technology). Sweden had promoted bioenergy crops in the 1970s and 1980s and implemented a carbon tax on energy production in 1991, which induced an almost full phaseout of fossil fuels in the district heating sector (Nilsson, et al. 2004). Germany established a Feed-In-Law in 1991 which guarantees a price for vendors of renewable electricity which enabled a rapid growth in both wind and solar industries

(Jacobsson and Lauber 2006). Despite Member-State differences in approach, and a relatively inactive European Commission (hereafter: the Commission) (up to recently), the EU as a whole has experienced a strong growth in renewable electricity production, thanks largely to the various support schemes and policy instruments to promote the deployment of renewable electricity, such as wind, solar, and biomass (Figure 5.1).

This chapter presents the various instruments and initiatives proposed and taken by the EU and its Member States to promote RES since it came onto the EU-policy agenda in the late 1990s. The analysis focuses on renewable electricity generation, and only briefly touches upon other facets of RES, such as biofuels for transport or the heating sector. It assesses and discusses what progress has been achieved by the EU and how far it is from having a common RES policy. Seeking to understand and explain the reluctance and mixed progress in RES, it examines both obstacles that the EU has faced in making progress and what considerations have motivated EU bodies and Member States in both furthering and impeding the creation of a common policy in this area. Based on this discussion, it discusses the prospects for further Europeanization of RES policy in the medium term future.

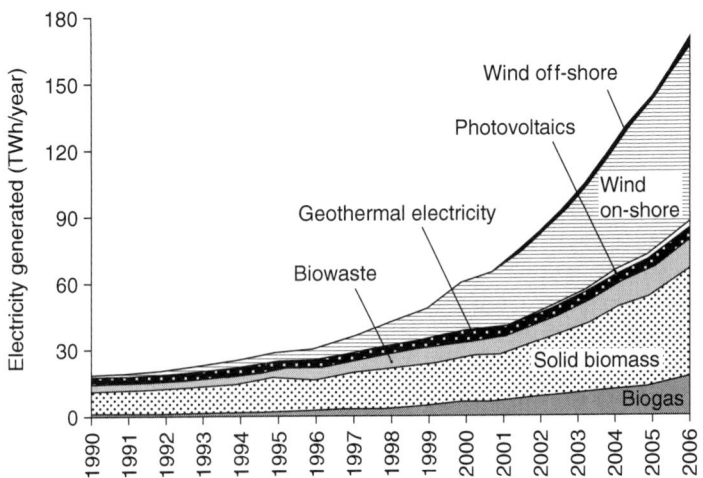

Figure 5.1 Growth in renewable electricity generation (in twh per year)
Source: Nilsson et al. 2009.

EU Policy Developments in Renewable Energy

Energy issues have always been part of the EU-policy discourse, but they did not take a front seat on the agenda until the 1990s. At first, the focus was on developing the internal energy market, and the first market package was put in place in the mid-1990s (CEC 1996). The Commission did not really consider renewable energy promotion as a policy priority until 1997, when a White Paper was released (CEC 1997), in view of developing a first RES directive. In these first deliberations, it was clear that the Commission strived for a harmonized European policy based on a market approach. The ideas for a harmonized market-based policy-instrument were further developed in a 1999 Working Document (CEC 1999). However, the wide variety of policy measures already in place at the national level, and the different experiences made with these, rendered the political debate about policy measures a difficult one. The first RES Directive 2001/77/EC on the promotion of electricity produced from RES was adopted after several years of negotiations involving debates on harmonization of national support systems, country targets, and the definition of RES (CEC 2001; Rowlands 2005). It set an overall indicative target of 22 percent electricity from RES by 2010, and included individual targets for each Member State. Tradable Renewable Electricity Certificates (TRECs) were mentioned in the directive but Member States resisted both harmonization of national support systems and a common system. No agreement was reached about a common instrument (Lauber 2007).

The debate about what policy measures were effective continued in the EU, and many Member States continued on their own paths, although clearly inspired and learning from each other (Busch and Jörgens 2005). Operating support is currently the most important support mechanism although many other policy instruments are used at the national level including modifications to the permitting procedure for new and enhanced installations, tax rebates, R&D support, and investment support (capital subsidies). Within operating support, two principal measures are currently used: the feed-in tariff (FIT) and the TREC (CEC 2008a) (see Table 5.1 for a summary comparison).

Generic market-based instruments such as TREC under a quota obligation have been implemented in seven Member States. This type of instrument typically fixes a quantity of RES to be achieved

Table 5.1 Summary comparison of FIT and TREC

	The FIT	The TREC
Support constituency	Favored by the majority of Member States—implemented in 18 MS, RES industry, green NGOs	Favored by many parts of the Commission and some Member States—implemented in 7 MS, most major power utilities, industrial organizations
Pricing mechanism	Differentiated tariffs, above 50 Ec for photovoltaic and below 10 for wind, fixed for a time period	A uniform (but fluctuating) certificate price set by market conditions
Outcome	Deliver large quantities of RES—also those that are early stage and more expensive	Deliver large quantities of the most cost-efficient RES technologies.
Market effect	Should promote competition between suppliers of a specific production technology	Should promote competition between different production technologies
Type of market efficiency	Dynamic efficiency	Static efficiency

and facilitates this by issuing green certificates that can be traded TRECs. TREC systems were introduced in countries such as the United Kingdom (UK), Sweden, Italy, and Belgium in the early 2000s. Technology-specific support measures coupled with the obligation of distributors to purchase renewable electricity at fixed prices (depending on technology)—so-called feed-in tariffs or premiums (FITs)—have been implemented in 19 Member States. Spain and Germany are two of the major EU countries deploying FIT. From an economic theory point of view, the two systems are not that different; the FIT system fixes the price and lets the market set the volume, whereas the TREC system fixes the volume and lets the market set the price.

While Member States were busy implementing their national approaches through the 2000s, the Commission kept arguing for a harmonized policy framework, which would be better aligned with the internal market policy. Not much happened, however, until 2006, when the EU's top leadership started to take a profound interest in renewable energy issues. As will be discussed later, this interest was fuelled by both energy security and climate change concerns. The result was that between 2006 and 2008, renewable energy met an ever-increasing policy interest and activity. For instance, in 2006 during the UK presidency it became, for the first time, part of the agenda at the European Summits (the meetings of the heads of government). There was significant political pressure to ramp up the EU energy and climate policy. In March 2007, the European Council reached a landmark agreement on an overall binding 20 percent renewable energy target for the EU by 2020, along with targets of 20 percent reduction in greenhouse gas emissions, and a 20 percent increase in energy efficiency. They requested the Commission to develop a policy proposal for how this would be achieved.

In January 2008, the Commission presented the draft directive "on the promotion of renewable source of energy" replacing the 2001 directive (CEC 2008c). This was part of a larger climate and energy package which also contained the new Emissions Trading System (ETS II), provisions on energy efficiency, and support for developing carbon capture and storage technologies. The proposed RES directive contained national targets for renewable energy shares, provisions for trade in "Guarantees of Origin" ("GOs") of renewable energy (a mechanism similar to the TREC system), and targets for renewable energy in transport (including biofuels). The overall binding 20 percent renewable energy consumption target for the EU by 2020 was allocated to different Member States (Figure 5.2). The target for renewable energy in transport was set to increase the share of renewable energy, including hydrogen, electricity from renewable sources of energy, and biofuels, to 10 percent by 2020. Sustainability criteria for biofuels for transport (but not for biomass energy more generally) were added to ensure that the production and supply chain of biofuels is sustainable. It included criteria for minimum greenhouse gas emissions savings compared with conventional fuels, as well as criteria against the cultivation of energy crops for such fuels on land that is currently covered by forest or where endangered species live.

According to normal regulatory procedure, the proposal was coprocessed in the European Parliament and the Council. The Council, in the formation of the Heads of State, and the European Parliament passed the directive in December 2008. During the processing of the proposal, the most significant change was that the proposed common policy instrument of GO trading was abandoned. Instead, GOs would be used purely for verifying compliance with targets and a flexible mechanism was put in place for statistical cooperation. These so-called statistical transfers, which can only be conducted under the condition that the selling Member State has reached its interim renewable targets, can also be applied in cases where Member States cooperate on joint projects (European Parliament and Council of the

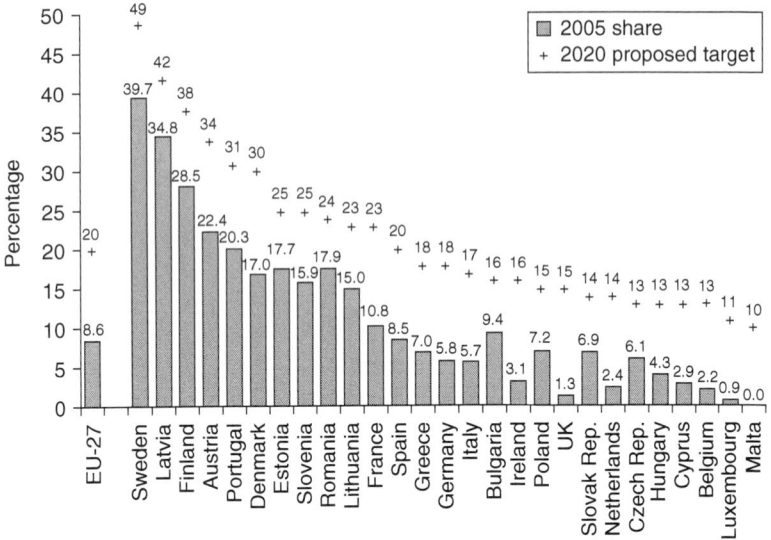

Figure 5.2 Renewable energy use and goals for 2020 in the climate and energy package of 2008

European Union 2009). One other important change was to loosen the sustainability criteria concerning greenhouse gas emissions savings—rendering the target easier to achieve (European Parliament and Council of the European Union 2009).

Assessment: EU Progress toward a Common RES Policy

The brief account above shows that the progress of the EU in the area of RES policy is ambiguous. On the one hand, there are many signs of progress, both in terms of policy development and in concrete achievements in RES growth. First, the EU has, at the level of its Member States, taken strong actions to promote RES, and many Member States have been active for over two decades, leading to significant growth in RES production and industries. Second, there has also been a certain centralization and power shift to Brussels in the new RES directive compared to the old one. One might claim that the EU has achieved a common policy in terms of the objectives for renewable energy, including binding quantitative targets up to 2020. Although environmental groups have argued that the climate and energy package is too weak to resolve Europe's energy and climate problems, the 2006 to 2009 developments on renewable energy, including the Council decisions in May 2007 and December 2008, are indicative of a very strong progress in the area. The EU has through these decisions established a common policy on RES, in terms of binding targets for each country and commitments to pathways toward these targets. In this sense, considering the lack of constitutional mandate, the Commission has been successful in pushing Member States toward promotion of renewable energy as a policy objective.

However, the EU is still far from having a common policy in the RES area. The instruments and approaches deployed in Member States have not been much coordinated. The EU has not, despite the best intentions from in particular the Commission, been able to harmonize, nor develop a common instrument such as happened with for instance greenhouse gas mitigation with the EU ETS. As a result, there are potentially important inefficiencies in how EU RES growth is being advanced. The Commission has, unsuccessfully so far, advocated harmonization with a flexible market regime based on quotas and trading. Important Member States and increasingly important industrial and environmental interests have resisted such policies and successfully challenged the effectiveness of trading systems compared to technology-specific support measures through FIT (CEC 2008a). As already noted the debate is unresolved between those that advocate a market-based trading mechanism of certificates or Guarantees of Origin; and those that advocate the use of fixed pricing such as FIT (Midttun and Gautesen 2007).

Provided that the EU pushed hard for policy harmonization in the 2001 directive and then again in the 2008 directive, failing both times and caving to pressures from Member States, it must be deduced that the EU is relatively far from developing harmonized or common RES policy-instruments. That a harmonized RES policy is not realistic in the foreseeable future is confirmed by interview respondents in Brussels. Member States are seemingly increasingly wedded to their national support systems. As expertise and interest groups build up around them they have become institutionalized over time, and there is currently little to suggest that the Commission will regain the force it had in the 1990s for pushing through internal market reforms in this area (Nilsson, et al. 2009).

Drivers and Impediments toward the Creation of a Common RES Policy

The overall positive progress on RES policy can be attributed to a wide range of drivers. Substantial policy drivers can be found that are related to all three "pillars" of energy policy:

- The energy security issue, growing on the agenda in the 2000s not least due to the Russia–Ukraine gas disputes in 2006 and in 2008, but also in the face of increasing oil prices and an increasing sense of vulnerability and resource competition with growing economies such as China.
- The internal market issue, that is the wish to expand the competency of the EU into the energy domain and secure a competitive and efficient energy supply for European industries and consumers.
- The climate change issue, where the EU has set upon itself to be a global leader in climate change mitigation, setting an example and paving the way for others to follow.

These fundamental and "slow" drivers notwithstanding, the processing and adoption of the RES directive in 2008 was a remarkably speedy one. Several more practical and short-term factors played into this. First, the institutional setup with the revolving six-month presidency played a role. France saw the climate and energy package as a prestige project that it wished to conclude during its presidency (July–Dec 2008). Without it, the legacy of the French presidency would have been far weaker on the whole. President Sarkozy decided to lift the issue to the Summit level (the gathering of the European governmental heads) rather than the "normal" Council level (the formation of the energy ministers) and was able to secure a deal despite strong skepticism on behalf of several Member States. Raising the political stakes to this level rendered it more difficult for skeptics to block or stall the process. Another crucial factor was the time constraint. European Parliament elections were due in June 2009, and a new Commission would be installed in autumn 2009. If the decision had not been taken by June 2009, the negotiation process would have had to restart, with delays of at least a year. This would then render impossible a strong European position at the United Nations (UN) climate change talks in Copenhagen in 2009, a meeting for which much hope was pinned at the time.

Third, the package proponents in the Council and Parliament were concerned about the agenda and interest of the incoming Czech presidency (for the first half of 2009) as they had voiced concerns about it during Council discussions and the Czech government was generally seen as both "Euro-skeptical" and skeptical to climate change mitigation.

In other words, there were both long-term agendas, and short-term politico-institutional factors enabling the rapid overall progress of the renewable energy agenda in the EU. How, then, can we understand the lack of progress in developing a common policy? The immediate explanation is that influential Member States such as Germany and Spain opposed a common instrument, and along with them came other countries who had put in place FIT systems, and the new RES-based industries (wind power industries etc.) that have grown dependent on these systems. The Spanish and German systems have in fact induced a substantive increase in renewable electricity as well as helped create a new industry. The two countries also account for most of the growth in European wind power capacity over the last decade, accounting for 21,000 MW and 12,000 MW installed wind capacity, out of the total EU capacity of 48,000 (EUROSTAT 2009). In Germany, who put in place their Feed in Law already in 1990, renewable sources today account for ca. 15 percent of the electricity supply. Spain's current system of FIT was put in place in 1997 through the Electric Power Act 54/1997, and updated in the Royal Decree in 2004. The current premium for wind is 40 percent of the average electricity tariff, and for solar 250 percent (Ragwitz and Huber n.d.). Complementary measures such as regulations requiring new housing to install solar panels provided additional triggers for the rapid expansion. In 2008, Spain accounted for 41 percent of the world market of installed solar power, installing 2,460 MW out of the world total 5950 MW (Germany installed 1,860 MW and the rest of Europe 310 MW) (Solarbuzz LCC 2009). Thus, there were strong new business interests at stake who defended the FIT system, working both through Member States and through renewable lobby organizations such as European Renewable Energy Council (EREC)—the umbrella organization of the European renewable energy industry, and European Renewable Electricity Federation (EREF)—an organization for independent power producers that exclusively produce renewable electricity; groups that, according to a Commission official, were "very good at getting their point across."

Aside from, and to some extent underlying, these interest-based explanations, there are also more ideational mechanisms at play. The reason for the Commission to push for a TREC system is of course that it in the Commission's view represents the most internal-market compatible approach. Since the 1990s, market efficiency considerations lie more or less at the heart of the Commission's raison d'être. Following a market efficiency logic, TRECs held the promise to deliver RES in the most cost-effective way possible. However, this is yet debated, not least because comparisons between systems are difficult to make. Through their designs, the measures are pursuing partly differing objectives and are based on different policy perspectives. The TREC approach is primarily concerned with market efficiency by way of inducing the delivery of the renewable electricity technology that has the lowest production cost into the system, whereas the FIT approach is concerned with building up new industries and technologies and helping them onto the market. Sweden's TREC system, started in 2003, has been criticized for not inducing growth in wind power but merely converting existing boilers to biomass-based generation (consistent with the theory—the cheapest option). Indeed, in the first round, most of the certificates were allocated to existing production capacity, where there was a great deal of unexplored capacity in combined heat and power production. Nonetheless, as it has become clear that the system will be extended another ten years, investors have become more confident, and recent figures demonstrate that wind power investments have been taking off very rapidly. One can expect there to be some truth in the theoretical assertion that the TREC system induces a stronger competitive pressure between different generation technologies to stimulate cost-efficient designs. Such a pressure is not present in the feed-in system where revenue is secured. Therefore, proponents of TREC argue that maintaining FIT systems for too long may slow down technology development and forego efficiency potentials. Proponents of TREC emphasize the economic efficiency of the system—the ability to deliver the least expensive green electricity and induce a competitive market between different technologies. Proponents of FIT, on the other hand, emphasize how it induces investor confidence as a result of the fully predictable revenue stream from the fixed price, and that support levels can be adapted to the specific needs of different technologies and nurturing new industries by way of providing long-term stability to protect niche markets (Fouquet and Johansson 2008). In the FIT system the competitive pressure lies not between technologies but *within* each power generation technology, for instance between different equipment manufacturers and suppliers, although due to production capacity constraints the last few years, this pressure has been rather weak.

Thus, the debate over RES policy instruments, and in particular the divide between those that advocate FIT and those that advocate TRECs, is also a debate about framing and what objectives are the most important ones on the agenda. From this perspective, another explanation emerges: the European policy agenda has in recent years been dominated not by the internal market but by concerns about innovation, employment, industrial growth and security. As these concerns have taken over, this played into the hands of those advocating national support systems in general and FIT systems in particular. This pattern manifested clearly in the Council deliberations over the new directive between January and December 2008. Although opinions of Member States on the TREC/GO issue were far from aligned as the Council began its process, a positive tone toward TREC/GO was maintained. For examples, the press release of the Council in February 2008 concluded that "the importance of trade in guarantees of origin has been underlined as a flexible instrument which should enable and not hinder Member States to reach their targets." (Council of the European Union 2008). However, at the top of the agenda now was the issue of competitiveness—not the advancement of the internal market. In addition, problems with wind-fall profits not only from ETS but also from GO trading had been acknowledged by the Commission in its impact assessment (CEC 2008b). The concern for industrial competitiveness played out in favor of national support schemes and against GO trading, as national support schemes were seen as more important drivers for industrial growth and innovation. Several GO friendly countries were turning more negative or becoming uncertain about the merits of the system (in particular given the provisions in the proposal creating legal uncertainty). The overall picture of positions at the time show that the opposition was rising, with many governments viewing the proposal as too uncertain (Nilsson, et al. 2009). Formerly strong GO proponents like the UK agreed that the Commission's proposal was problematic and instead worked toward an alternative voluntary mechanism together with, for example, Poland and Germany. As noted earlier, in December 2008 the Council and Parliament agreed on the new RES directive without the mandatory GO trading.

Summing up the key obstacles against harmonized or common policy instruments, the key aspect is that national governments that cut a lot of ice in the EU-policy arena have invested in and institutionalized support systems. A growing range of actors, such as environmental NGOs and renewable energy industries of different types, have developed high stakes in the continuation of FIT systems. These groups formed alliances with powerful Member States such as Spain and Germany, and many other supporting countries. Their positions and arguments were underpinned by experts and analysts that took a growing interest in innovation and early market support. As the overarching political agenda of the EU switched away from internal market efficiency to issues of security, competitiveness, and innovation, it played further into the hands of those advocating against harmonization (Toke 2008).

Prospects for Future Progress in EU RES Policy

European RES policy is still only in what might be considered the "take-off" phase. As Member States are being pushed to deliver on the targets up to 2020, there is no doubt that strong policies will need to be developed in the coming years. However, this is unlikely to occur through harmonization any time soon—renewable policy-instruments will remain a national affair in the short to medium term. The Commission's own working paper (CEC 2008a) showed a shift in its thinking as regards instrument harmonization; "…harmonization of support schemes remain a long term goal on economic efficiency, single market and state aid grounds, but that harmonization in the short term is not appropriate. By adopting best practices or combining national support schemes Member States can continue to reform, optimize and coordinate their efforts to support renewable electricity" (p. 17). Clearly, modifications to FIT, TREC, and other systems will be made but on the whole, Member States appear prepared to continue on their trodden paths, and FITs are become increasingly popular. For instance, the UK introduces a system of FIT for certain technologies alongside its more generic TREC system. Finland has recently opted for a FIT system. At the time of writing, Norway (not an EU but an EEA [European Environment Agency]member) is reluctantly contemplating joining Sweden in a joint TREC market.

Both FIT and TREC have contributed to considerable market expansion, the emergence of learning networks and growing political strength of industry associations for suppliers and owners of renewable energy. Such institutional change has induced European leadership in RES. However, it should also be noted that this leadership comes at a cost, as it implies politically orchestrated transfers of resources between stakeholders (i.e. from electricity consumers or tax payers to renewable industries). Costs have been significant both in FIT and TREC systems. The systems are therefore contingent on strong political support.

Therefore, in the short and medium term, further Europeanization of RES policy appears unlikely. What are the more long-term future prospects for a common EU RES policy? Based on the perspectives discussed in this chapter, future advances will depend on the development of four sets of variables, discussed briefly below.

The Relative Prominence of Overarching Policy Agendas in the EU

As competitiveness and economic concerns are ever increasing compared to 2006 and 2007, and United Nations Framework Convention on Climate Change (UNFCCC) negotiations keep stumbling, a further tightening of the European energy policy toward climate-policy goals appears unlikely. One question is whether or not climate has a particular status in the public opinion (which has not been a topic of this chapter). This momentum also depends on developments in climate science and observed impacts around the world. But on balance it seems that after agreeing on the "Package" the EU-policy machinery has turned to implementation mode—maintaining targets but not going much further. This will shape also the level of ambitions in RES policy. Of course, RES policy is shaped also by other agendas, at EU, national and local levels, including innovation and competitiveness, and these, combined with security concerns, may become more important than climate change in driving RES-policy developments in the future. The internal market agenda, which has dominated the European integration project as well as much of the world's economic policies since the 1980s, has come under increasing attack not least in the wake of recent economic turmoil globally. In particular those concerned with competitiveness have begun to advocate more strongly that their end objective is not always compatible with free markets. Instead, innovation policies and security policies may be as critical to the achievement of a competitive Europe. As a result, the interest in public initiative and publicly funded programs is increasing across layers of society, among politicians, businesses, NGOs, energy analysts, and even mainstream economic analysts. Here the renewed Lisbon strategy and what Europe is doing in its Lead Market and green economy initiatives may entail RES policies more on the innovation and technology-support side. In any case, the near future is likely to hold a more balanced approach to market promotion than in the past, including possibly a further relaxing of state-aid rules, as well as further and more variety and fragmentation in Member-State initiatives, rather than common policies based on internal market efficiency concerns.

The Institutional Relationship between Member States and the EU

At the institutional level, as regards the balance between Europeanization and Member-State autonomy, the recent patterns of RES policy and the Commission's own conclusions suggest that a continued considerable discretion will be left to Member States about how best to promote renewable energy. This includes a relaxation of state-aid rules, which have become increasingly generous over the last few years (Flåm 2009). The European integration project moves forward in jumps and impasses, but lately the momentum has considerably stalled, following the failure to get positive outcomes when posting the new constitution to public referendum. It appears unlikely that much more competency will be moved to the EU level unless the advocates can tie in such a movement to the supply security agenda. (It should be noted that although advocates of national autonomy have played the supply security card, it can be argued that an advancement of supply security is actually rather contingent on stronger European integration.)

The Relative Influence of Different Interest Groups with a Stake in RES Policy

Concerning the role and relative influence of different actors, the recent European RES-policy development shows an interesting and at least partly new pattern of advocacy power to smaller niche organizations with specialized interests (such as renewable energy producers) at the expense of the large incumbents with their more principled arguments (such as Business Europe) (Nilsson, et al. 2009). Also the major power producers have lost some ground, from a previously very privileged market position. In the case of RES, this new advocacy pattern played out in favor of national interests and against the internal market and Europeanization process, which tends to benefit the larger players. One reason may be that as the complexity of policy is increasing, the larger players have increasing difficulties forming a clear position, as they represent diverging interests on particular topics. Niche groups that can capitalize on agendas, such as new and renewable energy producers, will continue to have a strong voice in European energy policy.

New Empirical Evidence about the Merits of Different Support Measures

Much of the political debate about policy measures has so far been informed by modeling results and principal arguments. Economic modeling, performed for instance in the Commission's own impact assessments demonstrated benefits from efficiency gains from TREC instruments (CEC 2008b). However, empirical evidence from a wide experience of RES policy across Europe is now building up (see, for example, Bergek and Jacobsson 2010). This chapter has not studied this evidence in detail, but the Commission's own review of the performance of support schemes stresses that support schemes need to be adapted to a competitive internal electricity market, and also that well-adapted FIT regimes have generally been the most efficient and effective support schemes (CEC 2008a). Experiences with FIT had proven that they helped build up new industries and quickly reach results. However, the findings and the underlying definition were contested by internal-market advocates. For instance, the Commission defined efficiency by comparing support costs to generation costs, rather than looking at the full cost of the support; "The closer the level of support is to the generation cost, the more efficient a support mechanism is in terms of covering the actual costs. If the level of support is below the generation cost, which is the case in many of the Member States, it is not effective [sic!] as it is too low to trigger substantial investments in renewable electricity generation" (p. 9). There is clearly a need for further research and evidence about the real impacts of different instruments.

Conclusions

EU progress on RES policy is mixed. On the one hand, the last decade has witnessed a very rapid engagement with RES issues at the European level, and the EU has established relatively ambitious and binding targets for Member States in the medium term. On the other hand, the EU has not been able, despite its best intentions, to establish a common RES policy-instrument. Thus, the process of Europeanization of RES policy is there, but may be characterized as "hesitant" (Wettestad, et al. 2011).

Both the progress and the obstacles can be explained by long-term factors about what agendas are important and how these shift over time, and by short-term factors about what interests and what actors cut the most ice in the decision making process. As regards agendas, RES policy received a boost as it responded to all three pillars of energy policy heralded both by the Commission and by most Member States—security, climate, and cost. The advancement of European RES policy in 2007 and 2008 was in particular a result of the coupling of the climate change and energy security agendas. Brussels policy entrepreneurs were able to capture the prominence, media attention and political salience of the climate change concern, and couple it to the supply-security concerns emerging due to, for instance, Russia's foreign policy agenda, and draw upon analytical and political support from the rapidly growing interest groups and coalitions relating to renewable energy production.

Paradoxically, at the same time as these factors advanced RES policy in general, they undermined the Commission's wish to deepen the European harmonization of policy by advancing internal-market compatible policy-instruments. The overarching EU strategic agenda shifted away from internal market concerns to concerns over security, innovation and competitiveness, which impeded the advancement of the common policy-instrument. The debate is of course still on-going as to whether policies that nurture development, learning effects and market diffusion of RES technologies in a protected environment are better for European innovation and industrial development than harmonized market-based policy-instruments intended to ensure efficient market-based resource allocation (Nilsson, et al. 2009).

Regarding actors and interests, the role and power of the Commission in setting the agenda appears to have diminished over the examined time period and strong Member States have recovered the power of initiative. In addition, new interest groups have emerged with successful advocacy strategies, often forming alliances in unexpected combinations.

The future prospects for EU RES policy depends on the development of different agendas, institutional relationships in the European policy-making system, actors and interests, and the gathering of new evidence about the effectiveness and efficiency of different policy measures. The combined picture suggests that further harmonization is possible but that a common instrument, in particular one based on the TREC approach, is unlikely in the short-to-medium term.

Acknowledgments

The paper draws upon and synthesizes findings from three years of research on European energy and climate policy change from a combined institutional and multilevel actor perspective. The research was prepared within the framework of the CANES (Climate Change Altering Nordic Energy Systems) project funded by the Norwegian Research Council and Norwegian and Swedish industry, and implemented in collaboration with the Fritdjof Nansen Institute in Norway.

Works Cited

Bergek, A. and S. Jacobsson. 2010. Are Tradable Green Certificates a Cost-Efficient Policy Driving Technical Change or a Rent-Generating Machine? Lessons from Sweden 2003–2008. *Energy Policy.* 38: 1255–1271.

Busch, P. and H. Jörgens. 2005. The International Sources of Policy Convergence: Explaining the Spread of Environmental Policy Innovations. *Journal of European Public Policy.* 12: 860–884.

CEC. 1996. *Directive 96/92/EC of the European Parliament and of the Council of Dec. 19, 1996, Concerning Common Rules for the Internal Market in Electricity.* Brussels: European Commission.

CEC. 1997. *Energy for the Future: Renewable Sources of Energy, White paper for a Community Strategy and Action Plan. COM(97)599.* Brussels: European Commission.

CEC. 1999. *Electricity from Renewable Energy Sources and the Internal Electricity Market. Commission Working Document. SEC (99) 470 final.* Brussels: European Commission.

CEC. 2001. *Directive 2001/77/EC of 27 September 2001 on the Promotion of Electricity Produced from Renewable Energy Sources in the Internal Electricity Market.* Brussels: European Commission.

CEC. 2008a. *Commission Staff Working Document: The Support of Electricity From Renewable Energy Sources.* Brussels: European Commission.

CEC. 2008b. *Impact Assessment: Document Accompanying the Package of Implementation Measures for the EU's Objectives on Climate Change and Renewable Energy for 2020.* Brussels: European Commission.

CEC. 2008c. *Proposal for a Directive on the Promotion of the use of Energy from Renewable Sources.* Brussels: European Commission.

Council of the European Union. 2008. *6722/08 PRESS RELEASE 2854th Councilmeeting Transport, Telecommunications and Energy Brussels, 28 February 2008.*

European Parliament and Council of the European Union. 2009. *Directive 2009/28/EC of the European Parliament and of the Council of 23 April 2009 on the Promotion of the use of Energy from Renewable Sources and Amending and Subsequently Repealing Directives 2001/77/EC and 2003/30/EC.* Brussels: European Commission.

EUROSTAT. 2009. *Energy, Transport and Environment Indicators.* Luxemburg: EUROSTAT.

Flåm, K. 2009. EU Environmental State Aid Policy. Wide Implications, Narrow Participation. *Environmental Policy and Governance.* 19: 336–349.

Fouquet, D. and T. B. Johansson. 2008. European Renewable Energy Policy at Crossroads—Focus on Electricity Support. *Energy Policy.* doi:10.1016/j.enpol.2008.1006.1023.

Jacobsson, S. and V. Lauber. 2006. The Politics and Policy of Energy System Transformation—Explaining the German Diffusion of Renewable Energy Technology. *Energy Policy.* 34.

Lauber, V. 2007. The Politics of European Union Support Schemes for Electricity from Renewable Energy Sources. in L. Mez. *Green Power Markets: Support Schemes, Case Studies and Perspectives.* Brentwood, CA: Multi-Science Publishing: 9–30.

Midttun, A. and K. Gautesen. 2007. Feed in or Certificates, Competition or Complementarity? Combining a Static Efficiency and a Dynamic Innovation Perspective on the Greening of the Energy Industry. *Energy Policy.* 35: 1419–1422.

Nilsson, L. J., B. Johansson, K. Åstrand, K. Ericsson, P. Svenningsson, P. Börjesson and L. Neij. 2004. Seeing the Wood for the Trees: 25 years of Renewable Energy Policy in Sweden. *Energy for Sustainable Development.* 8: 36–50.

Nilsson, M., L. J. Nilsson and K. Ericsson. 2009. The Rise and Fall of GO Trading in European Renewable Policy: the Role of Advocacy and Framing. *Energy Policy.* 37: 4454–4462.

Ragwitz, M. and C. Huber. not dated. *Feed-In Systems in Germany and Spain: A Comparison.* Karlsruhe: Fraunhofer Institut.

Rowlands, I. H. 2005. The European Directive on Renewable Electricity: Conflicts and Compromises. *Energy Policy.* 33: 965–974.

Solarbuzz LCC. 2009. Marketbuzz 2009. Available at www.solarbuzz.com/Marketbuzz 2009.htm.

Toke, D. 2008. "The EU Renewables Directive—What is the Fuss about Trading? *Energy Policy.* 36: 2991–2998.

Wettestad, J., P. O. Eikeland and M. Nilsson. 2011. EU Climate and Energy Policy: A Hesitant Supranational Turn? *Global Environmental Politics.* In press.

Chapter Six

Energy Savings and Efficiency

Jørgen Henningsen

In June 2005, when introducing the European Commission's Green Paper on energy efficiency (EC 2005), then energy commissioner Andris Piëbalgs declared energy efficiency to be the top priority during his term as commissioner. This was no bad choice. The Barroso Commission (2004–2009) would be the last commission to have an impact on the European Union's (EU's) compliance with its Kyoto commitment, and the recent enlargement to include ten new Member States was a strong reminder of the huge potential, still unexploited, in energy efficiency. In addition, the Green Paper correctly observed that within the EU-15, a lot of low-hanging "energy efficiency fruit" remained on the trees. And this, despite energy efficiency having been part of the EU's "Energy and Environment" program since the early 1990s. In quantitative terms, the Green Paper estimated that 20 percent of Europe's gross energy consumption was "wasted" unnecessarily.

As happens so often in politics, however, events have taken over. Beginning in early 2006, reinforced in 2007, and culminating with the Commission's 2008 Energy and Climate Package (20–20–20: 20 percent reduction in greenhouse gas emissions, 20 percent renewable energy, and 20 percent improvement in energy efficiency) and the subsequent Council and parliament decisions on the package in 2008 and 2009, energy efficiency has been put on the back burner in favor of more glamorous policies such as renewable energy, emissions trading, and energy security of supply. Nevertheless, energy efficiency is still fully alive, to a large extent thanks to legislation proposed by the earlier Prodi Commission (1999–2004) but only slowly working its way through the cumbersome process of Council and Parliament negotiations and subsequent implementation (or nonimplementation) in Member States' legislation. Still, there is no evidence that energy efficiency has managed to make the quantum leap that would be justified by virtue of its being the most cost-effective policy option to reduce CO_2 emissions and improve energy security of supply.

In principle, energy efficiency is part of the EU's overall 20–20–20 strategy, to be attained by 2020. Where the greenhouse gas and renewable energy objectives have been translated into binding legislation, however, this is not the case with the energy efficiency objective. It is not difficult to explain why. First, the 20 percent target is to be achieved against a business-as-usual scenario, something that is difficult, if not impossible, to quantify. Second, energy efficiency cuts across virtually all economic sectors (industry, power production, appliances, buildings, transport, etc.), some of which are partly covered by other pieces of legislation. The result is that energy efficiency ends up as the second priority (if at all a priority), and it should be no surprise if some five to ten years in the future, we will see another Green paper on energy efficiency discussing how to pick the low-hanging fruit.

The Energy Efficiency Action Plan

In October 2006, the Commission presented an Energy Efficiency Action Plan as a follow-up to the 2005 Green Paper on Energy Efficiency (EC 2006). The plan exemplified the fact that it is easier to identify the efficiency improvement potential than to prescribe the measures that will turn the potential into reality. In fact, much of the plan simply reported on measures already proposed or agreed or measures following previous decisions to review existing policies or directives already in force. The annex listed 57 specific actions to be carried out in the course of the remaining years of the (first) Barroso Commission, a number that by itself should raise some suspicion of a lack of focus. Analysis by Commission Directorates-General led to the expectation that implementation of the action plan would deliver a 13 percent reduction in gross energy consumption by 2020 relative to business-as-usual projections. This was probably an optimistic expectation, and it was subject to the uncertainty of calculating future energy consumption using business-as-usual assumptions.

The action plan covered a number of areas. Among the most important were the following.

Appliances and Other Energy-Using Equipment

Inclusion of appliances and other energy-using equipment was particularly important because energy efficiency requirements for them are considered internal market legislation and, as such, are subject to full EU harmonization. It was also important because existing EU-legislation in the area stopped well short of requiring levels of energy efficiency for different types of appliances. In fact, much of the existing legislation reflected a desire to protect producers of less efficient appliances rather than the subsequent users. Whereas one might expect the market to favor energy-efficient appliances because of their lower cost of use, experience has shown that the price of an appliance weighs more heavily in purchasing decisions than the expected cost of using it.

The action plan identified 14 groups of appliances for which the Commission would propose new or reinforced minimum energy performance standards during the period 2007–2008. Insufficient allocation of resources for the work has made the timing slip, but the assessment, that this was, so far, the most important part of the action plan, remains valid. In the meantime, the actual implementation of the performance standards continued to be done through the 2005 "Ecodesign" Directive (2005/32/EC).[1]

Services and Energy End-Use Efficiency

This part of the action plan was limited to making a reference to the directive on Energy End-Use Efficiency and Energy Services (2006/32/EC), which is discussed below.

Buildings

The Energy Performance of Buildings Directive (2002/91/EC) has so far had little impact on the overall energy consumption in buildings within the EU.[2] This failure is partly due to the directive's limited scope (new buildings and major renovation and only buildings of more than 1,000 square meters) and partly to the fact that implementation is still left to a great extent to Member States. In addition, enforcement is slow and insufficient. The EU institutions do not have to go very far to observe the sad state of affairs. Brussels, like former socialist Member States, is full of poorly insulated houses.

The problem does not lie with the Commission. How to improve the energy performance of the hundreds of millions of houses and apartments throughout the EU, under completely different climatic, infrastructure, and economic conditions, is virtually impossible to put in a single formula, even one with considerable flexibility. The inconvenient truth is that even a modified directive with a broader scope than the one presently in force is unlikely to have much impact on energy consumption in buildings unless individual Member States make it a national policy priority. For this reason, the potential 11 percent reduction in total final energy consumption identified in the action plan is likely to remain only a potential for years to come, which is regrettable.

Energy Transformation

The action plan expressed confidence that improved energy efficiency in the power production sector would be taken care of by the emission trading scheme (ETS), which is discussed below. The fact that the action plan said nothing about the energy intensive industries covered by the ETS would lead one to believe that the Commission shared the same optimism on the achievements of the ETS in this sector.

Transport

By 2006, the Commission had determined that the automobile industry was unlikely to be able to deliver the necessary efficiency improvements to achieve the promised goal of 140 grams of CO_2 emissions per kilometer (g/km) by 2008/2009. Subsequently, the Commission proposed, and Council and Parliament agreed to, binding standards for CO_2 emissions (and thereby energy efficiency) by passenger cars up to 2020.

Nevertheless, it is important to recognize that, while the agreed target was not achieved, the energy efficiency of European passenger cars has improved much faster over the last ten years than that of cars in most other markets, such as the United States. Adopted legislation is likely to continue to promote this trend, but it is uncertain whether the lower penalties for exceeding the limit values, insisted on by the Council, will mean that car manufacturers (and buyers) will prefer to pay the penalties rather than shift to more efficient vehicles.

The action plan further announced the intention to include aviation in the emission trading scheme, a step that has now been taken and which will be operational from 2012. This development is unlikely, however, to have any significant impact on aviation energy efficiency over and above what will already happen because of concern in the sector over high fuel cost. The issue is further dealt with in the section on the ETS.

Regrettably, the action plan said nothing about energy efficiency in heavy-duty vehicles (trucks and buses). The potential for energy savings in this area is less than that with passenger cars, but it is still too large to ignore.

Energy Efficiency in the New Member States

The action plan had very little to say about what to do to address the often very inefficient use of energy in the new Member States. It is obvious that this is generally not a priority for the governments of those countries, but it is nevertheless an area that could potentially deliver both economic benefit and meaningful employment. Nevertheless, not a single specific action out of the 57 proposed was aimed at the new Member States.

The Directive on Energy End-Use Efficiency and Energy Services

Another important development in 2006 was the adoption of a new directive on Energy End-Use Efficiency and Energy Services (2006/32/EC).[3] In principle, this directive could be a cornerstone in EU energy efficiency legislation. It replaces the 1993 SAVE Directive and requires action on the part of Member States, both to set energy savings targets (although only indicative ones) and to ensure that final energy consumption is measured and paid for by the consumer (but only if it is not too difficult or expensive). The directive addresses public as well as private energy consumption, and it obliges to some extent companies delivering energy to consumers to promote savings in final energy use. Not least, it obliges individual Member States to develop national Energy Efficiency Action Plans (EEAPs) and to update these on a regular basis.

Whereas the scope of the directive responds to calls made from many sides for many years for stronger EU legislation on more efficient end use of energy, the fact that the directive contains few substantive measures that are sufficiently precise and binding to allow the Commission to take Member States to court should limit the enthusiasm. The directive might well end in the category of EU legislation where success is mainly observed in those Member States that would have taken the measures anyway. It is beyond doubt that close monitoring by the Commission will be essential, something that might well consume considerable resources.

The first round of national EEAPs, due by mid-2007, was not encouraging. Most were late and few went beyond putting on paper what was already in the pipeline in the different capitals. Few plans, if any, reflected serious government involvement across ministries on the issue.

Of course the final judgment on the merits of the directive should not be based on reports due less than 18 months after the legal text is finalized. A much better test will be the 2011 reports, but under present economic conditions one can fear that governments will content themselves with the decline in energy consumption resulting from the slowdown of the economy, rather than moving more ambitiously on energy efficiency. Press reports on the promotion of the "green new deal" are not encouraging (e.g., Lean 2008).

Energy Efficiency in the Emission Trading System

Another potential source of improvement in energy efficiency is the EU's ETS. The ETS is described elsewhere in this volume, so only the more specific potential achievements of ETS with regard to energy efficiency in the sectors covered by the scheme will be addressed here.

First, it is important to recognize that the purpose of the ETS is to achieve cost-effective CO_2 emission reductions, not necessarily to promote energy efficiency. Nevertheless, the Commission has, such as in the EEAP and at numerous less formal occasions, promoted the view that the ETS is *the* measure to ensure the achievement of energy efficiency in the respective sectors. Since it has been demonstrated that energy efficiency in industry is among the most cost-effective means of reducing CO_2 emissions, one would expect demonstrable effects on industrial energy efficiency. Yet this is not really the case.

In order for the ETS to deliver on energy efficiency, it is necessary that the system work according to intentions, including by delivering a sufficient CO_2 price. But how would one judge whether a given CO_2 price is sufficient?

Here comes the second observation: A given carbon price has a very different relative impact on the actual cost of using coal or natural gas. Approximate price levels in October 2010 were as follows: 70 euros per ton of coal, 150 euros per 1000 cubic meters of natural gas, and 15 euros per ton of CO_2. Adding the cost of the respective CO_2 emissions increases the price of coal by 60 percent, but adds only 15 percent to the price of natural gas. Presently the relatively high coal prices and lower gas prices, 15 euros per ton of CO_2, may be sufficient to encourage a shift from coal to gas, but it is unlikely to have any significant impact on the efficiency of new gas-fired power plants, let alone the improvement of existing ones.

A similar argument applies to the energy-intensive industries. In the few instances where coal is used as an industrial fuel, the ETS may provide some additional incentive to improve energy efficiency, but not in the broader use of natural gas. This differential impact would change, of course, if CO_2 prices were higher. Even at 30 euros per ton, however, CO_2 would add only 30 percent to a gas price of 150 euros per 1000 cubic meters, so the effect would still be modest at best.

There are three reasons why the ETS is unlikely to provide the incentive needed for significant energy efficiency improvements in the industrial sector. The first is that the CO_2-price is unlikely to be high enough. Adding the economic downturn and the possible life-extension of German nuclear power plants to what one could reasonably expect to be the assumptions underlying the Commission's January 2008 proposal for extending the ETS after 2012 points to a declining price level in the years to come. The second reason is that even a price of, say, 30 euros per ton of CO_2 does not add sufficiently to the fuel price to cause a significant difference. The third is that most industries require a payback time of two or, at most, three years in order to justify investing in energy efficiency. Not many projects will pass that hurdle because of a modest increase in the energy cost due to the CO_2 price.

This last point is the real obstacle to effectively using economic instruments more broadly to promote energy efficiency, and it reflects a problem that extends well beyond the ETS. It is a general observation that enterprises, public authorities, or private citizens are not likely to pay up front for lower future energy costs unless the up front payment is recovered over a very short period: usually less than three years, often even less than that. Thus we are presented with a paradox. It is increasingly being accepted that global climate change is the most serious environmental problem mankind has ever faced. Nevertheless, policy responses are in many cases limited to actions that deliver a comfortable profit to those expected to act. One might ask where our urban air-quality policy would be today if no reduction measures from car emissions had been required unless they were profitable.

A Horizontal Assessment

This description of recent developments in EU policy on energy efficiency is not exhaustive, but it should provide a realistic flavor of the ambitions, directions, and challenges. It shows a policy area that enjoys a high level of recognition of its potential, but which can still claim only modest achievements. It is an area subject to subsidiarity discussions, since many of the potential measures (buildings, small and medium-sized enterprises [SMEs], taxation issues, etc.) are predominantly of national concern, and yet are often not given, at the national level, the attention that would be expected in an area of importance for a common EU energy policy. Add to that the ideologically charged discussion of the virtues of the ETS as an overarching policy to achieve the EU climate policy objectives, and it is no surprise that the achievements so far fall short of the potential.

The more important question, however, is how much progress we can expect in the future. Is it possible to have justified expectations of significant energy efficiency improvements in the EU over the next ten years? The answer is "yes." We will certainly see an improvement. Appliances of all sorts to be sold over the next ten years will definitely be more energy efficient than those that are being replaced. Automotive fuel efficiency will continue to improve, although not necessarily as much as the recently adopted legislation might indicate. New buildings will certainly be more energy efficient than those being torn down.

Does this mean that, by 2020, most of the "low-hanging fruit" will have been picked? Certainly not. If the low-hanging fruit today represents 20 percent of energy end use, by 2020 it will most likely still be above 15 percent. This seeming paradox is partly due to the inability of the ETS (in its present form) to promote energy efficiency in the sectors covering roughly 50 percent of total CO_2 emissions and thus also roughly 50 percent of energy consumption. But it is also due to the fact that there is insufficient overall policy drive outside the ETS sectors to make energy efficiency a priority. And, finally, technological development generates new low-hanging fruit. In a different area, renewable energy, we have seen how wind energy has moved from being an expensive ("high-hanging fruit") technology to become virtually competitive with most other sources of electric power in the span of a decade. High-efficiency light bulbs offer another example.

Key to the modest expectations for the penetration of available energy efficiency technology in the coming decade is the lack of push from the policy areas that ought to drive improved energy efficiency: climate change and security of supply. Contrary to what has been stated by the Commission, repeated by most EU-leaders, and believed by the media, EU climate policy is at best ambitious only in the long term (2050). Certainly in the short term, it is inconsistent with a 2050 target of 80–95 percent reduction in greenhouse gas emissions, as agreed by the EU in the fall of 2009. In order to be consistent with the 2050 target, the 2020 target of a 20 percent reduction should be much more ambitious. When the Commission proposed its 20–20–20 package in January 2008, it was perfectly well aware that collective EU emissions were already well below 1990 levels, by around 7 percent in 2006. This achievement was largely due, however, to the 2004 enlargement, since the new Member States had emissions significantly below their 1990 levels thanks to the collapse of their production base from socialist times. The Commission also had reason to expect that by 2010 (the central year in the Kyoto period 2008–2012), EU-15 emissions would be 8 percent below 1990 levels (including some contribution from collective development mechanism [CDM] projects) and that EU-27 emissions would be around 5 percent lower than that because of the situation in the new Member States. Recent data from the European Environment Agency show a dramatic fall in 2009 emissions, taking total EU-27 emissions more than 17 percent below 1990 levels, or more than necessary to meet the 2020 target of a 20 percent reduction if one takes into account the possibility of achieving around 5 percentage points of the reduction through CDM projects.

Whereas the 20 percent reduction target was never ambitious, recent developments have removed any consistency with any of the long-term targets, be it a 60–80 percent or an 80–95 percent reduction by 2050. It is also difficult to imagine that the present climate and energy policy offers much of a driver for the innovation hoped for by the Commission in its "Europe 2020" development strategy. Political action is greatly needed.

This state of affairs will have important implications for future energy efficiency developments. Apart from those subject to legally binding legislation (appliances), the push for initiatives will be reduced, if not disappear altogether. Within the ETS system, carbon prices would be expected to fall and not to have a big impact, since even present prices are already too low to deliver much of one. Outside the ETS sectors, governments will find it less demanding to meet their national 2020 targets, and the urgency to do something about energy consumption in existing buildings or in SMEs (not covered by the ETS) will evaporate. This development obviously runs contrary to the idea of a "green new deal," of which investment in a climate friendly (and more energy efficient) economy is a cornerstone.

The lack of ambition in the EU climate policy has a couple of potentially perverse effects as far as energy efficiency is concerned. One is in relation to renewable energy. The fact that the renewable energy targets are legally binding gives renewables the upper hand over energy efficiency. The renewables energy policy is the only really ambitious part of the 20–20–20 package, and it cannot be concluded that it alone will be enough to deliver on the otherwise unambitious targets for greenhouse gas emissions and energy efficiency. In this case, we would run the risk that much of the fully developed energy efficiency technology will remain on the shelves of the respective companies, and that much-needed further technology developments will not take place. Similarly, one can fear that the considerable prestige invested by the Commission in the ETS will make the Commission feel less inclined to push for the full implementation of the 20 percent improvement in energy efficiency, since this might lead to a further weakening of the CO_2 prices and thus cast doubt on the environmental efficiency of the system.

As far as energy security of supply is concerned, the recession has also changed the outlook considerably. Coal and gas have turned into a buyer's market and will most likely remain so for several years, and the outlook for the oil market is that only in 2012 at the earliest will oil consumption be back at 2007 levels, thus providing some breathing space relative to the global shortage previously expected around 2015. Security of oil supplies in particular, however, remains a concern due to constantly rising consumption in several developing countries and the fact that global discoveries have kept up with just one-third of global consumption. Thus it is unlikely, in spite of good reasons in the medium term, that concerns about energy security of supply will provide sufficient momentum in the short term to promote energy efficiency beyond its present, relatively moderate level.

Conclusion

Energy efficiency is anchored, but not solidly, in EU energy and climate policy. Energy efficiency is likely to improve over the next decade, but it will not come anywhere close to taking advantage of the technical potential for cheap or even profitable energy/CO_2 reductions. If the new Barroso Commission, which took office in 2009, is to be serious about the medium- to long-term CO_2 reduction needs, it will have to review the recently adopted energy and climate legislation as a matter of urgency, not least in light of the impact of the economic recession. Leadership in the area of energy efficiency need not be expensive. In fact, it is more likely to be profitable for the EU if correctly designed.

Notes

1. Directive 2005/32/EC of the European Parliament and of the Council of July 6, 2005. *Official Journal of the European Union*, no. 191 (July 22, 2005): 29–58.
2. Directive 2002/91/EC of the European Parliament and of the Council of December 16, 2002 on the energy performance of buildings. *Official Journal of the European Union*, no. 1 (Jan. 1, 2003): 65–71.
3. Directive 2006/32/EC of the European Parliament and of the Council of April 5, 2006. *Official Journal of the European Communities*, no. 114 (April 27, 2006): 65–85.

Works Cited

European Commission (EC). 2005. *Doing More with Less: Green Paper on Energy Efficiency*. Luxembourg: Office for Official Publications of the European Communities. June 22. COM (2005) 265 final.
European Commission (EC). 2006. *Communication from the Commission. Action Plan for Energy Efficiency: Realising the Potential*. Brussels, October 19. COM (2006) 545 final.
Lean, Geoffrey. 2008. A "Green New Deal" Can Save the World's Economy, Says UN. *The Independent* (October 12).

Part II

National Perspectives

Chapter Seven

French Energy Policy within the EU Framework: From Black Sheep to Model?

Sophie Méritet

The debate over the creation of a common European energy policy has been going on for a number of decades. Right from the start, the first common institution of the original six countries of the European Union (EU) was the European Coal and Steel Community (ECSC) in 1951. It was followed in 1957 by the European Economic Community (EEC) and the European Atomic Energy Community (known as Euratom). The founders of the EU were aware of the strategic character of energy. After years of slow drift, the question of pooling energy stakes is again at the heart of European policy making. The discussions on a common energy policy have been recently brought back into the spotlight by the evolution of energy market fundamentals, climate change constraints, and security of supply priorities (especially the management of relations with some suppliers like Russia).

A complex equation must be solved: provide the EU[1] with secure and inexpensive energy (which is a strong element of competition), and reduce at the same time greenhouse gas emissions. The current European dependence on imported energy resources is increasing further and the energy sector has entered into a turbulent period in terms of prices and security of supply. These factors create a number of risks and uncertainties in the European energy landscape. They also create a need to think about a common strategy over the long term. They raise the fundamental question of future prices and the availability of energy. Dealing with tendencies toward "national economic protectionism," the European Commission (hereafter: the Commission) in March 2006 presented the the Commission's Green Paper—European strategy for secure, competitive, and sustainable energy (EC 2006a) that provides a basis for discussions on European energy policy. Looking at the diversity of the energy situation within the EU, the idea itself of a common policy was unrealistic a few years ago.

Nevertheless, a shared vision has always existed among the Member States for the creation of a single energy market. A convergence on energy goals in the long term is obvious, but a divergence in the means to reach them still exists. The Commission reacts quickly as soon as there is a risk of collusion between energy actors. However, it stays prudent on the definition of the energy mix, which is out of its field of competences. Today, it is not clear that Member States would like to engage in discussions on a common energy policy with a common energy mix. There are still a lot of areas in which countries do not want to deal with sensitive issues at the supranational level preferring instead to retain their national sovereignty.

In the European energy markets integration process, France has sometimes been referred to as the "black sheep," with its national energy model built on strong state intervention, two energy champions (state-owned firms Electricité de France [EDF] and Gaz de France-Suez Gulf Power Company [GDF-Suez][2]), nuclear power as the main source of electricity, and the French defense of the concept of "public service." At the same time, France is less dependent on energy imports compared to other Member States. The country acted decisively in the 1970s to limit its dependence on fossil fuels and now it is well positioned to deal with fuel costs and global warming. France is one of the European countries that emits the least greenhouse gases. However, France is also facing the same international demands and developments with the same risks and uncertainties as other European countries. It needs to diversify its energy mix and improve its security of supply. How can France define its national energy policy within the emerging European context? What could be the role of France in the creation of a common European energy policy? As the French energy model does not fit neatly into all aspects of a nascent European policy (e.g. deregulation process, renewable energy development), France has been under pressure to adapt. When the French energy policy was defined in 2005, the challenge was to protect national interests and take into account the European process. The highly strategic energy sector was, and is still, at the core of numerous debates. France is demonstrating that nations can successfully address their energy vulnerabilities, but its example also illustrates that today no single energy option will be the cheapest, cleanest, and safest.

This chapter focuses on the main French concerns related to energy policy within the EU context. It is divided into three related parts. The first section "The French Energy Situation in the EU" presents the French energy situation to understand the national constraints compared to other Member States in the EU. The second section

"The French Energy Policy: Priorities and Instruments" analyses the French energy policy model in more depth with its objectives and new instruments. The final section "French Energy Challenges in the EU Framework" discusses the French energy challenges in the European framework, and more precisely with the nuclear power park. Two current and major issues will be presented to explain the ambiguous position of France in the EU. On the one hand, the French regulated tariffs are considered as anticompetitive by European authorities. The "nuclear rent" management and the dominant position of the French utility are at the heart of the debates. On the other hand, the EU has the possibility to become the world leader in fighting climate change opening the nuclear option to Member States. This chapter focuses on the French energy challenges and the general attitude of France toward a common energy policy. France has been evolving gradually from its position of "black sheep" to an interesting position of protecting its national interests while still complying with the European energy-environment objectives and therefore perhaps presenting itself as a model for other Member States to emulate.

The French Energy Situation in the EU

The history of European nations and their respective energy reserves have implied a very high level of energy diversity throughout the EU. When comparing Member States, it is surprising to notice the differences that exist, depending on the energy mix, the industrial organization, the role played by the state, the dependence on imports, the technology choices and so forth. In France, the history of energy policy has always been characterized by a very strong intervention of the state. Public firms, or those controlled by the state, allowed the development of the French energy sector. They played a major role in its modernization, in the promotion of independence and in security of supply. The French nuclear program, launched shortly after the first oil crisis in 1973, is a good example since nuclear power covers approximately 40 percent of the French current energy needs (whereas in 2008 the world's total share of nuclear power in primary energy consumption is about 7 percent). This very "hexagonal" and state-oriented vision has to change with the globalization of energy markets, the integration process of the EU, the multiplication of uncertainties, the new climate changes challenges, and also with the financial constraints facing states for energy investments. France, like other European countries, has to find solutions for its energy dependence. Its energy mix underlines its national choices and priorities (Méritet 2008).

French Energy Resources and Dependence

In 2008, the French population represented 1 percent of the world population (around 65 million inhabitants), its gross domestic product (GDP) constitutes 4.7 percent of the world GDP and its primary energy consumption (258 Mtoe[3]) is about 2.3 percent of world energy supplies. But it has only 0.01 percent of the known world fossil fuel reserves (23 Mtoe).[4] In contrast to several European countries that benefit from raw materials (coal in Germany and Spain, natural gas in the Netherlands, etc), France is poor in energy resources. It does not possess many immediately available energy resources. Since the end of the 1970s, French coal production has fallen from 40 million tons per year to less than 3 million tons per year. The last coal mine closed in 2004. Similarly, with natural gas the field at Lacq supplied between 6 and 7 Mtoe of gas per year contributing up to 15 percent of France's primary energy production and now provides less than 1 percent of the national production of primary energy. Oil production has barely exceeded 3 Mtoe per year and presently stands at less than 1.5 Mtoe per year (around 1.8 percent of its total oil consumption). Therefore, the country is used to importing all its needs in fossil fuels. The French nuclear program was a response to the oil crises. France, like other industrialized countries, reacted to the two oil crises with measures in favor of the security of supply that deeply modified its national energy mix. In 2009, France has 58 nuclear power reactors with an installed capacity of 63 GW (it is the second largest park in the world after the United States). Since 1973, the priority is clearly the security of energy supplies with regard to the availability and the costs/prices of energies. Therefore, the French energy policy has given priority to the development of a national energy supply, most notably nuclear power and renewable energies.

Today, the EU is more vulnerable due to the increasing dependence on energy. If nothing is done, energy dependence will reach 70 percent by 2030: 90 percent of oil needs and 80 percent of natural gas consumption will have to be covered by imports (EC 2006a). This increase of import dependence can be explained by the imbalance between European reserves (0.6 percent of oil reserves in the world and 2 percent for natural gas) and its economic needs. Primary energy production in Europe is forecast to decline while demand is going to increase. Energy dependence is a key issue in the EU: National production of fossil fuel is decreasing and imports are growing considering that fossil fuel still represents three quarters of the energy consumed. France still imports half of its consumption of primary energy, against nearly three quarters before the nuclear program. In 2008, France produced 138 Mtoe and consumed 258 Mtoe. Thus, it has an energy independence of 50 percent against 26 percent in 1973. With no real fossil fuel reserves, France needs to import energy resources[5] even if the nuclear program plays its role and some measures have been implemented to limit the energy consumption as well as initiatives adopted to promote renewable energies.

France is the world's seventh largest consumer of energy with 258 Mtoe in 2008 behind for example Germany (311 Mtoe). With 3.9 toe consumed per inhabitant, France is above the average of the EU 27 (3.5 toe).[6] Until recent years, France's economic growth, rising population, growth in road transport of passengers and goods, and domestic electricity use, together with the requirements of major industrial consumers of energy (steel, chemicals, paper, cement, etc.) have all contributed to a sustained increase in energy consumption. The most significant increase is unfortunately in the transport sector (from 20 percent in 1973 to 31 percent in 2006), while the industrial sector share decreased (from 36 percent to 24 percent in 2006) and the residential and services sectors have remained stable (43 percent). This trend is unacceptable for economic and environmental reasons (energy costs, security of supplies, climate change...). The French government has therefore been implementing corrective measures for several years and reinforced them in the last energy law of 2005. One crucial element is the need to change the different energy uses and especially in transport where oil, a nonsubstitutable fuel, represents the largest energy source used. The increase of consumption in the transport sector goes beyond energy security of supply, it also implies industrial policies, the regional planning with city mass transportation territory management with city mass transportation, tax policy, social issues, and of course the competitiveness of the French economy.

The Energy Mix in the EU

The energy mix choice is made at the national level in the European framework. There is a convergence on the criteria to develop, but some differences exist between Member States. Looking at the countries in the EU, the diversity of the national energy mix is the most obvious difference: 27 countries each with its own unique energy mix. In certain countries like Greece, energy consumption relies exclusively on imported oil and coal. In France, the diversification is higher with reliance on nuclear, hydroelectricity, natural gas, and oil. Some states are almost completely dependent on energy imports, like Portugal. The new member countries further accentuate this picture of energy diversity with a strong dependence on Russian gas supplies (especially Hungary) and/or the use of coal (like in Poland).

France is neither an oil and gas exporting country nor is it a producing one. During the 1970s energy crises, it assessed its vulnerability to oil imports and its lack of gas and coal reserves. France decided that nuclear power was the best option. Between 1973 and 2008, its primary energy consumption evolved: coal now represents only 5 percent (16 percent in 1973), oil share 34 percent (68 percent in 1973), gas consumption doubled (from 7 percent in 1973 to 15 percent today), electricity consumption was multiplied by ten (from 4 to 42 percent) and renewable energies represent 5 percent of the total. There was a massive development of electric usage. The government is trying now to make consumers understand that available cheap energy is a thing from the past. From 10 percent of the final consumption in 1973, the total electricity consumption increased (mainly residential and tertiary) to represent 23 percent at present. Today France represents 17 percent of the world's nuclear activity with 58 reactors

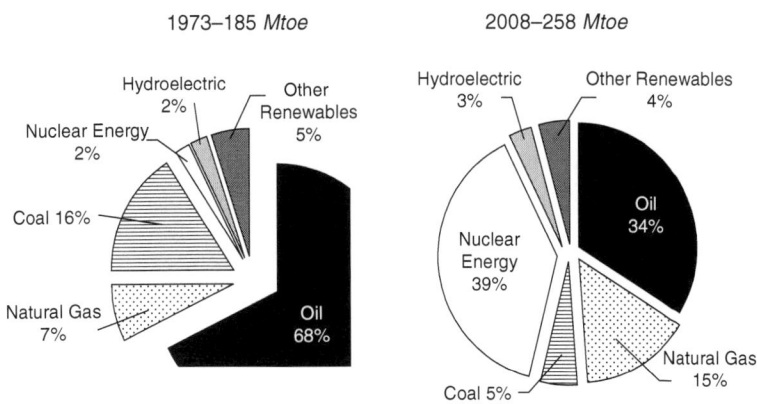

Figure 7.1 The French energy mix in 1973 and 2008 (in percent)
Source: BP Statistical Review of World Energy and DGEMP.

Table 7.1 Primary energy consumption in 2008 (in mtoe and in percent)

Countries	Total (Mtoe)	Oil (%)	Natural Gas (%)	Coal (%)	Nuclear (%)	Hydro (%)
Bulgaria	20.1	26.9	14.6	**37.0**	17.7	3.7
Czech Republic	43.3	22.9	18.0	**44.0**	13.8	1.2
Finland	26.8	**39.4**	13.3	12.6	20.3	14.4
France	257.9	35.7	15.4	4.6	**38.6**	5.6
Germany	311.1	**38.0**	23.7	26.0	10.8	1.4
Greece	34.6	**61.9**	10.9	24.8	—	2.3
Hungary	24.7	31.3	**43.7**	11.3	13.6	—
Netherlands	91.4	**50.9**	38.0	10.1	1.0	—
Poland	97.4	25.5	12.8	**61.0**	—	0.7
Portugal	22.6	**60.7**	18.3	13.9	—	7.1
Spain	143.9	**53.6**	24.4	10.1	9.3	2.6
Sweden	46.7	31.1	1.8	4.2	31.1	**31.7**
United Kingdom	211.6	37.2	**39.9**	16.7	5.6	0.5
EU 27	1728.2	**40.7**	25.5	17.4	12.3	4.1
US	2299.0	**38.5**	26.1	24.6	8.4	2.5

Source: BP Statistical Review of World Energy (2009).
Note: For each country, the highest percentage has been set in bold.

and 78 percent of the electricity produced is from nuclear power (450 billion kWh of 574 billion kWh). A strategy of a full-fledged fuel cycle was chosen by France.[7] Most of the reactors started between 1980 and 1995 (49 units). The lifetime of a third of the current operating nuclear power plants will end around 2020. In 2007, France started a third-generation EPR reactor (European Pressurized Water Reactor[8]) that should be operational in 2012.[9]

National Energy Priorities in the EU

National energy priorities continue to dominate European energy debates. The strategic energy sector remains linked to national considerations. Among the numerous debates, one is especially in the middle of all discussions: the nuclear option. Member States' positions used to be extreme on this subject, but some governments seem to have had a change of mind. Certain countries are interested in nuclear energy development (like Finland which built the latest nuclear power plant in operation in Europe), which limits fossil fuel imports and the emission of carbon dioxide (CO_2). France is not the only Member State to use nuclear energy,[10] but it is Europe's most enthusiastic advocate. The nuclear program is vital for France in its search for energy independence. The nuclear option is gaining ground again and a number of governments are opening the debate (United Kingdom and Spain) while other governments are looking to protect their coal industry (Germany and Poland). Government policies are changing, impacting also the energy mix. Italy and Germany are for instance revising their position on nuclear energy: Germany was organizing the closing of its nuclear power plants and Italy voted for a "no" to the nuclear option.

At the same time, some Member States have decided to proceed further with the use of renewable energy sources than that laid out in European directives (Denmark, Germany, etc.). In March 2007, at the European level, leaders accepted the target of 20 percent of renewable sources in energy consumption by 2020 (in exchange for flexibility on each country's contribution to the common goal). At a climate change summit, the EU adopted a long-term strategy for energy policy and climate change, called the "20-20-20," Climate action and renewable energy package: cutting the CO_2 emission by 20 percent from the 1990 level by the year 2020, developing renewable energy sources (20 percent share in the EU energy mix), and promoting energy efficiency (20 percent improvement). In response to the new Renewable Energy Directive, one of the first and most important steps in 2009 will be for the Member States to develop their renewable energy action plans.

France is among the group of countries in favor of the wording "non CO_2 emission resources or technologies" instead of "renewable energies." In this country, a balance still needs to be found between relying on nuclear power with low electricity generation costs and renewable energies that need to be subsidized to help their development. The breakdown of consumption of renewable energies in 2007 was the following: biomass still represents 58 percent (mostly wood) followed by hydroelectricity with 28 percent, then, waste 6 percent, wind and photovoltaic 1 percent, heat pumps 2 percent, biogas 1 percent, biofuel 3 percent, and other 1 percent (DGEMP 2008). Thanks to all the measures taken by the government, the French market is among the leading ones in terms of progress to develop renewable energies (Observ'ER 2009). The share of renewable energies in primary energy consumption[11] is still low at 7 percent, compared to an EU average of 7.5 percent in 2007.[12] Compared to the other countries, France was responsible for 9.5 percent of the CO_2 emissions in the EU-15 in 2007 (Germany 20.7 percent and UK 13.5 percent).[13] Per inhabitant, the country is the 11th highest in the EU-15 with six tons of CO_2 (12.7 for Finland, 10 for Germany, and 8.1 for EU-27). It is also among the last group of countries in the EU-15 in terms of CO_2 emissions per unit of GDP. France does not heavily emit CO_2 emissions thanks to the use of nuclear power, but the oil consumption for transportation is still increasing and the renewable energies (other than hydropower) need to be developed.

Energy intensity, a measure of the relationship between energy consumption and national economic production, varies between the 27 Member States. For instance, in 2006, the energy intensity varied from 125 for Denmark and 300 for Luxembourg (in Mtoe, 1995 prices). The new members present energy intensities higher than those in the older Member States.[14] The potential for improvement is very high because their emissions of greenhouse gases per inhabitant are higher than the European average. The structure of the French economy is more directed toward the services sector than other industrialized countries, which gives it a comparative advantage in the energy intensity (150 for France). Moreover, since the 1970s, France has made efforts to control energy consumption: Between 1982 and 2006, the annual improvement of energy intensity was 1.1 percent.

Considering its energy situation in the EU, the challenge for the French government and administration was to define a new national energy policy, more in line with the European framework yet not neglecting its own interests.

The French Energy Policy: Priorities and Instruments

Like all the other Member States in the EU, France has always had its own, distinct energy policy. After World War II, the energy sector appeared clearly as a highly strategic one. For many decades, the government has decided on the energy policy in the name of the nation. With the process of European integration, some governments lost a part of their sovereignty but not in this sector. The Commission gives recommendations on energy policy, even if a true common energy policy does not yet exist (at least not before the first step in the implementation of the third energy package). Member States are still responsible for the definition and implementation of their own national energy policy. France defines its own national energy policy but has to take into consideration new European constraints. The complementarities and the differences between national energy vision and the European one are helpful to understand the EU energy position and the possible development of a common policy.

Objectives of the Energy Act of 2005

A year before the publication at the European level of the Green Paper in 2006, France issued its national energy law. At present, French energy policy is defined by the Energy Act of 2005,[15] which emphasizes French interests through four priority axes. The first two apply to most of the European members. Even if they are shared at the EU level, the last two are more specific to France as they underline a higher degree of state intervention. The comparison between the French law and the European point of view is interesting. The timing was perfect to highlight the French position in the European debate. In this bill, the French energy priorities are expressed in the form of four major objectives:[16]

- *"To contribute to national energy independence and guarantee security of supply."*

As France has very limited energy resources, meeting its energy needs involves a risk that should be managed proactively. This objective is formulated on the short and long terms relevant to quantity and price. There is a double goal: to limit the exposure of the French economy to fluctuation in energy prices (in particular developing national energy production) and to ensure the availability of sufficient capacity to cope with problems of energy shortages (electricity blackout, lack of gas storage…).

- *"To protect human health and the environment in particular by fighting against climate change."*

Energy consumption and production can have a major impact on the environment, mainly the emission of green house gases, but also the emission of pollutants and the production of radioactive wastes. One key purpose of the French energy policy is to control the changes in environment protection with CO_2 emission and ensure that the risks of the nuclear sector are properly managed. In addition to this energy bill and within the framework of its Kyoto commitments, the "Plan Climat" in 2004, decided on measures to save nearly 15 million tons of carbon equivalents per year by 2010 (which means a quartering of CO_2 emission by 2050).

- *"To ensure competitive energy prices."*

The price, quality, and availability of energy are determining factors in France's competitiveness. This goal relies on the national nuclear program that allows France to have a low electricity generation cost for households and industries. France is keen to maintain its economic advantage in terms of the cost of production and the "public service" missions.

- *"To guarantee social and technical cohesion by ensuring access to energy for all."*

It is important that the energy policy provides everyone, and in particular the most deprived in society, with access to a quality energy source at a competitive price. Solidarity but also taxation, regulated tariffs, and public service missions, such as, for electricity, the obligation of supply, the equal treatment of customers, and so on are all part of the French way of managing energy.

Means and Instruments to Achieve the Energy Policy Goals

To reach the four goals of the energy bill, the French government employs four means: 1) control of the energy demand through a series of incentives and programs (including an energy saving certificate scheme [White Certificates], standards, and tax incentives); 2) diversity of the energy mix (by increasing the use of renewable energies and keeping the nuclear option open); 3) development of energy grids and storage capacities (to improve the safety of France's energy supply); and 4) research and development on energy (to meet long-term challenges in terms of energy intensity and consumption of renewable energies).

To provide a framework for these decisions "four goals and four means," the Energy Act of 2005 laid down quantitative objectives:

- a quartering of CO_2 emissions by 2050;
- an average reduction of final energy intensity of at least 2 percent per year from 2015, and 2.5 percent from 2015 to 2030:
- a production of 10 percent of energy needs from renewable energy sources by 2010; and
- a use of biofuels to a level of 5.75 percent by the end of 2008 and 7 percent in 2010.

In this new energy law, the government decided to implement some tools to help to reach the objectives of energy security of supply and more especially for electricity which is strategic.[17] The French government has put in place two specific instruments to regulate the market so as to ensure the security of electricity supply. The first tool is the "multiannual objective contracts" signed with the company of the public distribution system (Réseau de Transport d'Electricité [RTE]) and with the companies that fulfill public service missions.[18] Electricity and gas public utilities[19] status are very precisely defined by French law: their definition remains however rather broad but typically French with their "public service" missions. Each year, their cost is measured by the national regulatory commission. The second instrument is "multiannual programming of investment in production" (PPI[20]) which lays down objectives of capacity to be installed by primary energy sources. The PPI defines the need in electricity capacities and allows the government, if these capacities are not built, to call for tenders. Therefore, the French state has not given up all its prerogatives in terms of electricity investments.

To reduce France's energy dependence, it has been decided to promote energy savings and to invest in nuclear electricity generation and renewable energies. These options provide a reliable long-term supply without greenhouse gas emissions, and nuclear energy ensures stable electricity prices. They also correspond to French energy priorities. It was also decided in 2004 to begin to build an EPR model to have the option of eventually using this technology to replace the present generating facilities but also to support these facilities. The law of June 13, 2006 defines guidelines on nuclear transparency and security. In addition, the law on the management of radioactive materials and waste was published on June 29, 2006. French public opinion seems to be more positive toward nuclear energy compared to other countries (or for some analysts more realistic?). In parallel, since 1974, France has implemented energy saving measures. A tax credit for energy saving and renewable energies was reinforced in 2006.[21] An energy saving certificate scheme has been also implemented. The principle of energy saving certificates is based on an obligation imposed on energy sellers by the public authorities to generate energy savings over a given period. To develop renewable energies, several support programs have been put in place. Among them, the systems of obligatory purchase by the European Development Fund (EDF) and the other electricity distributors of electricity generated by renewable energies have given new impetus to renewable sources, such as wind power. Renewable energies benefit from the tax credit since 2005. This procedure has been a great success, since the solar energy market for heating has experienced spectacular growth.

For several decades, France has been striving to diversify its energy mix and to make its energy supply secure. The government chose nuclear power to ensure national independence and environmental protection at a stable and competitive price. The most recent energy laws reinforced its national goals by giving new tools and quantitative objectives. In reaction to the Green Paper in 2006, France made its own proposals public in a memorandum circulated to EU finance ministers. The French memo is relatively close to the Commission's Green Paper but places more emphasis on nuclear power and research in next generation nuclear power stations. As a founding member and a very significant player in the EU, the role and position of France is critical to the development of a common policy. Nevertheless, compliance with the European framework calls for adjustments to the French mindset and policy approach. The two positions are not so remote: the main goals are the same, some national priorities are underlined and the means may be different.

French Energy Challenges in the EU Framework

While France tries to implement its energy policy, the government has to face several challenges linked to the European integration process and energy market fundamentals. In terms of European energy policy, it is worthwhile trying to understand the French position, as it relates to energy companies' status and state intervention. Some of them are indeed at the core of very animated discussions. At the same time, the energy-environment challenge of the EU puts France in a good position. The nuclear option would appear to be a key factor in the debate.

France and the European Energy Deregulation Process

European law goes beyond the notion of "state" and the construction of the single market must be done through competition.

European requirements are a shock for the French culture of *dirigisme* ("colberto-jacobine" state interventionism). They imply major changes of electric and gas industries and, more generally, of all network industries. European regulations imply a complete separation between competitive activities (generation, purchase and supply of gas and electricity) and regulated activities (transmission). Networks are regarded as opened "essential facilities" with third-party access supervised by an independent authority of regulation. The directives of 1996 (electricity) and 1998 (natural gas) initiated the deregulation process and the directive of 2003 provides for the total opening up to competition. Since July 2007, all consumers have the choice of their energy suppliers. This process has raised strong opposition from certain members of the French parliament, who demanded the renegotiation of the directive. Indeed, this opposition reflected several refusals at once: the refusal of Europe, of the markets, and of competition. The French political community is conscious of these stakes but is still attracted by the maintenance of a mainly illusory and expensive public intervention policy and forgets that the fundamental word is "European" and not "Franco-French." It is true that politicians are confronted with an electorate attached to the status quo. Employees of public companies stand by their privileges, consumers are against changes and afraid of competition, and companies talk about delocalization to obtain regulated tariffs. It is not easy to explain to French citizens that GDF-Suez will supply electricity, that EDF will supply gas, and that in spite of the nuclear park, the French pay an over CO_2 cost and that the electricity prices will be the same as that generated from coal in Germany.

The Commission launched two procedures against France: one for the nontransposition of whole directives and the other one for state aid. Regulated electricity tariffs are considered as subsidies and therefore it is state aid because EDF is still a state firm. According to the Commission, these artificially low tariffs give an economic advantage to some companies and distort competition in the European single market. The Commission asks for the end of regulated tariffs[22] and the development of market prices through competition. The state intervention on prices and tariffs for electricity and natural gas are under scrutiny. Traditionally, the prices of oil products were administered prices. It is still the case for gas and electricity, at least for certain categories of customers. Is it time to free up these prices? With the deregulation process, the main question is how much "flexibility" can the government give to energy prices. For some people this question should not even be raised because energy prices should be competitive and not state regulated. For other people, it is inconceivable that French consumers should not benefit from the nuclear rent. A change in policy would be problematic from a social and political perspective in France today.

There is not a European energy policy yet. Nevertheless, there is a common competition policy that is applied to the European energy market. At the EU level, an energy price convergence is expectedly not an energy mix convergence.[23] What are the challenges for France? France is not ready to lose the benefits of its choices: nuclear power gives the country very low electricity generation costs. This policy involved closing all the coal mines at a huge social and economic cost particularly for the end users. Today French electricity is sourced mainly from nuclear and hydro: the cost of electricity generation is no longer dependent on fossil fuels. It is complicated to compete with the state owned French utility, with its very low production costs not linked to oil prices. The challenge for the government is to find a solution to let French consumers go on benefiting from nuclear low costs while respecting European directives.

In the energy sector inquiry (EC 2006b), the dominant positions of historical companies were already limiting the entry of new actors and hence the benefits of competition. In France, it is hard to compete with EDF's production cost based on nuclear power plants, which are almost all fully amortized. Consequently there are no real new entrants at least for the base load production due to the cost advantages of this historical actor. The national fear is that the Commission will pass a new directive imposing a maximum of market shares for historic companies in their domestic market. To avoid that, competition needs to exist in France otherwise it will lead to the dismantling of EDF. The French utility has been gaining market shares all over Europe for several years but its competitors cannot really penetrate its historical market. Some countries reacted passing some "reciprocity laws" limiting the access of EDF to some assets. The EC called the French government to task for unfair competition, but with a stronger Competition Commission, the threats could become reality.

With limited European interconnections and the refusal of some countries to build nuclear plants (which appears today the most competitive electricity generation technology), French nuclear enjoys a "scarcity rent" from the difference between European price and complete cost of French nuclear power plant generation. On the European market, the price is set to the marginal cost which is the production cost of the last plant called (it is often a natural gas or coal thermal unit). This price is almost always higher to the French cost of production because French nuclear power plants are not often the last units called. European electricity prices are superior to French regulated tariffs (which are linked to the cost of production of the French mix hydro-nuclear power). Competitors cannot increase their market shares in France: they cannot compete with the economic advantage of EDF. The theoretical solution is easy: new entrants need to have access to French nuclear power plants. This issue raises a multitude of questions with the main one being the regulated tariff of access to nuclear assets. In reality it will be compulsory to define an "access tariff": nuclear power plants could be considered as "essential facilities" built under the monopoly position of EDF. In the Champsaur Commission report (Champsaur 2009), the debate is open on the development of competition in the French electricity market with the nuclear rent. Two solutions are being currently discussed[24] 1) to tax the nuclear which means to increase the cost of production of EDF and use the rent (to do what? by whom?); and 2) to allow competitors to have access to nuclear asset (limited in time and in space) with a regulated price fixed by the French Energy Regulatory Commission (CRE[25]). The price should be close to the "economic cost" of nuclear. Competition will be on the supplier margin. There will be no more regulated tariffs "downstream" but a regulated tariff "upstream."

The Champsaur Commission recommends keeping the regulated tariffs for residential consumers on condition that they reflect the cost.[26] In France, the current regulated tariffs are too far from the cost of electricity generation in new power plants to be built. If the authority needs to build new capacities, the power plants have to be profitable which is not the case with the current level of prices.[27] Regulated tariffs do not give the correct incentives for firms to invest and for consumers to choose. During the summer 2009, the president of EDF asked[28] for a 20 percent increase of the electricity tariffs over three years (2 or 3 euros more per month on each energy bill).[29]

After the Champsaur report, a law called NOME (Nouvelle Organisation des Marchés Electriques) was supposed to come into force on July 1, 2010, three years to the day after the opening of retail market. However, its review under the assembly for the fall 2009 has been postponed to spring 2010, leaving some doubt about the date of its effective implementation. The project law NOME, is the next step of opening electricity markets to competition in France. It largely reflects the findings of the report of the Champsaur Commission . Discussions of the project bill are currently underway by French parliamentarians. It may therefore be subject to change. The law theoretically programs the disappearance of regulated tariffs for professionals (not households). The law also included new measures on rent sharing between nuclear suppliers. EDF will thus be forced to sell electricity to its competitors at a price lower than it currently does. The maximum volume and the price would be set annually by the ministers in charge of economy and energy, after consulting the Commission de Regulation de l'Energie. The law is likely to fundamentally change the structure of the electricity market in France. The historical player, EDF seems to be scared by this project bill: it is a direct threat to its dominant position in the French electricity market and it will allow the increase of market shares of its competitors (Poweo, Direct Energy, etc.). Very powerful unions are against this project law that would "destroy the French energy system." At the dawn of this great debate, a question on everyone's mind is: how will the exchange of nuclear capacity work and what is its long-term viability?

The debate over the management on the French nuclear rent and the organization of the energy market is just beginning. In the United States, Joskow and Schmalensee (1983) warned us that the deregulation process will take time: "If deregulation is to play a role in helping to improve the efficiency with which electricity is produced and used, it must be introduced as part of a long-term process that also encompasses regulatory and structural reform" (p. 221). For France, it could take ten years until the new electric capacities are built and running. Will the Commission have the patience to wait?

France and the European Climate Change Constraints

Europe has the potential to become a key actor in the area of energy and climate change in the 21st century. Climate change findings have recently revealed that the current energy-environment equilibrium is unsustainable. In this area, the incentives to cooperate are obvious. The protection of the environment introduces issues that have to be managed at a global level rather than the European level in the old continent. In the EU, actions are underway to build a sustainable energy future. Cooperation and solidarity are possible and can be successful as it is already for environmental questions. The European process also leads to collective agreements. Member States showed solidarity with the European trading system. They succeeded in setting up the first market of emission permits for CO_2. This market is a major step in the direction of greenhouse gas emissions reduction and might even eventually lead to a single energy market. (See Jørgen Wettestad's chapter 4 in this volume).

The Green Paper published by the Commission in 2006 does not quite reflect a truly common European energy policy but it highlights a certain number of principles on which the Member States agree to build the future energy system. These principles stress three key areas: 1) to improve the energy efficiency; 2) to diversify the energy mix; and 3) to ensure the security of supply. These principles are accompanied by precise national objectives with regard to: energy saving, development of renewable energies, and security storages. Nothing is obviously indicated on nuclear power but each country preserves its freedom of choice. One cannot at the same time reduce the gas emissions and close the door to nuclear power as pointed out by L. de Palacio, the former energy commissioner.

In a carbon-constrained world, in which the European countries are committed to reach their Kyoto targets,[30] an increase of coal fired power generation in the absence of carbon capture and storage is not a viable option. The only real alternative is to have nuclear power generation with some renewable energy. During a European summit in March 2007, a new step was made: a binding target of 20 percent for renewable fuels has been set in exchange for flexibility on each country's contribution to the common goals. References to the national energy mix have been added. It is one of the most ambitious packages on energy security and climate change protection. In an attempt to balance the pro and anti nuclear power countries, it is recognized that nuclear may also play a role in Europe's drive to cut greenhouse gas emissions. Under pressure from several new members, the EU agreed that individual targets would be allowed for each of the 27 Member States. These new members rely heavily on cheap coal and oil and are reluctant to switch to more costly environmentally friendly alternatives. The economic competitiveness of the countries and the whole EU is in question.

In the Kyoto protocol, France agreed to stabilize its greenhouse gas emissions at their 1990 level by 2008–2012 (Germany must reduce by 21 percent and UK by 12.5 percent). Compared to other Member States, France has small margins of maneuver. To comply with this objective, the *Plan Climat* in 2004, the energy bill of 2005, and the nuclear energy laws in 2006 were launched. For France, nuclear power is an answer to energy needs, climate change, and fears of energy supply disruption, but skeptics counter that it is too costly and dangerous to be viable. Within this framework, France can evolve from its role of "black sheep" and better fit into the emerging policy of the EU. French and European energy policies can be compatible and are not necessarily so different after all.

Conclusion

In spite of the energy diversity of the EU, a common vision has always been shared by all the Member States over energy development for the future. The single energy market is still the main common goal. The publication of the Green Paper in 2006 reaffirms the principle of solidarity between the countries in the EU. EU energy policy is a basket of a number of policies that are concerned with energy markets and energy issues. The last energy and environment packages represent a considerable compromise agreement that would make Europe the world leader in the fight against climate change.

What are the incentives to cooperate? Completion of the internal market, environment protection, and security of supply are the common energy battles that call for a common solution. Unity of the 27 member countries appears as the only means to meet the energy challenges of the 21st century. The European Trading Scheme shows that Member States can work together in the same direction in terms of environmental protection. Why should this not also be the case for energy policy? Energy policy still remains the responsibility of Member States, and decisions vary from one country to another.

A consensus exists on the need to reduce oil usage, develop liquefied natural gas, develop nuclear power in parallel with renewable energies, and keep faith in market mechanisms to decide on choices while some "garde-fous" need to be there too. Within a context of rising energy prices and growing world demand for fossil fuel, there is not just one energy source solution. An energy mix is clearly needed. The Europe of energy does not exist yet, but several Member States are actually able to reach certain common positions in energy policy. More flexible forms of integration are necessary to achieve commitments on a regional or functional basis. The entry of the EU institutions into the making of an EU energy policy is recent and shaky. The Member States have always had and still have strong political and legal rights to define and implement autonomous energy policies. What we may need today is a Schengen[31] area for energy. For some analysts, this kind of agreement would allow legal binding cooperation between Member States. It could represent an intermediate step toward harmonization and a common energy policy. It would give greater legal flexibility than is present under the Lisbon Treaty allowing each Member State to enter or not into a new area of European common policy built on formerly kingly rights and powers of Member States. Freedom of choice has always been appreciated by French people!

To move from a shared vision to a European energy policy, large steps are necessary but could be accelerated by a common foreign energy policy. Foreign policy relates to dialogue with the large exporting countries (Russia,[32] OPEC), with the big consumers (the United States, China, Japan, India) and also with the poorest countries (where more than one billion individuals do not have access to electricity). It would permit the EU to speak with a "single and unified voice" in international energy negotiations. Up to now, France like Germany or UK has its own position linked to its energy culture (state intervention, vertical integration, unions...), history (domestic resources, former colonies...)...The globalization of energy-environment problems makes the multiplication of the international dialogues in bilateral or multilateral forms essential. Even the "conservative party" in the UK one of the most euro-skeptical countries thinks it is compulsory to have a European energy policy to assure security of supply and fight against climate change. It is maybe through these two main issues that the development of a common policy will be possible with the support of the biggest Member States. What compromises can be identified and reached between Paris and the EU so that both "speak as one" on energy and environmental questions? That is the current challenge faced by the French government. France needs to figure out how to be part of the European process while still protecting its national ideas. France could and would like to play a significant role and even try to be a model in the EU. The debate over the new French project law is a step toward the compliance to European regulation. Some national fears need to disappear (end users, Unions...) and certain national advantages need to be highlighted (nuclear plants competitiveness, CO_2 emissions, renewable energies, white certificates...). Thus, France might evolve from "black sheep" to an energy model based on better energy intensity, energy independence, low electricity costs, energy capacities storages, and low emissions. France just needs to figure out how to deal with its long history of state intervention in energy sectors. At a stage when the process of European integration is at a standstill, the debate about energy issues is part of a larger debate about the nature and destiny of the EU. The European energy market is moving ahead, albeit slowly with its recurring national protectionisms, obstacles, and contradictions. Nonetheless it aptly reflects and represents our future as "United in Diversity."[33]

Notes

1. Today, the EU-27 members are Austria, Belgium, Bulgaria, Cyprus, the Czech Republic, Denmark, Estonia, Finland, France, Germany, Greece, Hungary, Ireland, Italy, Latvia, Lithuania, Luxembourg, Malta, the Netherlands, Poland, Portugal, Romania, Slovakia, Slovenia, Spain, Sweden, and the UK.
2. GDF-Suez is the result of the merger between Gaz de France and Suez Gulf Power Company in 2008.
3. Mtoe equals Million of tons oil equivalent.
4. Almost all the data on the French energy situation are official data from the French administration, source: DGEMP web site www.developpement-durable.gouv.fr, Direction Générale de l'Energie et des Matières Premières which is the general directorate for energy and raw materials in France.
5. The official forecasts are a doubling of imports by 2025.
6. Data are from the International Energy Agency (IEA).
7. France is one of the few countries where all fuel cycle facilities are found: conversion, enrichment, fabrication, reprocessing, and recycling of nuclear materials.
8. The European Pressurized Reactor (EPR), is the third-generation Pressurized Water Reactor (PWR) developed under Franco-German cooperation.
9. France has also devoted research programs to the fourth generation technology (sodium cooled fast reactor). Those units should be operational by 2040.
10. 47 percent of the nuclear electricity in the EU is generated solely by France, but for example, the UK owns 19 reactors (12 GW), Sweden 10 reactors (9 GW), and Germany 17 reactors (20 GW), etc.
11. Looking at the objectives of 2020, the share of energy from renewable sources in final consumption of energy in 2007 was 10.3 percent and the target is 23 percent.
12. The leaders are Sweden with 31 percent, Latvia 30 percent, Austria 23 percent, and Finland 23 percent—usually countries that use a lot of hydropower.
13. The EU-15 was responsible for 82 percent of the total of CO_2 emissions of the EU-27 in 2007.

14. The 7th new members from EU-15 to EU-25 presented energy intensities until 1400 for Estonia and Latvia.
15. Planning Act 2005-781 of July 13, "Loi d'Orientation sur l'Energie" loi n°2005-781 of July 13, 2005 is available on the website of the French administration: www.legifrance.fr.
16. The titles of the four goals are the original titles from the law with strategic words.
17. With regards to petroleum products, France meets EU and IEA obligations on strategic stocks. For natural gas, some similar measures to electricity have been implemented.
18. The right of access of users to services, the equality of their treatment which is synonymous with the refusal of all discrimination and the continuity of service in time and space are virtues consubstantial with the traditional definition of the French concept of public service.
19. According to the law, the status of EDF and GDF-Suez were changed to become corporations with a gradual opening of their capital whilst keeping them within the public sector.
20. PPI stands for Programmation Pluriannuel d'Investissements.
21. For example from 40 percent to 50 percent for energy production equipment using a renewable energy source and certain types of heat pump.
22. In June 2007, the Commission opened an investigation on standard regulated tariffs and return tariffs for large and middle size industrial consumers (not private consumers). French consumers can buy their electricity either on the free market or on the regulated market (standard regulated tariffs) set by the state. Customers who left the regulated market can ask for a special state administrated return tariff (Tarif Réglementé Transitoire d'Ajustement de Marché TARTAM) below the market price. Already 10 percent of large consumers benefited from this offer.
23. It is interesting to remember the market coupling of some power exchanges. The market coupling of APX, Belpex and Powernext will create a single electricity market in the three countries with a single price, only differing when there is insufficient interconnection capacity available on the Belgian—French or the Belgian—Dutch border. The three exchanges thereby provide a better quality of price formation and a greater liquidity in the coupled markets.
24. The Champsaur Commission has a preference on the second solution.
25. CRE stands for Commisison de Regulation de l'Energie.
26. Regulated tariffs exist in other European countries. Some of them are considering removing them, because they are not compatible with the deregulation philosophy.
27. Up to now, only two EPR prototypes are planned (for up to 40 of similar design). The price paid by consumer should not be set on EPR costs because EPR is not yet the marginal unit (it will be when all units will be changed). The new capacity in France should be the EPR which will be in operation in several years (ten years) and its cost is projected to be 55

euros / MWh (without transport and distribution costs) compared to the 30–40 euros / MWh in regulated tariffs in 2008.
28. The level of regulated tariffs is decided by the government after consultation with EDF and the CRE.
29. In July 2009, the government authorized an increase of 1.9 percent for private consumers.
30. Under the Kyoto Protocol, the EU agrees to reduce its emissions by 8 percent from level of 1990 by 2012.
31. The Schengen agreement allows EU citizens to travel within the Schengen area without being subject to police controls. The agreement was included in the Treaty of Amsterdam in 1997. Today 24 countries are in the Schengen area not all the EU countries are in and some non EU countries are in.
32. Member States showed solidarity during the Russian Ukrainian gas crises at the beginning of 2009.
33. It is the motto of the EU.

Works Cited

BP Statistical Review of World Energy. 2008 (2009). BP web website available at http://www.bp.com/productlanding.do?categoryId=6929&contentId=7044622.
Champsaur, P. 2009. *Rapport de la commission sur l'organisation du marché de l'électricité*. Available at http://actionnaires.edf.com/fichiers/fckeditor/File/Finance/investors/2009/090424-RapportChampsaur_vf.pdf.
DGEMP. 2008. Available at www.developpement-durable.gouv.fr.
EC. 2006a. European Commission Competition DG Sector Inquiry on the Gas and Electricity Market. Art 17 Regulation 1/2003. Preliminary Report. Bruxelles.February 16, 2006. Available at http://ec.europa.eu/comm/competition/antitrust/others/sector_inquiries/energy/execsum.pdf.
EC. 2006b. *Green Paper: European strategy for secure, competitive and sustainable energy*, European Commission Competition DG. Bruxelles. Available at http://ec.europa.eu/energy/green-paper-energy/doc/2006_03_08_gp_document_fr.pdf.
Joskow, P. and R. Schmalensee. 1983. *Markets for Power.* MIT Press.
Méritet, S. 2008. *French Perspectives in the Emerging European Union Energy Policy*. Energy Policy. no.35: 4767–4771.
Observ'ER. 2009. *The State of Renewable Energies in Europe*. The Eighth EuroObserv'ER Report.

Chapter Eight

Germany and EU Energy Policy: Conflicted Champion of Integration?

John S. Duffield and Kirsten Westphal

Germany is critical to the development of a common European Union (EU) energy policy. It is by far the largest energy user of the 27 Member States, accounting for approximately 18 percent of total energy consumption in the EU (BP 2010). It is also a substantial energy producer, ranking second in the production of coal (after Poland) and second in nuclear electricity generation (after France). Finally, Germany plays a crucial role by virtue of its central geographical location, which puts it in the middle of regional natural gas and electric power distribution networks.

Germany has traditionally been one of the most consistent proponents of European integration. It was one of the six members of the three original European communities and, along with France, has often been regarded as the "motor" of European integration. In more recent years, Germany championed monetary union and the enlargement of EU to include many of the Central European countries of the former Soviet bloc.

When it comes to recent developments in EU energy policy, however, Germany has exhibited much more ambivalence. It has backed some EU energy policy initiatives, especially those concerning climate change, renewable sources of energy, and energy conservation. But it has resisted others, such as the liberalization of the gas and electricity markets and the creation of a common external energy policy. And even in cases where Germany has been generally supportive of a common energy policy objective, is has often fought hard to put its own stamp on the details, such as the mechanisms for promoting renewable energy sources and the implementation of the Emissions Trading Scheme (ETS).

This chapter explores the mixed pattern of German support for a common EU energy policy over the past decade. It begins by describing Germany's energy situation at the beginning of the 2000s and the energy challenges Germany has faced in recent years. It then describes the key features of German energy policy over the same period and how these have played themselves out at the EU level. The next section explores the determinants of German energy policy and Germany's ambivalent attitude toward a common EU energy policy. The chapter concludes with a discussion of the implication of German policy for the future of EU energy policy.

Background

Germany's Energy Mix in 2000

As Germany entered the 2000s, its mix of energy sources had changed substantially since before the first oil shock in 1973. Oil continued to command the biggest share of Germany's primary energy consumption (PEC), at just under 40 percent. But this figure was down substantially from the peak of 57 percent, in the former West Germany, reached in the early 1970s (BP 2010). Virtually all of the oil consumed in Germany was imported, with nearly one-third coming from Russia (IEA 2002, 58). But this import dependence raised few concerns, since petroleum and petroleum products from one foreign supplier can be substituted relatively easily by those from another.

Next came coal, which accounted for just over a quarter of Germany's PEC, a figure that had been fairly steady since the mid-1990s. Coal, especially brown coal (lignite), generated more than half of Germany's electricity, while hard coal was used in steel production. Although domestic coal production had declined as inefficient mines were closed, especially in the former eastern states, it still provided for about two-thirds of German coal consumption.

Third on the list was natural gas, which had met about 22 percent of Germany's energy needs since the mid-1990s. Germany was not entirely dependent on gas imports, producing about 20 percent of its consumption at home. But most imported gas arrived via fixed pipelines from just three countries—Russia (45 percent in 2002), Norway (27 percent), and the Netherlands (22 percent)—and could not easily be replaced in the event of a supply disruption (AGEB 2010; IEA 2002, 76).

Nuclear power plants accounted for 30 percent of electricity production in 2000. At the time, Germany had 19 operating commercial nuclear reactors, but none had come on line since 1988, and the former East German reactors had all been shut down for safety reasons (IEA 2002, 111).

Bringing up the rear were renewable sources of energy. These accounted for just 3.4 percent of PEC and 7.3 percent of electric power generation in 2000. But the contribution from renewable sources was growing rapidly, having doubled since 1990. In 2000, Germany was the world leader in wind power production and had the highest installed solar electric capacity in Europe (IEA 2002, 91–92).

General Goals and Challenges of German Energy Policy in the 2000s

German energy policy has been guided by three primary goals:

1. economic efficiency, especially in the form of affordable energy prices (*Wirtschaftlichkeit*);
2. environmental protection and sustainability (*Umweltverträglichkeit*); and
3. security of supply (*Versorgungssicherheit*).

Economic efficiency has been perhaps the most constant goal of postwar German energy policy. During the second half of the 1980s and most of the 1990s, its achievement did not seem particularly problematic. Energy, and especially oil, prices were generally low. In the late 1990s and 2000s, however, it became a matter of increasing concern as oil prices rose more or less steadily.

In comparison, environmental sustainability is a relatively new goal. It first appeared in the 1970s in the form of worries about the safety of nuclear power plants and the disposal of nuclear waste. Since the late 1980s and 1990s, however, increasing attention has been devoted to the closely related challenges of climate change and reducing greenhouse gas emissions, much of which are attributable to energy consumption. Public concern about climate change reached a crescendo in 2007, with the publication by the United Nations (UN) Intergovernmental Panel on Climate Change of its Fourth Assessment Report, but the issue has often dominated the German energy policy agenda in recent years.

In response, the government has adopted a series of ambitious goals and programs. In 1995, it established a goal of cutting CO_2 emissions by 25 percent over the period 1990–2005. And at the end of the 1990s, it agreed to reduce its greenhouse gas emissions by 21 percent (compared to 1990 levels) within the EU Burden-Sharing agreement under the Kyoto Protocol (IEA 2002, 38). In 2000, the government adopted a comprehensive National Climate Protection Programme, and the Integrated Energy and Climate Programme (IECP) approved by the government in 2007 was largely, if not entirely, aimed at the addressing the problem of climate change (Duffield 2009). As Chancellor Angela Merkel stated, "with this program, we are taking on the central challenge of the 21st century, climate change" (Bundesregierung 2007). The government offered to reduce Germany's CO_2 emissions by a breathtaking 40 percent below the 1990 level by 2020, conditional, however, on the EU achieving a 30 percent reduction over the same time period and other states committing themselves to similarly ambitious goals.

After spiking in the 1970s and early 1980 as a result of the oil shocks, concerns about energy security remained largely dormant during the next two decades. Even Germany's increasing reliance on energy imports, which reached 60 percent of total consumption in 2000 (IEA 2002, 28), raised few alarms. German officials emphasized that the country's energy supplies were highly reliable. Russia, like the Soviet Union before it, could be counted on for promised deliveries of oil and gas, and Germany possessed large petroleum stockpiles and gas storage facilities that it could draw upon in the event of an emergency.

Thus, energy security did not regain prominence as a policy issue until the beginning of 2006. The occasion was the gas dispute that erupted that January between Russia and Ukraine. Over the next several years, additional events raised further questions about Russia's dependability as an energy supplier.

Key Elements of German Energy Policy in the 2000s

How has Germany sought to promote its energy policy goals and address the corresponding challenges in the past decade?

One major thrust of Germany policy, which dates back to the 1970s, has been to reduce energy consumption by increasing energy efficiency. Germany had long maintained substantial excise taxes on most fossil fuels, and in 1999, the government introduced a new "eco tax" on motor fuels, heating fuels, and electricity, which was gradually raised over the next four years and was intended in large part to encourage energy savings. Early in the 2000s, the government quickly implemented EU directives on energy labeling of appliances and the energy performance of buildings, and it established a program to provide financial support for building renovations that improved energy efficiency and reduced CO_2 emissions. The 2005 grand coalition agreement established the ambitious objective of doubling energy productivity by the year 2020 compared with 1990, which would require annual increases of around 3 percent.

A somewhat newer but equally important component of German policy has been the promotion of renewable energy sources, especially for electricity production. The use of renewables could serve to reduce both greenhouse gas emissions and fossil fuel imports. The first major step was the 1991 Electricity Feed Law, which obliged power companies to buy all the electricity generated from wind, hydropower, biomass, and solar energy in their distribution areas at a price, or feed-in tariff, based on the end-use cost to consumers. The 2000 Renewable Energy Act extended coverage to additional renewable sources, such as landfill gas and geothermal energy, and revised the feed-in tariff formula to reflect the cost of each technology and to provide long-term certainty for both developers and users (IEA 2002, 93–94).

As a result of these incentives, German renewable energy output grew at an annual rate of 12 percent between 2000 and 2006 (IEA 2007, 65). Thus Germany was able to meet its initial goals of generating 12.5 percent of its electricity and 4.2 percent of total energy consumption from renewable sources by 2010 well ahead of schedule. That rapid progress prompted the "Black-Red" grand coalition (2005–2009) to establish even more ambitious targets for renewable energy sources for 2020: at least 20 percent of electricity generation and at least 10 percent of the total energy supply. The coalition also introduced a biofuels obligation that would rise to 6.75 percent of the fuel supply in 2010, exceeding the corresponding EU target of 5.75 percent, and then to 8 percent in 2015 (IEA 2007, 72).

While consistently promoting energy efficiency and renewables, recent Germany energy policy has been less consistent in other areas. One has been the issue of energy market structure. The German government has frequently expressed support for competitive energy markets, largely as a way of holding down energy prices. But it has also supported the establishment and maintenance of large national energy companies that could use domestic market power to increase their leverage in negotiations with foreign energy companies, such as Gazprom (Buchan 2009, 16). Thus when the Federal Cartel Office rejected the merger of one of the four dominant electric utilities, E.On, with the leading natural gas supplier, Ruhrgas, it was overruled by the Federal Ministry of Economics (BWMi)[1] (Müller 2007, 32–33; Westphal 2007, 100). For domestic political and social reasons, the government also maintained subsidies for hard coal production, although in 2007 an agreement was reached to phase them out over the following decade.

Inconsistency has also characterized Germany policy toward nuclear power, despite the widespread revival of interest in nuclear power—the so-called nuclear renaissance—that concerns about climate change and energy security have occasioned in a number of other countries. The Green party grew out of the nuclear protest movement in the 1970s, and the Social Democratic Party (SPD) had opposed nuclear power since the mid-1980s. When these two parties formed a "Red-Green" coalition government (1998–2005), one of their top priorities was to wean the country off of nuclear power. In 2000, the Red-Green government reached an agreement with the electrical utilities, formalized in a 2002 law, to phase out all nuclear power plants by limiting their effective lifetimes. No new plants could be constructed, and the last operating facility would go out of service around 2022 (Westphal 2009a).

Many outside the government, including the opposition parties, questioned the wisdom of the nuclear phaseout, which would deprive Germany of a carbon-free energy source and potentially increase Germany's dependence on energy imports. And when the center-right Union parties (CDU/CSU) formed a grand coalition with the SPD in 2005, some of its leaders called for at least extending the lifetimes of the existing nuclear power plants. Still, the SPD held firm, insisting that there be no change in the policy as a condition for joining the new government. The 2009 election of a CDU/CSU-Liberal "Black-Yellow" coalition, however, created a new opportunity to revisit the phaseout, and in September 2010, the government called for a temporary extension (12 years on average) of the lifetimes of the remaining 17 power plants (BMWi/BMU 2010).

A final important aspect of German energy policy that has seen changing emphasis has been the external dimension. The Red-Green coalition, headed by Gerhard Schröder, emphasized building and maintaining bilateral ties with Russia (see the contribution by Grätz in this volume). It promoted in particular the construction by a consortium of Russian and German energy companies of a natural gas pipeline under the North Sea that would link Germany directly to Russian gas supplies. In the view of one experienced observer, "Germany has asserted that it reserves the right to work out its long-term energy security with Russia on a bilateral, mutually beneficial, pragmatic footing—and that it brooks no outside or third-party intervention (Bhadrakumar 2006)."

Although led by a former Schröder protégé, Frank-Walter Steinmeier, the foreign ministry in the subsequent Black-Red grand coalition placed more emphasis on multilateralism. The overall goal was to promote greater dialogue among producer, consumer, and transit countries in order to emphasize their common interest in stable and predictable energy trade. Steinmeier repeatedly called for the creation of a system of cooperation energy security, which, he argued, would help to build mutual understanding and trust. And with regard to Russia in particular, the new government's principal approach was to try to embed Russia in a multilateral rule-based framework for trade and investment based on liberal principles of market access. The foreign ministry hoped to induce Russia to ratify the Energy Charter Treaty and its important transit protocol and, that failing, to replace the expiring EU-Russia partnership and cooperation agreement (PCA) with a new one that contained a substantial section on energy (Duffield 2009).[2]

Germany and EU Energy Policy in the 2000s: Implications of German Energy Policy

Recent Germany energy policy has had mixed implications for the establishment of a common EU energy policy. Overall, one could say that Germany has been at best ambivalent about developments at the EU level. In some respects, Germany has made EU energy policy a top priority, especially where doing so has been seen as a means of achieving Germany's goals of fighting climate change and, to a lesser extent, energy security. Indeed, energy policy was a special focus during the German presidency of the EU during the first half of 2007, which saw the adoption of a set of ambitious EU energy policy goals at the spring meeting of the Council (Silberberg 2006). Among the goals that Germany set for the presidency were

- Boosting energy efficiency;
- Promoting greater use of renewable energies;
- Completing the internal markets for gas and electricity; and
- Making the EU more visible as a player at the international level and putting its partnerships with key producer, transit, and

consumer countries on a solid and reliable footing (Silberberg 2006; Federal Government n.d.).

In other respects, however, Germany has resisted movement in the direction of a common EU energy policy. In this regard, there was little change from the previous decade, when the government was described as one of those most reluctant to see a European energy policy develop, preferring to retain autonomy in the pursuit of supply security (Jochem et al. 1996, 82). In the 2000s, Germany opposed the inclusion of an energy chapter in the proposed European constitution, when that ill-fated project was still being considered (Müller 2005, 178). Although an energy chapter was eventually included in the Lisbon Treaty, which stood in for the unsuccessful constitutional project, it nevertheless reflected Germany's consistent insistence that each Member State should be free to determine its own energy mix, a position that became only more rigid following the decision to phase out nuclear power plants. As one of the state secretaries in the Foreign Ministry argued shortly before the beginning of the German-EU presidency:

> Brussels must respect Member States' particularities, including the issue of their national energy mix. We are firmly convinced that enhanced energy cooperation at the European level, which we champion, cannot override Member States' decisions on the makeup of their energy sources. This especially applies to Germany's decision to phase out nuclear power in accordance with the coalition agreement (Silberberg 2006).

With regard to more specific aspects of EU energy policy, Germany has resisted many of the Commission's initiatives for liberalizing the gas and electricity markets. And the external aspects of German energy policy have often had the effect, whether intentionally or not, of making it difficult for the EU to speak with one voice on energy issues.

Areas of Support

Germany has been most supportive of EU initiatives in the areas of energy efficiency, renewable energy sources, and climate policy. Germany strongly endorsed the Commission's 2007 proposal to increase renewables and efficiency and to reduce greenhouse gas emissions all by 20 percent by 2020, and it has sometimes proposed even more ambitious goals. Likewise, the grand coalition's own 2007 IECP was viewed in large part as its effort to implement the EU's 20-20-20 in 20 goals at the national level.

Nevertheless, important differences have existed between Germany and the Commission over the details of these policies. For example, Germany's support for ambitious renewable energy targets has been conditioned on being able to maintain the use of feed-in tariffs, which have been viewed as very successful at promoting the development of renewable sources in Germany. Thus, on at least two occasions—at the beginning of the 2000s prior to the adoption of the 2001 EU directive on the production of electricity from renewable sources and again prior to the 2008 directive on the promotion of renewable energy sources—Germany has resisted Commission proposals to establish obligatory quota systems, which would mandate that certain quantitative levels be achieved by certain dates (Mahony 2007; see also Eikeland's contribution to this volume).

As Jørgen Wettestad points out in his contribution to this volume, Germany has also had an uneasy relationship with the ETS. In Wettestad's estimation, Germany's initial National Allocation Plan (NAP) for the first phase of the ETS (2005-2007) was only average and may even have involved an over allocation of emissions permits. Then in 2006, the German government proposed a reduction in its overall allocation for the second phase (482 million metric tons of CO_2) that was just 3.4 percent lower than in the first. The Commission found this inadequate and unilaterally cut the proposed allocation by another seven percent, to 453 million metric tons, a level that the government was eventually forced to accept (Müller 2007, 31). More recently, Germany has criticized Commission proposals to reduce substantially the total allowed number of permits, to begin auctioning permits (rather than continuing to give them away to industry and utilities), and to centralize the auctioning of emissions permits (rather than allowing each Member State to conduct its own auctions) (Phillips 2008; Wettestad in this volume). Germany has also sought to give generous emissions allowances to coal-fired power plants (IEA 2007, 12 and 29).

Areas of Resistance

Germany has exhibited even more ambivalence toward the EU's project to create a single internal energy market. The German government has frequently expressed its support for this goal. For example, during its 2007 EU presidency, the completion of the internal energy market was sometimes described as the government's "highest priority." In practice, however, Germany has put up considerable resistance to the proposals emanating from Brussels almost every step of the way (see also Buchan 2009, 21).

This resistance began in the 1990s, when the first EU directives on the electricity and gas markets were negotiated. Even then,

> in contrast to its professed free market approach to the energy sector, the German government has been rather ambivalent about the liberalization of energy utility markets both at home and in a European context. It has offered only halfhearted support to the Commission in its attempts to open up electricity markets while it was strongly opposed to similar moves in the gas sector (Jochem et al. 1996, 82).

For example, Germany opposed the Commission's proposal that third party access (TPA) to the electricity grids be regulated as a way of reducing hidden barriers to entry and instead insisted on including the option of negotiated TPA, which Germany alone exercised. As a result, the German market remained effectively closed to foreign suppliers (Buchan 2009, 22; IEA 2002, 108).

In the early 2000s, as the Commission prepared a second package of internal energy market directives, Germany opposed, unsuccessfully this time, the organizational separation of energy companies' transmission activities from their generation and supply activities, even though this arrangement, known as legal unbundling, is regarded as one of the weakest means for ensuring an open market (Eikeland in this volume; IEA 2007, 10). And when the second package, adopted in 2003, mandated that each country establish national regulatory agencies for gas and electricity, Germany was the last Member State to do so (Buchan 2009, 22). According to an IEA analysis, "The installation of a network regulator in 2005 signals Germany's acknowledgement that negotiated reform and internal regulation of the energy markets were unsuccessful (IEA 2007, 9)." Yet even then, the new Federal Network Agency (Bundesnetzagentur, or BNA) could devote only limited resources to energy regulation, since it was also responsible for other network industries (Buchan 2009, 47).

When further delays in the establishment of open energy markets prompted the Commission to develop a third energy package in the late 2000s, Germany once again sought to water down the provisions to the greatest extent possible. This time, the Commission called for full ownership unbundling as a way of breaking the stranglehold of the powerful, vertically integrated gas and electricity companies in countries like Germany. The German government, along with those of France and other countries whose gas and electricity markets are dominated by one or a small number of companies, however, expressed strong opposition to this proposal. As a result, the Commission was forced to resort to its fall back position of mandating the establishment of independent system operators (ISO) that "manage and operate transmission system assets without influence from transmission owners, but do not own the assets themselves (IEA 2007, 38)." Yet even this compromise was not deemed sufficient by Germany and others. They insisted instead that the third package include the option for an independent transmission operator (ITO), which would not establish as many barriers between the network owners and operators (Buchan 2009, 72).

Another aspect of the original Commission proposal that Germany successfully opposed was the so-called "reciprocity clause." As described in Eikeland and Grätz's contributions to this volume, this provision would have prevented companies from nonmember countries from controlling gas and electricity networks unless an agreement on mutual market access to the transmission assets in the potential investor's home country had been concluded (see also Grätz 2009, 77). Informally known as the "Gazprom clause," it was seen as being primarily aimed at requiring Russia to open its energy market and transmission networks to third parties in return for allowing the Russian state-owned gas company to invest in EU markets.

This last element of German policy toward the liberalization of the EU energy markets is linked to its approach to external energy relations in the late 1990s and 2000s. During the Red-Green coalition, Germany became the driving force for a renewed, special EU-Russia partnership (Westphal 2007, 105). As a practical matter, however, the government's external policy was characterized by a shift away from multilateralism to a more unilateral pursuit of national interests (Westphal 2007, 101, 111). The government's efforts to help German energy companies become internationally competitive and expand their activities abroad (as a way of enhancing Germany's energy security) had negative implications for the EU's attempts at promoting multilateral governance and common institutions in relations with Russia. The Schröder government's use of its strong personal ties with the Putin administration to promote German-Russian energy relations undermined the Commission's efforts to establish a common foreign energy policy and, paradoxically, limited the opportunities of the EU as a whole to diversify its energy supply and increase its energy security (Westphal 2007, 93, 112). This approach was perhaps most evident in the Schröder government's strong backing of the Nord Stream pipeline project, which would provide a direct link between Germany and Russian gas supplies.

The prospects for German support for a common external EU energy policy seemed to improve during the subsequent grand coalition. From the outset, Chancellor Merkel exhibited more skepticism toward Russia, an attitude that was only reinforced by the Russia-Ukraine gas conflict in early 2006. Meanwhile, Foreign Minister Steinmeier offered much rhetorical support for the development of a European external policy that would enable the EU to speak with a single voice. He placed considerable emphasis on getting Russia to ratify the EU's Energy Charter Treaty or at least to negotiate an energy agreement grounded in the principles contained in the unratified treaty (Duffield 2009). And as noted above, improving external energy relations was one of the goals of Germany's EU presidency in 2007. But these ideas were not accompanied by concrete proposals to increase either the EU's legal competence or its institutional capacity to conduct a common external energy policy. To the contrary, Germany never relinquished its prerogatives to act unilaterally in this area.

Determinants of German Energy Policy

How are we to explain and understand Germany's mixed record of support for a common EU energy policy in recent years? A logical place to begin is with general societal preferences. Of particular relevance in this context is the high level of concern about the environment that has characterized German society, although this environmentalism has, paradoxically, cut both ways. On the one hand, acute concerns about climate change have done much to motivate significant efforts by governments of all political stripes to promote energy efficiency, renewable sources of energy, and reductions in greenhouse gas emissions at both the national and European levels. On the other hand, widespread concern about nuclear power, ranging from ambivalence to outright opposition, underlay the Red-Green coalition's decision to phase out nuclear power and the inability of any government to facilitate the construction of new power plants. These policies, in turn, have created an obstacle to cooperation with EU partners on some energy issues and reinforced Germany's determination to maintain national autonomy over the choice of energy sources.

Arguably, however, an even more important determinant has been the structure of the energy economy, especially those aspects concerning electricity and gas. Ironically, as the EU has sought to increase competition in the gas and electricity markets, those industries have been concentrated in fewer hands in Germany. The number of major supraregional gas companies that owned the major pipeline systems and accounted for most of Germany's gas imports declined from six to as few as four during the 2000s (IEA 2002, 73–74; IEA 2007, 99). Similarly, electricity generation and transmission have been dominated by just four supraregional companies—E.On, RWE, Energie Baden-Wuerttemberg (EnBW), and Vattenfall—that control about three-quarters of the country's generation capacity and have accounted for an even higher percentage of the electricity actually produced (IEA 2007, 127). These companies have divided Germany into four regions in which they act as quasi-monopolies (Müller 2007, 29).

Two characteristics of the major energy companies have underpinned German resistance to the creation of a common EU energy policy. First, as suggested above, they are vertically integrated. Not only do the Big Four electricity companies produce and transmit most of the electricity, but they also dominate retail supply and distribution, in part through cross-ownership of municipal utilities and in part directly (IEA 2007, 30; Müller 2007, 29). Such vertical integration furthers the narrow commercial interests of the companies themselves. But some have argued that it also serves the national interest, by enabling German companies to compete with other national champions in the EU and by increasing their leverage in negotiations with foreign suppliers (see also Eikeland's contribution to this volume). In any case, the German electricity and gas companies have strongly lobbied at the national and EU levels against such measures as legal and ownership unbundling in order to maintain their profitable vertically integrated corporate structures as well as their oligopolistic market structures.

The other important characteristic with implications for Germany's support for a common EU energy policy are the close ties that the gas companies have with Russia. Ruhrgas, now E.On Ruhrgas, is currently the largest foreign shareholder in Gazprom, with about 6.4 percent of the shares, and it has a strategic interest in maintaining close energy ties with Gazprom and in expanding into the exploration and production of Russian gas because it produces only five percent of the gas it sells. Likewise, BASF Wintershall has a history of various cross-ownership deals with Gazprom. Both companies hold long-term gas delivery contracts with Russia that extend beyond 2030.

These structural linkages between German and Russian companies created an alliance of interests that undermined, or at least weakened, the Commission's efforts to extend competition within and beyond the EU's borders (Westphal 2007, 105). The German gas importers prefer to minimize competition on the German market because of the vulnerability inherent in their long-term purchasing contracts from Gazprom (Müller 2007, 39). In addition, E.On Ruhrgas and Wintershall lobbied strongly for the Nord Stream project, in which they were junior partners to Gazprom, because it would strengthen their position on the international and EU markets (Westphal 2007, 111).

This discussion of the electricity and gas industries raises the issue of the relationship between business and government. The interests of the energy companies would not matter so much if they did not receive expression in government policy. In fact, however, many companies have enjoyed close links with, and presumably have exercised considerable influence over, at least parts of the government, and these ties may have grown even stronger during the late 1990s and early 2000s when the government was negotiating the first stages of the liberalization process and the nuclear phaseout (Westphal 2007, 105).

The energy industry has been one of the main constituencies of the Federal Ministry of Economics (BMWi). And as long-term energy policy analyst Friedemann Müller has argued, the close links between energy companies and BMWi have resulted in a conservative German policy toward the EU. In particular, the resistance of energy companies to EU energy market liberalization efforts has influenced the BMWi position in Brussels negotiations. In Müller's view, the BMWi reflexively defends the interests of the energy industry under almost any circumstances (Müller 2005, 177–78; see also Müller 2007, 33).

It is not just a matter of industry using its allies in government to do its bidding, however. The relationship is more complicated than that. While the companies seek to influence the government in order to promote their self-interest, many government officials view strong energy companies as serving German national interests.

A final factor shaping German policy has been differences in the orientations of the major political parties. The SPD has traditionally been more open to cooperation with first the Soviet Union and then Russia, while the CDU/CSU has been more wary. These differences were on display in the contrasting approaches of Schröder and Merkel, described above. In addition, the CDU/CSU has been more supportive of European integration and market liberalization. Thus the CDU/CSU-Free Democratic Party (FDP) government under

Helmut Kohl (1982–1998), which oversaw the implementation of the Single European Act and negotiated the Economic and Monetary Union (EMU), may have been more supportive of the initial steps toward the creation of a single energy market than was the following SPD-Green coalition.

Nevertheless, these differences should not be exaggerated. For example, since the 1970s, both major parties have tended to hold a more positive view of the Soviet Union/Russia than have other West European powers, such as France and Great Britain. Hence officials of all governments have insisted on the reliability of Russian gas supplies, and even the 2006 Russia-Ukraine gas conflict did not seem to call into question this basic tenet of German energy policy.

Conclusion

Germany has traditionally been a leading proponent of European integration. Yet in recent years, it has been ambivalent about, if not downright antagonistic toward, the creation of a common EU energy policy. Successive German governments have resisted or at least not supported some of the most central elements of EU policy, especially energy market liberalization and external energy relations.

This ambivalence has been grounded in large part in the structure of the German energy sector, which has been dominated by a small number of gas and electricity companies, and the particular interests of those powerful companies. Those companies have opposed various efforts to liberalize the gas and electricity markets and have sought to retain a free hand in negotiations with foreign suppliers such as Gazprom. In turn, successive German governments have tended to give voice to those commercial interests in negotiations at the EU level.

Even where German officials might see some advantage, such as lower energy prices, in supporting Commission initiatives, they confront a "chicken-and-egg" problem. Until the European energy markets are fully integrated and liberalized, the security of Germany's energy supply will depend to an important extent on the maintenance of strong national companies that can compete and negotiate on roughly equal terms with state-owned enterprises and powerful foreign energy interests. But as long as they exist, those same companies will lobby against further liberalization measures.

Nevertheless, the last couple of years have seen some developments that provide reasons for optimism. In 2008, several of the large

German energy utilities, including E.On, RWE, and Vattenfall, under pressure from the Commission for allegedly engaging in uncompetitive practices, decided to sell their transmission networks. This unexpected development raised hopes that other giant energy concerns, in Germany and elsewhere, would follow suit.

An even more recent development has brought German policy more in line with that of the other major EU Member States as well as the preferences of the Commission. In 2009, the national elections brought to power a new government that promised to review German energy policy, especially the nuclear phaseout decision. The following year, the Black-Yellow coalition prepared a new energy concept paper that called for extending the lifetimes of the remaining nuclear power plants (BMWi/BMU 2010).

In addition, the new energy concept suggests a greater degree of emphasis on pursuing Germany's energy policy goals at the European level. One of the longest (of nine) sections is devoted to the issue of energy supply in the European and international context. Other proposed steps include supporting the import of green electricity from third countries and pushing forward the creation of an integrated electricity market through new transmission lines in Europe and beyond. Nevertheless, it is too soon to tell whether these developments suggest more than minor adjustments in German policy, rather than a fundamental reorientation.

Notes

1. From 2002 to 2005, the BMWi was combined with part of the traditional Federal Ministry of Labour and Social Affairs to form a superministry known as the Federal Ministry of Economics and Labour (BMWA).
2. In 2009, Russia withdrew from the treaty (Westphal 2009b).

Works Cited

Arbeitsgemeinschaft Energiebilanzen (AGEB). 2010. *Evaluation Tables on the Energy Balance for the Federal Republic of Germany 1990 to 2009 (July).* Available at http://www.agenergiebilanzen.de/viewpage.php?idpage=227 (accessed October 26, 2010).

Bhadrakumar, M. K. 2006. Germany, Russia Redraw Europe's frontiers. *AsianTimes Online* (May 3). Available at http://www.atimes.com/atimes/China/HE03Ad01.html (accessed September 17, 2010).

BMWi/BMU. 2010. *Energiekonzept: Neun Punkte für eine umweltschonende, zuverlässige und bezahlbare Energieversorgung* (September 7). Available at http://www.bmwi.de/BMWi/Navigation /Service/publikationen,did=357316.html (accessed September 24, 2010).

BP. 2010. *BP Statistical Review of World Energy2010.* Available at http: //www.bp.com/productlanding.do?categoryId=6929&contentId=704462 2 (accessed March 15, 2011).

Buchan, David. 2009. *Energy and Climate Change: Europe at the Crossroads.* New York: Oxford University Press.

Bundesregierung. 2007. *Startschuss für Energie- und Klimaschutzkonzept* (July 3). Available at http://www.bundesregierung.de/nn_774/Content /DE/Archiv16/Artikel/2007/07/2007-07-03-energiegipfel.html (accessed September 24, 2010).

Duffield, John S. 2009. Germany and Energy Security in the 2000s: Rise and Fall of a Policy Issue? *Energy Policy.* 37(11): 4284–4292.

Federal Government n.d. *Europe – succeeding together.* Presidency Program, January 1 to June 30, 2007. Available at http://www.eu2007.de/includes /Downloads/Praesidentschaftsprogramm/EU_Presidency_Programme _final.pdf (accessed September 20, 2010).

Grätz, Jonas. 2009. Energy Relations with Russia and Gas Market Liberalization. *International Politics and Society.* 3/2009 (July): 66–80. Available at http://www.fes.de/ipg/index_e.htm.

International Energy Agency (IEA). 2002. *Energy Policies of IEA Countries: Germany 2002 Review.* Paris: International Energy Agency.

International Energy Agency (IEA). 2007. *Energy Policies of IEA Countries: Germany 2002 Review.* Paris: International Energy Agency.

Jochem, Eberhard, Edelgard Gruber, and Wilhelm Mannsbart. 1996. German Energy Policy in Transition. In *European Energy Policies in a Changing Environment.* Ed. Francis McGowan. Heidelbert: Physica-Verlag. 57–87.

Müller, Friedemann. 2005. Germany and Energy Security Policy: Technical versus Political Modes of Intervention. In *Germany's Uncertain Power: Foreign Policy of the Berlin Republic.* Ed. Hanns Maull. New York: Palgrave Macmillan. 169–184.

Müller, Friedemann. 2007. *How to Security Reliable Energy Sources in Germany.* "U.S. and German Approaches to the Energy Challenges." AICGS Policy Report 29. Available at http://www.aicgs.org/docments /pubs/policyreport29.pdf (accessed May 30, 2008).

Phillips, Leigh. 2008. "EU climate proposals hurt industry." *Euobserver.com.* Available at http://euobserver.com/19/26498 (accessed July 21, 2008).

Silberberg, Reinhard. 2006. *A Preview of Germany's EU Presidency: The Status of the Federal Government's Preparations* (October 4). Available at http://www.auswaertigesamt.de/diplo/en/Infoservice/Presse /Reden/2006/061004SilberbergEuropa.html (accessed September. 24, 2010).

Westphal, Kirsten. 2007. Germany and the EU-Russia Energy Dialogue. In *The EU-Russian Energy Dialogue: Europe's Future Energy Security*. Ed. Pami Aalto. Farnham, UK: Ashgate. 94–118.

Westphal, Kirsten. 2009a. At the Crossroads: Germany's Peaceful Nuclear Program. In *Nuclear Energy in the Gulf*. Ed. Emirates Center for Strategic Studies and Research (ECSSR). Abu Dhabi: ECSSR.

Westphal, Kirsten. 2009b. *Taking Medvedev at His Word: The Russian President's Proposal for an International Energy Accord and the Energy Charter Treaty*. SWP Comments 24 (October). Available at http://www.swp-berlin.org/en/produkte/swp_aktuell_detail.php?id=11388 (accessed October 25, 2010).

Chapter Nine

The UK and EU Energy Policy: From Awkward Partner to Active Protagonist?

Francis McGowan

This chapter examines the way in which the British government has shifted its stance on the details and scope of a common energy policy in the European Union (EU). That shift has been highly significant: more or less from the moment of membership, British politicians and officials were wary of transferring authority over energy matters to the European level. A combination of domestic political divisions over its participation in the European Community and the desire to retain control over the resources of the North Sea meant that British governments were quite hostile to the development of a more coordinated European approach to energy matters. This reluctance to engage persisted over the subsequent decades with regard to most aspects of energy policy, the principal exception being in the area of market liberalization (a policy innovation where the United Kingdom [UK] was an early adopter). In an echo of the UK's traditional "economistic" motivation for participating in European integration, Conservative—and later Labour—governments were forceful supporters of the European Commission proposals to increase competition in the energy sector (though other Member States were, at least initially less enthused).

Over time, the choreography surrounding EU policy—and the nature of the UK's participation in it—has changed. Some of the states that were opposed to, or ambivalent about, liberalization have become supporters of open EU energy markets. Moreover, the agreement on increasing competition in the sector has coincided with a broadening of the energy policy agenda. European institutions have embraced the climate change issue along with revived worries over energy supply security, using them to renew the case for a common energy policy. The New Labour government was increasingly supportive of such a policy, pushing it forward during its 2005 presidency and broadly backing the specific measures over the following years. At the time of writing, this support for EU-level policy seems to have survived the change of government in 2010.

The continuity between New Labour and the current coalition of conservatives and liberals also extends to some rethinking about the means and ends of energy policy: after many years of leaving energy decisions to the market, the British government appears to have recognized the limitations of such an approach and the need for state intervention to rectify market failures. It remains to be seen how this will influence its preferences at the EU level where the Commission remains strongly committed to market solutions. Both changes seem to stem at least in part from the same change in circumstances, however: the country's shift from being a net exporter to becoming a net importer of energy.

This chapter explores the changing priorities and principles underlying the UK's stance on European energy policy. The chapter begins by providing an overview of the UK's energy balances and of the development of national energy policy. On this basis it then examines the UK's role in European energy policy in terms of how it has influenced and has been influenced by European initiatives. The paper reviews the evolution of policy from the period before the UK joined the European Communities to the present day. This historical dimension is appropriate given the mix of continuity and change in the British approach and the way in which a variety of factors—from the geological to the ideological—have acted as catalysts and constraints in UK-EU energy relations. The chapter concludes by considering what has driven the changes in the UK's position. Has it been the result of more *communautaire* spirit on the part of the government? Has it been due to recognition that markets cannot address some of the major challenges facing the energy economy in the UK or in Europe? Or is it a reflection of changed national priorities? Just as the UK's national interest was once expressed in a defense of energy sovereignty and opposition to anything more than a limited European energy policy, it may be that its preferences have adapted to new circumstances in which collective action may serve Britain better.

The UK's Energy Endowment: Resources and Policy

As with any other Member State, an assessment of the UK's position on European energy policy has to take account of the evolution of its own policy priorities. This in turn requires some understanding of how the UK's energy endowment has developed over time.

Unique among Member States in the postwar era, the UK enjoyed for a number of years a surplus of energy resources, producing more than it consumed. Its status as a net exporter was furthermore reinforced by the diversity of fuels at its disposal: as was said by more than one commentator, Britain was an "island of coal floating in a sea of oil and gas."[1] In the last decade, however the country's self-sufficiency has been eroded and the UK has returned to being a net importer of energy. Moreover, the balance of fuels has shifted over time in response to changing market and environmental conditions. Table 9.1 summarizes the changes over time.

The coal industry was at the heart of the UK's energy economy for many decades but has been in relative and increasingly absolute decline over the postwar period. While historically dominating the country's energy balances, changing demand patterns and the growth of oil consumption meant that between 1948 and 2009, coal's share of primary energy supply fell from around 90 percent to around 14 percent (with the market now almost entirely focused on power generation). Moreover, whereas historically British demand for coal was overwhelmingly met from national supplies, in the last two decades the share of imports has increased substantially. British coal production was by European standards relatively cost efficient but consumers have been able to import from suppliers—outside the EU—whose costs are considerably lower. Many mines outside the EU were able to produce and export coal at much lower prices. As a result, in 2009, coal from British mines accounted for around 5 percent of the country's total energy needs.

At the same time as domestic coal entered a relative and absolute decline, the country became a significant producer of oil and gas. Consumption of oil had increased substantially over the postwar period while natural gas began to be supplied in the late 1960s. The discovery of large reserves off the British coast (particularly the North Sea) meant that the country was effectively able to meet most of its requirements for both fuels (though in practice the country continued to import crude oil and oil products). Between the end of the 1960s and the end of the last century, production of gas rose from under 1 percent to 27 percent of energy supply. Oil production began slightly later, rising from the equivalent of 26 percent of needs at the end of the 1970s to 60 percent at the end of the 1990s. In this century, however, production of oil and gas has not been able to keep up with demand and more recently has entered into a steady decline, with gas

Table 9.1 Energy production and supply in the UK

	1948	1958	1968	1978	1988	1998	2008	2009
Total Energy Production (m.tonnes oil equivalent)								
Coal	134.1	38.6	107.1	75.5	63.3	25.8	11.4	11.0
Oil	0.2	0.2	0.2	58.2	125.5	145.3	78.6	74.7
Natural Gas			1.9	36.2	42.1	90.2	69.7	59.7
Renewables						2.5	4.0	4.9
"Primary Electricity"*	0.4	1.3	7.0	10.3	17.0	24.0	13.0	16.5
Total	134.7	40.1	116.2	180.2	247.9	287.8	176.7	167.0
Total Primary Energy Supply (m.tonnes oil equivalent)								
Coal	128.0	129.2	100.7	73.3	69.6	40.9	37.9	31.0
Oil	14.3	40.6	89.7	97.0	84.0	87.1	83.5	79.4
Natural Gas			3.0	41.0	51.5	88.3	93.7	86.7
Electricity	0.4	1.3	7.0	10.3	18.1	25.0	13.9	16.7
Renewables						2.1	5.3	6.1
Total	142.7	171.1	200.4	221.6	223.2	243.4	234.3	219.9

Source: Digest of UK Energy Statistics.

Note: "primary electricity" is primarily nuclear. Hydroelectric contribution has been around 0.3/0.5 mtoe annually for most the period. Since 1996 wind generation has been included in the statistics, bringing the total renewable contribution to primary electricity to 1.1mtoe in 2008 and 1.3 mtoe in 2009.

output meeting only 76 percent of total gas requirements in 2009 and oil production just over half the levels of ten years earlier.

The UK has also been a significant producer of non-fossil energy. In the 1950s Britain was one of the pioneers of civilian nuclear technology. Over the following decades its share of total energy supply rose from less than 1 percent in 1958 to around 8 percent in the 1990s. The role of renewables has been relatively modest. Traditionally, it focused on large-scale hydroelectric capacity—mainly in the North of Scotland—but the country has lagged behind other parts of Europe in the development of other renewable energy sources. While renewable production has been rapidly increasing in recent years, it has been from a low base—it is now around 3 percent of total primary supply—and remains an underexploited resource.

Managing this energy endowment has been the primary objective of national energy policy. As in most European states, energy policy has been primarily a supply side affair with relatively little attention paid to managing demand. There have been initiatives to foster greater energy efficiency—particularly in the wake of the energy crises—but the resources and commitment of officials and politicians have tended to favor investments in energy production (Chesshire 1986).

Before the 1980s, the country's energy supply industry was almost entirely in the public sector (oil being a partial exception). For much of the postwar period until the election of Margaret Thatcher in 1979, British energy policy was largely conducted through the publicly owned firms created by the nationalization of the coal, electricity, and gas industries in the late 1940s. Nationalization and reorganization of these industries was relatively uncontentious, with a variety of justifications invoked (ranging from the building of socialism to the reaping of scale economies). As public enterprises they were deployed for a wider range of economic objectives than the core task of ensuring adequate supplies. Over the following years the energy industries were to be key players in economic reconstruction and retained a strategic aspect throughout the period of public ownership (Bending and Eden 1984; Cairncross 1985).

Prior to the energy crises of the 1970s, British energy policy focused upon setting a framework for the development of new resources (oil and gas) and technology (nuclear) while managing the rationalization of the coal industry. The oil shocks—and the return of a Labour government following a confrontation between the previous Conservative government and the coal miners in 1973/1974—changed the balance of policy. There was increasingly a perception of energy as a precious commodity, and the new government sought to increase the role of the state in the development of the North Sea resources as well as to foster new nuclear technologies and revive the coal industry. The policy had its successes (fostering offshore oil and gas development and managing a major conversion of domestic infrastructure from manufactured to natural gas) and failures (the management and development of nuclear power). As we will see, however, a primary consideration was to retain national control over the exploitation of these valuable resources (Cook and Surrey 1977; Department of Energy 1978; Department of Fuel and Power 1967).

When the Conservatives returned to power in 1979, energy policy began to change quite fundamentally. Hitherto, UK energy policy could be described as primarily concerned with the development of British energy resources with a view to meeting domestic energy needs but also with a view to fulfilling a number of broader economic objectives in promoting industrial, regional, and social policies, with publicly owned enterprises an important policy instrument. In 1993 (after nearly 15 years of Conservative rule), the government summarized its energy policy objectives as: to encourage competition amongst energy producers and to provide a regulatory framework to allow markets to work well; to commercialize energy markets in which the full costs of energy were borne by customers; to privatize the energy industries and support wider share ownership, to take account of the environmental impact of the energy sector and meet international commitments; to promote energy efficiency and safeguard health and safety (Department of Trade and Industry 1993). While some aspects and aspirations are common to both periods, a change of emphasis—away from government planning toward the market—is all too apparent.

While this transformation did not happen overnight, the government's approach to energy policy shifted steadily away from being one where it was the dominant player to one where more decisions were taken by privately owned firms operating in market conditions. One of Mrs. Thatcher's first energy ministers, Nigel Lawson, recalled in his memoirs that he "was determined to break the dirigiste mentality that pervaded both the Department of Energy and the nationalized energy industries" (Lawson 1992: 163). In a 1982 speech he outlined the change of direction, arguing that the government's principal task was to "set a framework which will ensure that the market operates in the energy sector with a minimum of distortion and that energy is produced and consumed efficiently" (Lawson 1982: 3). Such sentiments reflected the government's overall economic policy and its ideological commitment to private enterprise and competition. At the heart of the new energy policy was a nexus of policies involving the privatization of state owned energy companies, the opening up of the markets in which those companies operated and the establishment of regulatory frameworks to encourage competition, and to control prices where competition was not possible (Helm, Kay, and Thompson 1989).

The policy was a political success—boosting the government's revenues, enriching a number of small shareholders, transforming the ethos and corporate culture of the energy sector and creating a growth industry in privatization—though its broader economic impacts have been more contested. What were not perhaps clear at the time were the incentive effects of the combination of privately owned utilities and competitive energy markets. Although obtaining significant returns, the new owners had few incentives to invest, particularly in longer term, capital-intensive technologies. The coincidence of the privatizations with a sustained period of low energy prices and apparent surpluses in global energy markets eroded the perception of scarcity, which had defined energy policy since the 1970s. In the electricity sector, utilities lost interest in technologies such as nuclear power (whose reputation had been tarnished by revelations of poor economics during privatization and by accidents such as Chernobyl), and instead favored the development of gas power stations (Surrey 1996).

The other casualty was the coal industry. Following the strikes of the 1970s the Conservative party regarded the miner's union as the epitome of trade union power which they were committed to confront. Over the course of 1984 and 1985 the government faced off a prolonged strike over pit closures and restructuring. However, ultimately the most serious challenge to the sector came in the wake of electricity privatization when "the dash for gas" (the rush to invest in gas fired power stations) led to a further scaling back of the industry. While the issue became highly contentious—forcing the government to provide some additional supports for the industry—ultimately the effects were to accelerate a rationalization of the sector (the rump of which was privatized in the mid-1990s) (Parker 2000).

The shift from coal to gas was in part justified on environmental grounds. Over the 1980s the British government's reputation on environmental issues was poor—it was known as the dirty man of Europe for its tardiness in reducing emissions from power stations which were responsible for acid rain in other parts of northern Europe (Boehmer-Christiansen and Skea 1991; Weale 1992). From the end of the decade and throughout the 1990s, however, the government sought to reinvent itself as more responsive to environmental concerns (Department of the Environment 1990; Jordan 2000; Osborn 1997).

The return of the Labour Party to government did not mark a major shift in British energy policy. In opposition the party had been critical of many parts of the Conservative government's market based energy policy, at times even committing to renationalize the energy industries (Labour Party 1983; Labour Party 1987; Labour Party 1992). However, under the leadership of Tony Blair the party adopted a more "market friendly" approach to the economy, including the energy sector. Aside from a "windfall tax" on the electricity utilities and some refashioning of regulatory responsibilities to give greater weight to the interests of consumers and address social issues, governments since 1997 not only left the previous policy in place but enthusiastically embraced and advanced it. The government abandoned its commitment to public ownership in the sector and pursued the extension of competition in gas and electricity markets to all customers (Gray 2004; Labour Party 1997; Rutledge 2007).

New Labour's principal innovation was its pledge to deepen the commitment to an environmentally friendly energy policy, particularly in relation to climate change. While the Conservatives had launched some initiatives as part of their attempts to improve their environmental reputation, the integration of climate change into energy policy advanced to another level in the late 1990s. This reflected a growing acceptance of the significance of the threat and increased attempts to agree an international response, with the government becoming a strong advocate of market based instruments to drive the transition to a low carbon energy economy (Carter 2008).

Climate change concerns were important in the government's drive to redesign national energy policy after many years of neglect (Department of Trade and Industry 2003; Department of Trade and Industry 2007). While energy markets were still at the heart of the policy, the government also sought to encourage energy efficiency and renewables through a variety of mechanisms (Mitchell 2007; Politt 2010). As the country's energy self-sufficiency began to diminish, concerns over supply security also reemerged, particularly as international energy prices and worries over long-term availability of supplies increased (Lovell, et al. 2009; Helm 2005a; Scrase and MacKerron 2009). It has been in this context that the government sought to revive the fortunes of nuclear power. It is worth noting that the nuclear industry had been lobbying for many years for such a change but growing insecurity seems to have been the catalyst for a change of heart among senior politicians and officials. (Department of Business Enterprise and Regulatory Reform 2008). However, while private investors were now keener in principle to invest in nuclear, the market conditions were still seen as uncertain. In this and in other areas of energy policy it appeared that price signals and competition were working against investment in such risky and long-term options. As a result New Labour moved toward a more interventionist energy policy, which, while not a full circle return to the energy policy agenda of the past, marked a major shift (Wicks 2009).

Nor was it only New Labour that recognized the need for a change in energy policy. In the period before the election, the Conservative energy spokesman criticized New Labour for being too reliant on energy markets and stressed the importance of energy security and the need to intervene (EU Energy 2009). While its policy proposals in the run up to the election did not repudiate the past commitment to energy markets, it clearly signaled a more extensive role for government (Conservative Party 2010; MacKerron 2010). In effect, therefore, the Conservative-Liberal coalition government, which came to power in 2010, seems to be consolidating the reorientation that began in the last years of New Labour (HM Government 2010).

UK and EU Policy: Historical Evolution

British energy policy has been primarily defined by changes in its energy balances, particularly the availability of energy resources. Those considerations have been equally important in the conduct of its energy relations with other countries: The pursuit of the national interest in energy matters has entailed the maintenance of sovereignty over choices on energy resources. The UK's role in the development of EU energy policy has to be seen as one aspect of such energy diplomacy. Negotiations by politicians and officials with other Member States and institutions have been framed by this concern.

This concern with energy sovereignty has been compounded by two more general factors: the UK's liberal disposition on matters of economic policy and its ambivalence toward the wider project of European integration. The interplay between these two factors has been a characteristic of British relations with its continental neighbors for many years (at least since the Cobden Chevalier Treaty of 1860 and the embrace of free trade) (Marsh 1999). Since the creation of the European Communities in the 1950s it is notable that the British government reconciled itself to membership because of the perceived economic advantages of joining the "common market" (as well as in some cases a perception of declining global influence) (Aspinwall 2004; Young 1999). However, while it has largely embraced economic integration, the British political class has been more ambivalent about the political consequences of membership (George 1998; Gowland and Turner 1999). The issue has been a cleavage in British politics, between and within the major parties. The impact of "Europe" on domestic politics, moreover, has fed back into the way that governments position themselves in negotiations on European policies. As we will see, both factors have left an impact on the UK's negotiating position on EU energy policy as well as on EU energy policy itself.

From 1950s to Membership

Many reasons have been given for the failure of the British to participate in the negotiations for the European Coal and Steel Community (ECSC). The UK's aspirations to remain a major power (on the basis of its links to its commonwealth and colonies and its close relationship with the United States [US]) meant that it was not prepared to engage in a serious project of European integration (Young 1999). However for our purposes it is worth noting the response of Herbert

Morrison, a senior Labour politician, to the proposal. Upon hearing about the Community he declared that the government could not contemplate joining because "the Durham miners won't wear it" (quoted in Young 1999: 64; Dell 1995). The idea that the coal industry—not long nationalized in one of the most symbolic acts of the Labour government—would be subject to outside control was deemed to be politically unacceptable. At the time, of course, the inclusion of coal in the treaty was primarily related to its role in the steel industry—though the first steps toward a Community perspective on energy matters were made under the ECSC's auspices (Lucas 1977) and followed up after the creation of the European Economic and Atomic Energy Communities (EEC and Euratom) (Lister 1960; von Geusau 1975)—but the quote illustrates the tension between the prospect of integrating energy markets and satisfying domestic constituencies. With the UK remaining outside the Community for another 20 years, and energy scarcely a policy success story over the same period, however, such a prospect seemed fairly distant.

The UK cooperated with its European neighbors on energy matters in the framework of the Organisation for Economic Cooperation and Development (OECD), particularly in the aftermath of the Six Day war when the Organization became the focus for discussions on storing and sharing oil stocks (Shackleton 1978; Thorpe 2007). When new negotiations of membership of the Communities finally began in 1970, energy was not to be one of the principal sticking points. Most of the issues related to those energy sources covered by separate treaties: Euratom was relatively straightforward on energy matters (Shovelton 2000, 206ff) while coal was in some aspects more sensitive, with negotiations clouded by concerns over a possible loss of national control over the industry (Shovelton 2000, 204). As regards the acquis relating to energy, there was not much to negotiate about (not withstanding nearly 20 years of attempts to formulate such a policy). As the official history of the negotiations noted, energy was one of the European Community's common policies that was "fortunately still...relatively rudimentary though beginning to develop fast" (O' Neill 2000, 188).

Indeed, the UK's membership of the European Communities (hereafter: the Community)—at the beginning of 1973[2]—coincided with a renewed attempt by the Community to formulate a comprehensive energy policy. Proposals made in the late 1960s had been refashioned by the Commission in 1972 (Commission of the European Communities 1968; Commission of the European Communities 1972). However, neither set of proposals met with much enthusiasm from the existing Member States (particularly France). In discussions about the Commission's proposals shortly after accession, British government officials indicated that they shared the French goal of restricting the Commission's role in developing any policy (Foreign and Commonwealth Office 1973).

Britain and Europe in the Energy Crisis: An Opportunity Avoided?

As it turned out, an Anglo-French entente on energy matters did emerge but not in the way that was anticipated. Although there was growing concern in the early 1970s about the strength of the oil exporters—and some discussions on the need for a commensurate collective response from consuming countries (Foreign and Commonwealth Office 2005)—the manner in which the energy crisis emerged was a surprise (Yergin 1991). The 1973 Arab-Israeli war was accompanied by efforts by the Organization of Arab Petroleum Exporting Countries (OAPEC) to engineer a boycott against those countries that were supporting Israel, principally the Netherlands. While the Dutch looked to the support from their fellow Member States, the response of the British and French was less than wholehearted. The British in particular were anxious that the Community not do anything that would antagonize OAPEC (Hellema et al. 2004; 1975; Walton 1976).

Nor was it only the embargo which divided the Member States: the British and French were the first to seek bilateral agreements with the governments of exporting nations to ensure future supplies, in the process undermining the scope for a collective response by the Community (Connelly and Perlman 1975; Lucas 1977, 59). While there may have been a hope that the energy crisis could serve as an opportunity for the Community to rekindle a rather sluggish energy policy debate, this was not to be the case. Indeed, when the crisis was discussed at the Copenhagen summit in December 1973, progress on agreeing a common response was blocked by disagreements between Britain and Germany over the funding of regional policy (Lucas 1977, 59; *Times* 1973).

Central to British policy in this period was the desire to prevent the Commission from managing the oil market and to retain complete control over the North Sea energy resources. As the Commission put forward new proposals on energy in 1974, the UK's response was lukewarm. A paper prepared by the then energy minister Eric Varley provides a very clear statement of British opposition to an extensive Community policy. Noting that little progress had been made on energy policy despite the intentions expressed at the Paris 72 and Copenhagen 73 summits, the paper was responding to the Commission's 1974 proposals for an energy strategy (Commission of the European Communities 1974). Varley was candid in seeing little to gain from a Community policy especially given the country's likely self-sufficiency in energy resources. Those areas where international cooperation was needed were better pursued in wider fora (involving the US and Japan—effectively the emerging IEA [International Energy Agency]—or bilaterally (nuclear) (Cabinet Office 1974).

However the paper also recognized the dangers of adopting too hostile a stance as it would "generate ill will" (Cabinet Office 1974, 1) with other Member States and undermine the planned renegotiation of membership terms. On this point Varley echoed a senior official's view that it was necessary to pay some lip service to cooperation "if we are to get our own way on the things that really matter" (Prime Minister's Office 1974). Much of what the Commission proposed was unproblematic and could be supported, though the report argued that many of the objectives being set involved a "large element of wishful thinking" ranging from the optimistic to the unrealistic (Cabinet Office 1974, 1). The exception to this approach was the Commission's plans for the oil market, which Varley saw as an attempt to gain control of the country's resources. The UK was completely opposed to the proposals partly because it doubted the Commission's competence but mainly because it did not want to surrender sovereignty over such an important policy area. In particular, it opposed the creation of a new European Energy Agency, something proposed in various forms by the Commission and the French. (Cabinet Office 1974, 5).

British ambivalence was more publicly manifest at a Council meeting in the summer of 1974 when one of the principal opponents of membership of the Community—Peter Shore—led the British delegation in a discussion of energy and other matters. In what proved to be a rather embarrassing episode, Shore refused to back conclusions on energy policy, effectively unraveling the careful background diplomacy of the previous months. His actions—described in one newspaper report as his "finest hour as an anti-marketeer" (*Times* 1974a) antagonized the other Member States and the Commission but was relatively short-lived in its impact: within a matter of months the UK had lifted its objections and the resolution was passed by the Member States (*Times* 1974b). The episode nonetheless demonstrated how the domestic differences within the government on Europe spilled over into the conduct of particular policies.

In this period, the UK seemed to prefer the newly created International Energy Agency as its forum for discussing energy policy matters. As noted, it regarded an organization that embraced the other industrialized economies (particularly the US) as a better venue for discussing international energy problems. While this need not have been incompatible with the pursuit of a common energy policy, the decision of the French not to join the agency made coordination between the two organizations more difficult (Simonet 1975; Van der Linde and Lefeber 1988).

It would be wrong to attribute all the problems of developing a common energy policy in the 1970s to the reluctance of the British but they manifest particularly strongly the tendency of Member States to defend their own preferences. European energy policy for much of the rest of that decade and for the earlier part of the 1980s was primarily characterized by rather weak target setting initiatives (McGowan 1990) which presented few problems for the British government. However the UK was to eventually make a more significant contribution to European energy policy, which had the effect of making the policy itself more significant in its impact on Member States.

Britain and the Internal Energy Market: From the Exception to the Rule?

As noted earlier, the UK had embarked in the 1980s on a radical shift in its energy policy by giving much greater weight to the role of market forces in determining prices and investment and allowing competition to replace the model of a vertically integrated monopoly that had been regarded as the appropriate model for energy utilities. This was, of course, a part of a much more fundamental shift in the economic policy of the UK and other industrialized economies. Within Europe one of the factors underpinning—or even forcing the pace of—that liberalization process was the model of economic integration on which the EU was built. Although perhaps not apparent in the early period of the European Community, there was nonetheless a strong element of economic liberalism in the original treaties and this became apparent as the economic policy pendulum moved in the direction of the market (McGowan 2001, 76–81). The EC in particular emerged as a strong advocate of economic reforms based on removing barriers to trade amongst Member States and, under the leadership of Jacques Delors and a number of liberally minded Commissioners, sought to use Community law and legislation in pursuit of such reforms. In

1985 the Commission launched the Single Market initiative, a package of over 300 legislative measures designed to open up to competition those sectors which had hitherto enjoyed various forms of protection from competition (Moravcsik 1991; Young 1999).

The initiative, steered by the British commissioner Lord Cockfield, impacted only indirectly upon the energy sector but as it gathered momentum, the Commission proposed to extend the policy to the energy industries—sectors which it had considered to be "too difficult" to tackle, given the sensitivities and vested interests involved. A Commission communication on the Internal Energy Market was published in 1988 and laid out a program of market liberalization for sectors that had traditionally enjoyed privileged and protected positions, often national as well as natural monopolies (Commission of the European Communities 1988).

In pursuing such a policy there is no doubt that the British experiments made the Commission's strategy more feasible than it otherwise would have been. It effectively broke the taboo which considered the electricity and gas sectors as natural monopolies and made it harder for those Member States hostile to the proposals to have the proposals dismissed. Armed with the UK example (and the UK support) the Commission embarked on an extended debate to liberalize the EU electricity and gas markets. Yet in the early years of the debate, the British were arguably the only country to support the Commission. (This was also apparent at the industrial level where the industry association Eurelectric [The Union of the Electricity Industry]—mainly hostile at that time to liberalization—was obliged to publish a major policy document as the opinion of the "continental members" of the organization) (Eising 2002; Eurelectric 1991).

The negotiations on the liberalization of electricity and gas markets were drawn out over four phases of legislation and nearly 20 years of bargaining (the first transit proposals were made in 1989 and the final reforms were agreed in 2008). Over that time the UK was a key protagonist supporting the Commission's proposals—sometimes criticizing the reforms for not going far enough—and building up a coalition in favor of market opening (Department of Trade and Industry 1997, 14). Over time and as Member States pursued their own reforms the balance of opinion in the EU institutions duly shifted. Where there remained attempts to dilute or change reforms to favor the status quo, the British government was to the fore in arguing against such moves (not always successfully). The most recent instance of this struggle came in 2006 when the Commission published its proposals to bring about a full liberalization of the gas and electricity markets (the so-called third package) (Commission of the European Communities 2006). As part of these reforms the Commission proposed that the Member States apply a full separation of the different components of production, transmission, distribution, and supply of electricity and gas ("unbundling"). While previous reform packages had required companies to break up their vertically integrated structures the measures had not always been effective in ensuring a level-playing field that would encourage competition. The new proposals were opposed by those Member States—such as France and Germany—whose governments had retained close ties to their national energy utilities which had in turn maintained high levels of de facto integration. When these Member States proposed amendments to the reforms which substantially diluted the Commission's proposals the British and other pro-liberalization Member States sought to maintain the Commission's original plan but ultimately had to agree to the compromise (Wood 2008).

Given its fundamental role in supporting market reform at the European level, it is perhaps ironic that it was the British government that came under the scrutiny of the Commission's competition authorities for the way in which it planned to reorganize the electricity industry. The growing activism of DGIV (later DG-Comp [Competition Directorate-General]) was the other feature of EU-level liberalization in the last 25 years and in the process of energy liberalization, the Commission was keen to establish its competence to oversee the energy markets and ensure that they were compatible with EU competition rules. For the most part the Commission's interventions were directed at those least willing to reform. Ironically, however, it was often easier for the Commission to intervene in cases where changes were taking place than in those where incumbency was underpinned by inertia. Thus when the British government embarked on the most radical phase of its energy privatization policy, it attracted the attention of the Commission.

The proposals for privatizing the British electricity sector envisaged a fragmentation of the industry into a series of production and distribution companies and a set of contracts between these companies had to be established to underpin the industry as it shifted from public to private ownership. Moreover there needed to be special arrangements to underpin the country's nuclear power companies (whose lack of economic health had been revealed by the privatization process). The Commission investigated these arrangements, prompted in part by the efforts of British environmentalists who claimed the nuclear subsidies were contrary to EU rules. The Commission ultimately accepted the government's proposals but only after much debate (a number of Commissioners were opposed to nuclear energy) and after the UK government had limited the extent of the support it would give the sector (Commission of the European Communities 1995; *Guardian* 1990). According to some accounts, the then British competition commissioner Leon Brittan (formerly a member of the Conservative government) was central to ensuring that the Commission approval was obtained (Independent 1990).

This would not be the last time that the British government's treatment of its energy sector came under Commission scrutiny (the rescuing of British energy in 2002 and 2004 was perhaps the most sensitive intervention). However one has to remember that the Commission was becoming much more active in examining the conduct of governments toward the energy sector and its dealings with the UK were generally not as fraught as they were with other Member States. Moreover the UK government itself was prepared to complain to the Commission against what it saw as unfair competition in the energy sector in areas such as coal subsidies (Department of Trade and Industry 1997, 119) and delays in implementing legislation (European Report 1999).

Energy and the Environment: The Laggard Catches Up

While it is difficult to imagine energy liberalization being pursued and sustained without the support and advocacy of the UK, in other areas of European energy policy the UK was less of a pioneer. The 1980s were marked by a greater awareness of the environmental consequences of energy use and the development of stricter policies to limit its impact. As noted, initially the British government was slow to recognize the growing political significance of the environment and to accept the need for tougher controls. Even later on when it had agreed to EU regulations on controlling emissions and had adopted a greener hue in its own policy rhetoric, the UK remained skeptical about the direction of EU environmental policies as they affected the energy sector (Grant, et al. 2000).

This opposition was most clearly apparent from the early 1990s when the Commission sought to address the emerging challenge of climate change. Central to its strategy was a proposal for a carbon tax (later a carbon-energy tax). The plan enjoyed support from most

Member States (though the French were opposed to the "energy" component which they considered would penalize their nuclear industry). However the British were perhaps the most intransigent. As a government report from 1994 noted, the UK would meet its commitments on CO_2 reduction "without recourse to a carbon tax. It therefore does not need a tax at the national level and does not accept the case for one at EU level" (Department of Trade and Industry 1994, 82). Sustained British opposition through much of the 1990s effectively buried the proposal (as taxation matters required the unanimous support of Member States). Later, the UK's enthusiasm for market solutions allowed it to adopt a more positive approach to EU climate policy. In the wake of the failure of the fiscal option, the EU turned to the idea of emissions trading as a way of combating the use of fossil fuels and encouraging low carbon alternatives (an option the Commission had originally rejected). Since it had established a domestic system of emissions trading in 1999, the UK was broadly supportive of this new direction in EU climate policy (Skjærseth and Wettestad 2009; Wettestad 2005).

Developing a Community Competence in Energy

So far our discussion of the UK's role in EU energy policy has focused on a variety of initiatives that were proposed by the Commission on the basis of a variety of treaty provisions. The relatively more successful measures agreed in the last 20 years have been proposed under the legal bases covering the internal market (energy liberalization) or the environment (climate policy). Over the years there have been a number of attempts to develop a common energy policy or energy strategy which have sought to pursue and reconcile a variety of objectives (such as supply security, sustainability, and competitiveness) and render them into a coherent EU approach (McGowan 1990). Some advocates of a common energy policy, however, considered this approach to be too piecemeal and uncoordinated, arguing instead that a common and consistent response to the various energy challenges facing the EU required a dedicated treaty chapter. In the various Intergovernmental Conferences that were held over the 1990s, drafts of such a chapter were presented for consideration (European Commission 2000, 9; Laursen and Vanhoonacker 1994). Until 2004, however, they were abandoned because of a lack of consensus amongst Member States. It is perhaps no surprise that the UK was a consistent skeptic on the need for such provisions. In the negotiations for the Amsterdam Treaty, for example, the British government noted that it "would prefer a more flexible arrangement and remains doubtful about the need for any formalized process" (Department of Trade and Industry 1997, 15) such as an explicit treaty provision on energy.

Yet in the negotiations that resulted in the European Constitutional Treaty (and which in this respect were largely carried over into the Reform—or "Lisbon"—Treaty), the Member States agreed to the inclusion of an energy chapter. Such a provision could have been vetoed by the British government but while it was under pressure to do so from some parts of the British energy industry (notably in the offshore oil and gas sector) it chose not to do so (*Economist* 2003; European Voice 2003). The government claimed that it had ensured that the treaty provisions were limited in their scope (House of Commons Library 2004). The government was initially keen to argue that its agreement to an energy chapter constituted a relatively modest concession. However, it appeared to presage a more fundamental shift in the UK's view of the value of and need for a common energy policy.

The shift in the UK's stance was confirmed during its presidency of the European Council in 2005. Many issues contended for attention during the second Blair presidency (all the more important after its differences with other European powers during the Iraq war). As usual, the British government was keen to encourage other Member States to embrace economic liberalization. Yet in the preparations for an informal summit (at Hampton Court) on economic reform (where the usual market nostrums would be repeated) the British also put forward a paper calling for greater attention to energy cooperation among Member States. The paper—prepared by a British academic closely involved in the policy debate on British energy policy—identified a number of areas where European cooperation would be appropriate (notably on climate change and the development of energy networks and storage) (Helm 2005b). Later the British government was to refer to the "Hampton Court Agenda" as reinforcing the case for a European energy policy as laid out in the Lisbon Treaty (Foreign and Commonwealth Office 2007, 3).

Blair's advocacy of a European approach to energy policy was arguably an important contributory factor in reviving interest in energy policy. New Commission initiatives on energy policy had been expected but the British "u-turn" in favor of a collective response undoubtedly eased their progress. In any event, the case for such a response was reinforced within a matter of months when a dispute between Russia and Ukraine disrupted the flow of gas into some EU

Member States. Coming at a time when concerns about the price and availability of energy were increasing, the dispute underpinned the case for a common response, enhancing the supply security rationale for such a policy (McGowan 2008).

The Commission's proposals for climate and energy were developed over the course of 2006 and 2008—initial ideas were endorsed by the Member States at their Spring Summit in 2007 and agreement was reached on the legislation in late 2008. In most respects the UK played a broadly positive role in the negotiations - a fact acknowledged by the Commission President in a tribute to Blair (Agence Europe 2007). Even on those aspects where the UK was skeptical—principally a proposal to set binding targets for the development of renewable energy by 2020—it eventually acquiesced. Leaked government papers showed that officials were opposed to the setting of binding targets on the grounds that they would undermine the carbon price and blunt the effectiveness of carbon trading (and be very difficult for the UK to meet) (*Guardian* 2007). However, in the face of considerable criticism about plans to blunt the proposal, the British prime minister Gordon Brown reaffirmed the government's commitment to the overall policy. Other aspects of the proposal—such as a scheme for trading renewable energy "certificates of obligation"—were backed by the government but had to be diluted in the face of the opposition of other Member States (Nilsson et al. 2009; Toke 2008).[3] Why did the government not pursue its preferences on these matters? It may have been that a combination of bad publicity—for an ostensible supporter of renewable energy—and a possible defeat in any vote persuaded the government that it was not tenable either to oppose the principle of fixed targets or to insist on a comprehensive renewable trading system.

A bigger question, of course, is why the government embraced the principle of a broadly based—and binding—energy/climate policy. A number of factors may help us understand this change. One is the UK's desire both to be seen as contributing to a coherent European policy in an area where it had highlighted the need for national action and contribution toward international cooperation. Another may have been that it realized that there were limits to existing policies and that supportive interventions were needed. However, while these factors may well have played a role, perhaps the most important factor was the change in UK's energy circumstance. As it moved out of energy self-sufficiency it not only did not have a strategic advantage to defend but was also becoming more vulnerable to external disruptions and therefore more amenable to collective actions which might limit such risks.

Overall, the UK government appeared to recognize the value of an EU energy and climate policy. It shared and continued to push for market liberalization and broadly endorsed the objectives and instruments for tackling climate change. Even in those areas where it considered that EU proposals would be difficult and expensive to implement (as in the legislation setting binding targets for renewable energy supply) it was ready to adapt British policy. However, there remain limits to this newfound willingness to cooperate. Over the last year the Commission and some Member States have refloated the possibility of a carbon tax to discourage the consumption of fossil fuels in those areas not covered by the Emission Trading Scheme (ETS). The British have been to the fore in opposing such a proposal on the grounds that it would impinge on Member States' fiscal sovereignty. Since such a measure would require unanimity in the Council, it appears that the Commission has postponed making a proposal in this area (EurActiv 2010).

It seems that the Coalition government is maintaining the broadly positive stance of its predecessor toward EU energy policy. There had been expectations that a Conservative government would be less willing to cooperate with the EU. Relations with the EU had been a source of division for the party in the 1990s and 2000s, much as was the case for the Labour Party in the 1970s and early 1980s, and the issue appeared to have been resolved in favor of Euro-skeptics (Bale 2010). Even so, the Conservative leadership had indicated that in some areas cooperation in the EU was desirable and climate policy was one of those areas (MacKerron 2010). Once in power, the Coalition government seems to have adopted an apparently more positive line on the EU overall (*Financial Times* 2010; HM Government 2010), and this has been particularly apparent in the area of energy and climate policy. A notable development was the government's willingness to endorse a call for tougher carbon reduction targets of 30 percent by 2020 (Department of Energy and Climate Change 2010).

Conclusion

The UK's Damascene conversion to EU energy policy in 2005 has been as much an outcome of national interests as was its preceding reluctance. When the UK enjoyed a favorable energy balance, it was unsurprisingly less keen on policies that would encroach upon its ability to determine its own policy and particularly the allocation of energy resources. As its energy dependence has re-emerged, it has become keener on cooperative strategies. The government has had its difficulties with key elements of the policy—for example, the targets for renewable energy production—but, after an initially hostile position it seems to have acquiesced, accepting that the need for a strong political commitment to an EU-wide energy and climate policy takes priority over the details of how it should be implemented. However, while the first conversion may have eased the progress of EU energy policy, a second shock on the road to Damascus may prove rather problematic.

The same factors which endeared the British government to a more comprehensive EU energy policy have called into question the central plank of the UK's approach for nearly three decades. In that period the combination of plentiful energy supplies at home and abroad (which in turn impacted upon energy prices and perceptions of energy security) coincided with the government's pursuit of privatization and liberalization to create a new market driven energy policy. More recently, however, the UK seems to be rowing back from its enthusiastic endorsement of market based energy policy. The failure of the energy industries (particularly firms in the gas and electricity sectors) to invest in new capacity and the limited impact of carbon pricing as an incentive mechanism for producers and consumers seems to have prompted a rethink amongst those advising government and potentially those in government as well. Subsidies to foster new investment and a more interventionist role by government appear to be the order of the day. This shift in emphasis seems to be shared by the new government.

However, if the principal advocate of energy liberalization is backing away from such an approach in its domestic dealings, what are the implications for EU policy as a whole? For the moment it appears that the Commission remains committed to a market-driven energy policy (Commission of the European Communities 2010). If such a policy fails to deliver the anticipated results, however, the balance of policy may be rethought. If the UK is less assertive of the primacy of markets and less defensive of national sovereignty on energy policy, such a rethink would be relatively easier to attain.

Notes

1. Establishing the original source for this statement appears beyond the search capacities of the web. However it has also been quoted—without attribution—in such sources as IEEP (2005).

2. The UK's membership in 1973 followed more than a decade of attempts to join the Community. Most of these had foundered on the opposition of the then president of the French Republic—General Charles de Gaulle and it was only after de Gaulle's retirement that the prospects for British accession improved (Dinan 2004).
3. Advocates of trading in certificates claimed that such a system was market driven, cost effective, and compatible with the ETS. Critics argued that it would undermine those systems of support for renewable energy which had been most successful in promoting the technologies (Toke 2008).

Works Cited

Agence Europe. 2007. *Barosso Praises Tony Blair's European Commitment.* May 11, 2007.
Aspinwall, M. 2004. *Rethinking Britain and Europe.* Manchester University Press.
Bale, T. 2010. *The Conservatives: From Thatcher to Cameron.* Polity Press.
Bending, R and R. Eden. 1984. *UK Energy: Structure, Prospects and Policies.* Cambridge University Press.
Boehmer-Christiansen, S and J. Skea. 1991. *Acid Politics.* London: Belhaven 1991.
Cabinet Office. 1974. *EEC Energy Policy—Note by the Secretary of State.* May 7. C974) 38.
Cairncross, A. 1985. *Years of Recovery: British Economic Policy 1945–51.* London: Methuen.
Carter, N. 2008. Combating Climate Change in the UK Challenges and Obstacles. *Political Quarterly.* 79(2): 194–205.
Chesshire, J. 1986. An Energy-Efficient Future: A Strategy for the UK. *Energy Policy* 14(5): 395–412.
Commission of the European Communities. 1968. *First Guidelines for a Community Energy Policy, Memorandum presented by the Commission to the Council.* COM (68) 1040.
Commission of the European Communities. 1972. *Necessary Progress in Community Energy Policy, Communication from the Commission to the Council forwarded on 13 October 1972.* COM (72) 1200.
Commission of the European Communities. 1974. *Towards a New Energy Policy Strategy for the European Community.* COM (74) 550/final 2.
Commission of the European Communities. 1988. *The Internal Energy.* Market COM (88) 238.
Commission of the European Communities. 1995. *White Paper: An Energy Policy for the European Union.* COM (95) 682.
Commission of the European Communities. 2006. *A European Strategy for Sustainable Competitive and Secure Energy.* COM (2006) 105.

Commission of the European Communities. 2010. *Stock taking document: Towards a new Energy Strategy for Europe 2011–2020*.
Connelly, P. and R. Perlman. 1975. *The Politics of Scarcity—Resource Conflicts in International Relations*. Oxford: Oxford University Press (OUP).
Conservative Party. 2010. *Rebuilding Security—Conservative Energy Policy for an Uncertain World*. London: Conservative Party.
Cook, P L. and J. Surrey. 1977. *Energy Policy: Strategies for Uncertainty*. Robertson.
Dell, E. 1995. *The Schuman Plan and the British Abdication of Leadership in Europe*. Oxford University Press.
Department of Business Enterprise and Regulatory Reform. 2008. *A White Paper on Nuclear Power*. Command Paper 7296 His/Her Majesty's Stationery Office (HMSO).
Department of Energy. 1978. *Energy Policy: A Consultative Document*. Command Paper 7101, HMSO.
Department of Energy and Climate Change. 2010. *Joint EU Climate Change article by Chris Huhne, Dr Norbert Röttgen and Jean-Louis Borloo*. Available at http://www.decc.gov.uk /en/content/cms/news/EU_CC _article/EU_CC_article.aspx.
Department of Fuel and Power. 1967. *White Paper on Fuel Policy*. Command Paper 3438, HMSO.
Department of the Environment. 1990. *This Common Inheritance*. Command Paper 1200, HMSO.
Department of Trade and Industry. 1993. *The Prospects for Coal*, Command Paper 2235, HMSO, London.
Department of Trade and Industry. 1994. *Energy Report 1994: Markets in Transition*. London: HMSO.
Department of Trade and Industry. 1997.*Energy Report 1997: Shaping change*. London: HMSO.
Department of Trade and Industry. 2003. *Energy White Paper:Our Energy Future—Creating a Low Carbon Economy*. Command Paper 5761, HMSO.
Department of Trade and Industry. 2007. *Meeting the Energy Challenge: A White Paper on Energy*. Command Paper 7124.
Dinan, D. 2004. *Europe Recast: A History of European Union*. Basingstoke: Palgrave.
Economist. 2003. An Intergovernmental Tug of War. November 22, 2003.
Eising, R. 2002. Policy Learning in Embedded Negotiations: Explaining EU Electricity Liberalization. *International Organization*. 56(1): 85–120.
EU Energy. 2009. *UK Opposition Adopts Interventionist Energy Policy*. Issue 204. March 27, 2009.
EurActiv. 2010. *EU Carbon Tax Proposal Delayed*. June 25, 2010.
Eurelectric. 1991. Electricity Market.

Eurelectric. 1991. *Statement of the Continental Members of EURELECTRIC Relative to the Internal.*
European Commission. 2000. *Green Paper—Towards a European Strategy for the Security of Energy Supply.* COM (2000) 769.
European Report. 1999. *Commission Strongly Denies Reports over EDF Competition Case.* October 16, 1999.
European Voice. 2003. *Oil and Gas Industry Fights Energy Chapter.* December 4, 2003.
Financial Times. 2010. Cameron Steps Back from Euroscpetic Line. May 13, 2010.
Foreign and Commonwealth Office. 1973. *Telegramme 313.* February 23, 1973.
Foreign and Commonwealth Office. 2005. *Record of Meeting of the Oil Policy Committee.* January 21, 1973 found in "Documents on British Policy Overseas Series III, Volume IV."
Foreign and Commonwealth Office. 2007. *The Reform Treaty: The British Approach to the European Union Intergovernmental Conference, July 2007.* Command Paper 7174, London: HMSO.
George, S. 1998. *An awkward partner: Britain in the European Community.* Oxford University Press.
Gowland, D and A. Turner. 2000. *Reluctant Europeans: Britain and European Integration 1945–1998.* Harlow: Longman.
Grant, W., D. Matthews and P. Newell. 2000. *The Effectiveness of EU Environmental Policy.* Palgrave.
Gray, J. 2004. Blair's Project in Retrospect. *International Affairs.* 80(1): 39–48.
Guardian. 1990. EC Anti-Nuclear Forces Climb Down before Sale. March 29, 1990.
Guardian. 2007. Revealed: Cover-up Plan on Energy Target. August 13, 2007.
Hellema, D., C. Wiebes and T. Witte. 2004. *The Netherlands and the Oil Crisis—Business as Usual.* Amsterdam: Amsterdam University Press.
Helm, D. 2005a. The Assessment: The New Energy Paradigm. *Oxford Review of Economic Policy.* 21 (1).
Helm, D. 2005b. *European Energy Policy: Securing Supplies and Meeting the Challenge of Climate Change.* Available at http://www.dieterhelm.co.uk/sites/default/files/European_Energy_Policy251005.pdf.
Helm, D., J. Kay and D. Thompson. 1989. *Introduction: Energy Policy and the Role of the State in the Market for Energy.* The Market for Energy. Eds. D. Helm, J. Kay, and D. Thompson. Clarendon.
HM Government. 2010. *The Coalition: Our Programme for Government.* HMSO.
House of Commons Library. 2004. *The Treaty Establishing a Constitution for Europe: Part III.* "Research Paper" 4/75.

IEEP (Institute for European Environmental Policy). 2005. *Evaluation of the 22nd Report of the Royal Commission on Environmental Pollution—"Energy the Changing Climate."* London: IEEP.

Independent. 1990. *EC Test for Power Deal.* March 27, 1990.

Jordan, A. 2000. *The Europeanisation of UK Environmental Policy, 1970–2000: A Department Perspective.* "One Europe or Several? Working Papers." No 11.

Labour Party. 1983. *The New Hope for Britain.*

Labour Party. 1987. *Britain Will Win.*

Labour Party. 1992. *It's Time to Get Britain Working again.*

Labour Party. 1997. *New Labour: Because Britain DeservesBetter.*

Laursen, F and S. Vanhoonacker. 1994. *The Ratification of the Maastricht Treaty: Issues, Debates, and Future Implications.* European Institute of Public Administration (EIPA).

Lawson, N. 1982. *Speech on Energy Policy.* "Department of Energy Paper 51."

Lawson, N. 1992. *The View from No.11: Memoirs of a Tory Radical.* Bantam Press.

Lister, L. 1960. *Europe's Coal and Steel Community—An Experiment in Economic Union.* New York: 20th Century Fund.

Lovell, H., H. Bulkeley and S. Owens. 2009. *Converging Agendas? Energy and Climate Change Policies in the UK.* "Environment and Planning C: Government and Policy." 27.

Lucas, N. 1977. *Energy and the European Communities* London: Europa, 1977.

MacKerron, G. 2010. *Tory Energy Policy: Going Red While Going Green.* Parliamentary Brief. March 2010.

Marsh, P. 1999. *Bargaining on Europe: Britain and the First Common Market 1860–1892.* Yale University Press.

McGowan, F. 1990. Conflicting Objectives in European Energy Policy. In *The Politics of 1992.* Eds. C. Crouch and D. Marquand. Oxford: Blackwell 1990.

McGowan, F. 2001. *Social Democracy and the European Union: Who's Changing Whom?* In *Social Democracy: Global and National Perspectives.* Eds. Martell et al. Basingstoke: Palgrave.

McGowan, F. 2008. Can the European Union's Market Liberalism Ensure Energy Security in a Time of Economic Nationalism? *Journal of Contemporary European Research* 4(2): 90–106.

Mitchell, C. 2007. *The Political Economy of Sustainable Energy.* Palgrave Macmillan.

Moravcsik, A. 1991. Negotiating the Single European Act: National Interests and Conventional Statecraft in the European Community. *International Organization.* 45: 19–56. Cambridge: Cambridge University Press.

Nilsson, M, and K. Ericsson. 2009. The Rise and Fall of GO Trading in European Renewable Energy Policy: the Role of Advocacy and Policy Framing. *Energy Policy.* 37(11).

O' Neill, C. 2000. *Britain's Entry into the European Community: Report by Sir Con O'Neill on the Negotiations 1970-1972*. London: Routledge.
Osborn, D. 1997. Some Reflections on UK Environment Policy, 1970-1995. *Journal of Environmental Law*. 9(1).
Parker, M. 2000. *Thatcherism and the Fall of Coal*. Oxford University Press.
Pollitt, M. 2010. *UK Renewable Energy Policy since Privatization*. European Pipeline Research Group (EPRG) Working Paper 1002.
Prime Minister's Office. 1974. *Note to Prime Minister—EEC Energy Policy*. (C(74)38). May 8, 1974.
Rutledge, I. 2007. New Labour, Energy Policy and 'Competitive Markets. *Cambridge Journal of Economics*. 31(6): 901-925.
Scrase, J and G. MacKerron. 2009. *Energy for the Future*. Palgrave.
Shackleton, M. 1978. *Oil and the British Foreign Process*. Millennium. 7(2).
Shovelton, P. 2000. *The Other Communities*. In O'Neill. 2000.
Simonet, H. 1975. *Energy and the Future of Europe*. Foreign Affairs 53(3).
Skjærseth, J and J. Wettestad. 2009. The Origin, Evolution and Consequences of the EU Emissions Trading System. *Global Environmental Politics*. 9(2).
Surrey, J (ed). 1996. *The British Electricity Experiment*. London: Earthscan.
Thorpe, K. 2007. The Forgotten Shortage: Britain's Handling of the 1967 Oil Embargo. *Contemporary British History*. 21(2).
Times. 1973. EEC in Grave Crisis as Britain Matches Bonn Move on Regional Fund. December 19, 1973.
Times. 1974a. Britain Blocks Eec Energy Policy and Starts Row Over Sugar. July 24, 1974.
Times. 1974b. Britain Takes Its Brake Off EEC'S Energy Plans September 18, 1974.
Toke, D. 2008. The EU Renewables Directive—What is the fuss about trading? *Energy Policy*. 36(8).
Turner, L. 1975. The European Community: Factors of Disintegration. *International Affairs*.
Van der Linde, J. and R. Lefeber. 1988. International Energy Agency Captures the Development of European Community Energy Law. *Journal of World Trade*. 22(5).
Von Geusau, A. 1975. *Energy in the European Communities*. Leyden: Sijthoff.
Walton, A. 1976. Atlantic Relations: Policy Coordination and Conflict—Atlantic Bargaining over Energy. *International Affairs*. 52(2).
Weale, A. 1992. *The New Politics of Pollution*. Manchester UP.
Wettestad, J. 2005. The Making of the 2003 EU Emissions Trading Directive: Ultra-quick Process Due to Entrepreneurial Proficiency? *Global Environmental Politics*. 5(1).

Wicks, M. 2009.*Energy Security: A National Challenge in a Changing World*. London: DECC
Wood, J. 2008. Energy: EC's Unbundling Plans Diluted. *Utility Week*. June 13.
Yergin, D. *The Prize*. New York: Simon & Schuster 1991.
Young, H. 1999. *This Blessed Plot: Britain and Europe from Churchill to Blair*. Basingstoke: Pan Macmillan.

Part III

Cross-Cutting Perspectives

Chapter Ten

Rethinking European Climate Change Policy

Arno Behrens and Christian Egenhofer

European climate change policy has been designed to meet the requirements of a more efficient, greener, and more competitive economy. With domestic legislation in place comparatively early, the European Union (EU) has over several years assumed the role of a driving force behind international climate policies and negotiations. However, this link between domestic action and international leadership has recently been weakened. On the one hand, the economic crisis and related greenhouse gas emissions reductions have starkly reduced the ambitiousness of domestic greenhouse gas emissions reduction targets and thus also their model character for other industrialized and emerging economies. On the other hand, the failure to reach a legally binding, comprehensive, and ambitious climate change agreement in Copenhagen has put into question the influence the EU can assert on the international level. EU climate change policy needs to react to these developments in order to provide incentives for low-carbon energy investments required to fight global warming and its predicted impacts on Europe and indeed the world.

This chapter first gives an overview about the possible impacts of climate change on Europe before describing the current state of climate change policy in the EU. More importantly, the chapter assesses options for the EU to react to recent developments related to the economic crisis and the failure of the Copenhagen climate change conference in 2009. A special focus is placed on transport and the urgent need to address growing greenhouse gas emissions from this sector by means of a comprehensive policy approach. To conclude, concrete policy recommendations are made for the required framework for the transition toward a low-carbon energy system.

Impacts of Climate Change in Europe

According to the Intergovernmental Panel on Climate Change (IPCC) there is persuasive evidence that most of the temperature rise that has occurred over the past 100 years is attributable to human activity and in particular the increasing level of global greenhouse gas emissions. With an average temperature increase of about 1 degree Celsius since preindustrial times (EEA 2008), Europe experienced a higher temperature increase than the global average of about 0.74 degrees Celsius (IPCC 2007a). As greenhouse gas concentrations in the atmosphere continue to increase, the potential impact of greenhouse gas emissions on people and ecosystems may prove to be significant. For the next two decades, the IPCC (2007b) projects a global average temperature rise of about 0.2 degrees Celsius per decade across a range of emission scenarios. Again, projections suggest higher temperatures in Europe than the global average (EEA 2008). The consequences of further temperature increases may be serious for humanity and other forms of life on earth.

The effects on Europe have—among others—been analyzed by the European Commission (2009a) and even under the assumption that mitigation will be substantial, temperatures in various regions are estimated to increase on average by over 4 degrees Celsius by the end of the century. The highest temperature increases are expected in the Mediterranean region in the baseline scenario without mitigation.

As to the impacts of increasing average temperature on Europe, a recent literature review by Behrens et al. (2010) found that direct losses from extreme weather events are projected to increase considerably all over Europe.

Although there remains a lot of uncertainty about local and regional effects, it is clear that the repercussions will vary considerably across regions (see Table 10.1). Some effects could even benefit certain regions. Most of the positive impacts will be in northern Europe. This region could benefit from higher crop yields, an expansion of forest areas and enhanced forest-growth rates, an increasing number of tourist visits, and a net decrease in climate-related deaths.

While northern Europe will also have to bear some severe negative consequences (e.g. in the form of more frequent extreme weather events or coastal and river flooding), it is mainly the countries in the south, which are already economically disadvantaged, that will suffer most. Some of the most severe negative impacts in the Mediterranean include prolonged periods with temperatures above the comfort zone and the accompanying effects on human health and tourism, increasing

Table 10.1 Simplified summary of climate change impacts in Europe and their intensity

Climate change Indicators	Northern Europe	Central and Eastern Europe	Mediterranean
Direct losses from weather disasters	M(−)	M(−)	H(−)
River flood disasters	M(−)	H(−)	L(−)
Coastal flooding	H(−)	M(−)	H(−)
Public water supply and drinking water	L(−)	L(−)	H(−)
Crop yields in agriculture	H(+)	M(−)	H(−)
Crop yields in forestry	M(+)	L(−)	H(−)
Energy for heating and cooling	M(+)	L(+)	M(−)
Hydropower and cooling for thermal plants	M(+)	M(−)	H(−)
Tourism and recreation	M(+)	L(+)	M(−)
Health	L(−)	M(−)	H(−)

Source: Behrens et al., 2010.

Notes: H: High; M: Medium; L: Low; (+): Positive impact; (−): Negative impact.

water scarcity, droughts, forest fires, desertification, decreasing agricultural productivity, coastal flooding, and loss of biodiversity. One of the few positive outcomes will be the reduced likelihood of river flood disasters (which will be more frequent in central and Eastern Europe).

Impacts of climate change on Europe clearly show strong distributional patterns. Similar to the global context, where poorer developing countries are expected to suffer most, it is the poor regions in Europe that will be affected most. Hence, climate change further compounds the difficulties of these countries in achieving a level of welfare equivalent to the EU average. At the same time, the cumulative impacts of climate change on poorer countries will also affect northern European countries, as growing water scarcity and other repercussions in Mediterranean countries could pose social and security challenges through increasing risks of conflicts and migration pressures. Fighting climate change through domestic and international action is thus not only a matter of solidarity, but clearly in the self-interest of the EU and *all* of its Member States.

The outlined future impacts of climate change on the EU are a useful starting point for policy-makers when shaping effective adaptation (and mitigation) policies for Europe. Uncertainties, variability, and differences among estimates remain. Nevertheless, while the precise quantification of the economic consequences requires continuing research and may be impossible even at a later stage, the nature of the possible impacts and the geographical and sectoral differentiation appear to be sufficiently clear at this stage. The magnitude of the effects depends on the global emissions pathways, but it has been possible to approximate it from existing global mitigation efforts and it can be adjusted as the effects evolve.

EU Strategies for Climate Change Policies

As early as 1996, the EU adopted a long-term target of limiting global temperature increase to a maximum of 2 degrees Celsius above preindustrial levels. This was reiterated over the years, among others in the European Council of October 29/30, 2009 (Council of the European Union 2009). Limiting global warming to a maximum of 2 degrees Celsius above preindustrial levels—a level below which EU policy-makers believe that irreversible ecological damages may still be avoided—will require cuts in global emissions of at least 50 percent by 2050 relative to 1990 levels. According to the European Commission (2009b)—making reference to the Fourth Assessment Report by the IPCC (IPCC 2007a)—this would require developed countries to reduce their greenhouse gas emissions by 25–40 percent by 2020 and 80–95 percent by 2050 compared to 1990 levels. At the same time, developing countries would need to limit emissions growth to 15–30 percent below baseline by 2020 (European Commission 2009b).

The EU's position must be understood in the context of the multilateral climate change negotiations where the EU has traditionally played an important role. In the year 2001, the EU found itself catapulted into leadership after United States (US) president George W. Bush declared that the US would not take part in the Kyoto Protocol. Active EU diplomacy ensured that Japan, Canada, and Russia ratified the Protocol, which entered into force in 2005. To prepare for this, the EU has adopted numerous legal texts (directives, regulations, decisions, recommendations, and opinions; see Egenhofer et al. 2009) to fulfill its commitments. Among them have been policies to support renewable energy and to improve energy efficiency in buildings and transport. However, the centerpiece of EU climate change policy has been the EU Emissions Trading Scheme (EU ETS), which became operational in 2005. While these and other policies have focused on the implementation of the Kyoto Protocol commitments, in parallel the EU has been developing a new strategy to meet mid- and longer-term climate change objectives. The EU had realized that—in the absence of US engagement—EU leadership was indispensible for reaching a global agreement on climate change. At the same time, this leadership position is regarded as an opportunity for shaping the new regime in line with the EU's climate agenda. Other benefits include the reduction of energy import dependency and the possibility to gain leadership in low-carbon technologies.

The Energy and Climate Change Package

Although there have been several prior EU policy initiatives, the heart of its current greenhouse gas emissions reduction strategy is the energy and climate change package,[1] which was formally adopted on April 6, 2009. This package intends to achieve the EU's overall binding environmental targets, which were adopted by the European heads of state and government at their March 8–9, 2007 summit chaired by the German presidency (Council of the European Union 2007). There, leaders committed themselves to unilaterally reduce greenhouse gas emissions by 20 percent by 2020 compared to 1990 levels (up to 30 percent if other developed countries were to commit to comparable emissions reductions) and to increase the share of renewable energy in the EU's total energy consumption to 20 percent. While these two targets are binding, they also set themselves a nonbinding energy efficiency goal of reducing primary energy consumption by 20 percent by 2020 compared to projections.

The core elements of the energy and climate change package are the revised EU ETS,[2] in combination with the so-called "effort-sharing" decision[3] and the directive for the promotion of renewable energy sources.[4] The revised ETS-Directive strengthens the ETS by setting the goal of reducing greenhouse gas emissions by 2020 by 21 percent below 2005 levels in the covered sectors (representing some 40 percent of the EU's total greenhouse gas emissions). Emissions reductions outside of the ETS sectors are covered by the effort-sharing decision, which requires non-ETS sectors (covering some 60 percent of EU greenhouse gas emissions) by 2020 to reduce their emissions by 10 percent compared to 2005 levels. Efforts will be shared among Member States according to the principles of solidarity and equity, resulting in different (binding) targets for different countries. Taken together, both pieces of legislation will result in greenhouse gas emissions reductions of 14 percent compared to 2005, which is equivalent to a reduction of 20 percent compared to 1990.

The *renewable energy directive*,[5] on the other hand, creates a common EU framework for the promotion of renewable energy sources, with the aim to increase the percentage share of energy from renewable sources in the EU's final consumption of energy to 20 percent by 2020 (up from some 8.5 percent in 2005) and to achieve a 10 percent share of energy from renewable sources in each Member State's transport energy consumption. The directive sets for each Member State a national target for the overall share of renewable energy in gross final energy consumption, taking into account differences in starting points between Member States as well as equity and solidarity considerations. Each Member State will need to adopt a National Renewable Energy Action Plan, which was due to be notified to the European Commission (hereafter: the Commission) by June 2010. Although the directive provides for flexibility and cooperation mechanisms (e.g., statistical transfers between Member States, joint projects with third countries, etc.), most national targets will be reached through domestic action.[6] The directive also establishes common rules related to the access of renewables to the electricity grid and includes sustainability criteria for biofuels and bioliquids to ensure that they can be counted as renewable energy for the purpose of this directive.

Such an integrated approach to energy and climate change issues was necessitated by various changing conditions faced by the EU. With dwindling domestic resources and increasing dependence on energy imports—to a large extent on Russia—the EU and its Member States have been examining domestic and external policy options to move to a more sustainable and secure energy supply. This includes, amongst others, investment in renewable energy sources (for an assessment of the role of renewables for the security of European energy supplies, see Behrens 2010), pushing carbon capture and storage technology for fossil and other fuels and investment in nuclear energy in Member States that wish to do so. To drive down costs for these technologies, there is a need for large-scale deployment. The International Energy Agency (IEA 2008) makes the case, for example, that renewables (except wind) experience significant capital cost reductions for each doubling of capacity, such as 15–20 percent for photovoltaics and 20 percent for solar water heaters. This justifies proactive support policies for low-carbon technologies.

To offset expected price rises both for industry and domestic consumers, energy efficiency is a central piece, certainly for the transition period until new technologies and new fuels become available on a large scale. With increasing prices, reducing consumption gives a reasonable prospect for keeping the energy bill constant. Energy efficiency is an important component of the Commission's Second Strategic Energy Review—focusing on the security of European energy supplies—which was tabled on November 13, 2008.[7] Increasing energy efficiency is a strategic objective of the EU (20 percent by 2020) and related legislation has recently been strengthened or is under revision. For example, the recast of the Energy Labeling Directive entered into force in June 2010 and the recast of the Energy Performance of Buildings Directive in July 2010. Similarly, an evaluation of the 2006 Energy Efficiency Action Plan is ongoing and expected to be completed in early 2011.

Unlike the greenhouse gas reduction target and the renewables target, however, there is no binding target on improving energy efficiency in the EU. Given the sluggish improvements of energy efficiency in Member States, there seems to be increasing momentum for the Commission to table a proposal for a binding 20 percent target in the context of the upcoming new Energy Efficiency Action Plan. There is thus a chance that the currently indicative target of saving 20 percent of Europe's energy consumption compared to projections for 2020 could turn into a binding target in the future.

While the EU has started to address the climate change challenge with its energy and climate change package, it will require a global alliance to avoid dangerous climate change. Keeping in mind that the EU was only responsible for roughly 14 percent of global greenhouse gas emissions in 2007 (IEA, 2009a) and given that in the reference scenario, this share will decrease to around 9 percent until 2030 (ibid.), the EU's ability to have a direct effect on global greenhouse gas emissions is limited. This is well illustrated by the fact that EU *cumulative* CO_2 savings between 2008 and 2020 (with a 20 percent CO_2 emissions reduction target) would represent only 40 percent of China's *annual* CO_2 emissions in 2020. But even if all OECD countries were to reduce their greenhouse gas emissions to zero by 2030 (which is highly unrealistic), non-OECD countries alone would exceed global emissions levels in line with the 2 degrees Celsius threshold (IEA 2009b). Effective international climate change cooperation thus needs the involvement of developing countries, and especially of fast growing emerging economies.

The Failure at Copenhagen and its Implication for EU Climate Policy

The failure to reach a legally binding, comprehensive, and ambitious agreement in Copenhagen—in line with the 2 degrees Celcius target—has potentially severe consequences for EU climate change policy as well as for business. There is a risk that future EU policy may be stalled, reducing further the already low incentive for low-carbon investment (due to the economic crisis). In addition, it raises questions on the effectiveness of the EU's international negotiations strategy and especially on how the EU can defend its interests.

Several options are currently being discussed on how the EU can retain the credibility of its climate change policies together with leadership in international climate negotiations. One option could be to unilaterally increase the current 20 percent greenhouse gas emissions target to 30 percent as this might reinvigorate the EU leadership and infuse new dynamics into the global climate change discussion. In this way, the EU would document that it believes that a stringent unilateral target is in its self-interest, preparing the economy for the low-carbon future. While more affluent Member States tend to be in favor of such a move, this would almost certainly trigger very difficult discussions on burden sharing, finance, and competitiveness. There is also a fear especially in those Member States with a per capita Gross Domestic Product (GDP) below the EU average that due to their EU membership they are asked to reduce a multiple of what developing countries are asked to do. They are loath to contributing to large-scale finance transfers to developing countries, some of which are actually richer than them. And finally, an EU move to 30 percent would quickly erode the substantial excess allocation in the form of Assigned Amount Units (AAUs) under the Kyoto Protocol that these countries possess and are keen on selling internationally.

However, it should be noted that the recent financial crisis and the associated economic recession had a considerable impact on EU greenhouse gas emissions and that the current EU 20 percent reduction target may be substantially easier to reach than was assumed before the crisis. By and large, a 30 percent reduction target post crisis appears to be roughly equal to the 20 percent reduction target precrisis in terms of costs. Amann et al., (2009) for example, show that by 2020, EU greenhouse gas emissions could be almost 14 percent lower than was assumed precrisis (i.e., in 2008). Compared to 1990 emissions levels, this would mean a reduction of over 16 percent, which brings the EU relatively close to its target without further climate measures. An evaluation of the EU's current ambitions, for example, by changing the base year for greenhouse gas emissions reductions from 1990 to 2005, shows that the EU's 20 percent target compares poorly with the ambitions of other industrialized countries including the US (Egenhofer 2010). The EU will thus need to consider how credible a target is that represents little of a constraint for another decade. From this perspective it is difficult to see how the EU can avoid moving—relatively swiftly—to a 2020 target higher than the current 20 percent goal. This is in contrast to government's reflexes to avoid additional burden in times of economic crisis.

A second and currently more plausible option is to target specific sectors with integrated policies such as transport (see below), buildings, or agriculture, or by making the energy efficiency target legally binding. The upcoming EU budget review offers an opportunity to make available EU budgetary resources to assist those Member States with per capita GDPs below the EU average to accept to implement energy efficiency policies. Under either scenario there might be continuous calls for tightening the ETS cap, for example, by reducing offsets or even by adjusting the cap to ensure that the ETS delivers effectively. Incentives through price signals (in ETS sectors and by national carbon taxes) are seen as economically more efficient than regulation.

Regarding the international dimension of its climate policies, the EU's soft approach is often criticized. Given that this approach has largely failed in Copenhagen, the issue of introducing a carbon border tax is gaining some momentum. Indeed, carbon border taxes are the only credible and realistic option the EU has to defend its interests. Currently such a move is still highly controversial not only between but also within Member States and within the Commission not only because of potential implications for EU relations with China and India, the world trade regime and international relations, but also for European businesses operating internationally. However, from a purely economic perspective this would be a straightforward means of moving toward a global 'shadow' carbon price (see, for example, Gros and Egenhofer 2010). Precondition would have to be a 30 percent reduction target or more, 100 percent auctioning of allowances under the EU ETS and a national or EU-wide carbon tax for the nontrading sector, not a likely but a possible scenario. Importantly, the EU will need to take a position, or otherwise delegate the outcome of this debate to the US.

There is also another option for the EU to pursue pricing of carbon on the global level. By scaling up and reforming existing flexible mechanisms such as the clean development mechanism (CDM) and by creating new ones that allow the establishment of a global carbon price, the EU could regain leadership on the international level. But this would require the cooperation of other countries, notably developing countries, which is currently rather unlikely.

Another option and what seems to be chosen by the EU is to slog on by attempting to integrate the achievements of the Copenhagen Accord into the two United Nations (UN) negotiation tracks and then hope to achieve a legally binding global agreement. This assumes that a legally binding, comprehensive, and ambitious agreement is within reach in South Africa 2011 and that the Copenhagen Accord, as a kind of bottom-up pledge and review system is only a historical blunder on the way to a truly global agreement worth its name. This assumes also that the world as a whole is ready to discuss and agree on a final carve up of the remaining global carbon budget. These are bold assumptions, especially in the light that China and India have shown little appetite for anything other than "extreme" unilateral actions. The Chinese negotiation position has been remarkably consistent in rejecting any calls for legally binding commitments before (possibly) 2030 and China even has a major issue with international monitoring. In addition, the US continues to struggle even with a very modest domestic bill, let alone Australia or Canada.

This is where the EU's domestic and international agendas come together again. Under the assumption that a legally binding, comprehensive, and ambitious agreement in South Africa is within reach, the EU strategy will need to focus on managing the transition from an EU perspective, that is, by reinforcing incentives toward low-carbon investment. If such an agreement is not within reach, the EU will need to reflect on some of the international issues presented above.

Focus: The Need for a "Transport and Climate Change Package"

The transport sector is not only vital for European integration; it also constitutes an important component of the European economy. The sector contributes some 7 percent of GDP and more than 5 percent of total employment in the EU (European Commission 2009c).

Progressive European (market) integration, notably successive ways of enlargement have lead to a substantial increase in transport volumes in recent years. On average, passenger transport (pkm) increased by 1.7 percent annually since 1995—mainly driven by air and road transport, while freight transport (tkm) increased by 2.7 percent over the same period (ibid.)—mainly driven by road and sea transport. These developments have lead to an increasing recognition of the negative side effects of mass transport in Europe, including deterioration of infrastructure, land use issues, congestion, air and noise pollution, injuries and deaths, as well as substantial amounts of greenhouse gas emissions. The latter is of particular importance in the context of the EU's global climate leadership. Failure to address greenhouse gas emissions in transport will not only jeopardize the achievement of recently adopted EU emissions reduction targets, it would also hinder the industrial transformation of the transport sector.

While greenhouse gas emissions decreased in all sectors of the European economy since 1990, transport was the only sector that experienced continuous growth in emissions, which increased by some 36 percent[8] in the period between 1990 and 2007. As a result, the European transport sector is currently responsible for almost a quarter of all EU greenhouse gas emissions. The fastest growing modes of transport between 1990 and 2007 were civil aviation (+93 percent) and navigation (+51 percent), while in absolute terms the largest increase was in road transport (+29 percent). Road transport continues to contribute the bulk (71 percent) to transport greenhouse gas emissions and is responsible for some 17 percent of total EU greenhouse gas emissions (European Commission, 2010).

These figures clearly show that the transport sector will need to play a major role in the EU's climate policy. In order to meet the 2 degrees Celsius climate change target, by 2020 emissions from road transport need to decrease in absolute terms while increases in emissions in the aviation and maritime modes need to be halted. In the longer term, that is, until 2050, emissions from the transport sector need to decrease by up to 80 percent in order to achieve the global emissions reduction targets. Achieving these objectives will require a dramatic shift in the way people travel and in the way we move goods.

Reducing transport emissions will have additional benefits in terms of security of energy supplies. The transport sector today depends on up to 97 percent on hydrocarbon fuels, and mainly on oil. Biofuels and other renewables will not be enough to address vulnerability. The overall EU transport demand is projected to increase to such an extent (18 percent by 2020 according to the IEA) that the EU target of replacing 10 percent of transport fuel use with renewable energy sources—although creating an additional security margin—can only moderately reduce European dependence on oil. In a time where oil imports will continue to replace declining domestic oil production and import dependence will increase, a low-carbon transport strategy seems unavoidable.

There has been little progress in designing an integrated and strategic response to rising greenhouse gas emissions, security of energy supply issues and the transport sector's innovation challenge. European transport policy to date has largely been aimed at increasing efficiency, reducing costs, and increasing the speed of transport. But it has failed to take into account environmental considerations. The transport related elements of the energy and climate change package (including the "renewables directive," the "clean cars directive," and the "fuel quality directive") represent a step in the right direction but fall significantly short of an integrated strategy that sketches out a pathway to a low-carbon transport sector. To do this, Europe needs a "transport and climate change package" comparable to the aforementioned energy and climate change package. This package must give answers to fundamental strategic questions about what a sustainable EU transport system should look like and how it can be achieved. It may include setting concrete (binding) targets for the decarbonization of the transport sector. In addition, it should comment on the cost-effectiveness of alternative low-carbon transport options with the aim of building political consensus for their implementation.

The transport and climate change package needs to review a number of policies at EU but also Member-State level. The "polluter pays" principle will need to be applied across all modes of transport and will need to include responsibilities for greenhouse gas emissions. Pricing mechanisms need to reflect the true costs of transport. This also means that taxation will need to treat comparable fuels in a comparable way. The tax exemption of aviation fuels, in the fastest growing mode of transport, will thus need to be reconsidered. Another central policy area will be infrastructure. Upgraded and new transport infrastructure will be required to master the transition to a low-carbon economy in much the same way as smart grids will become the backbone for the energy sector's transition. In fact, road transport infrastructure and electricity grids will need to become more closely integrated because decarbonization of road transportation will not be possible without an increasing share of low-carbon electricity in transport. The decarbonization of the power sector and a strong commitment for innovation in the car and related industries are thus prerequisites for decarbonization of road transport. Although it looks likely that future road transport will rely on electricity, this is not to say that other alternatives to conventional combustion engines (e.g., hydrogen) should not be looked at. The largest challenge for decarbonizing the transport sector will be in international aviation and maritime transport because of a lack of technological options in the near future. Biofuels could play an increasing role, together with energy efficiency measures and demand reductions. The EU will need to take leadership aimed at reaching international agreements for reducing emissions from aviation and shipping. In addition, the expansion of the high-speed train network may help in the substitution of air and road travel. Given that transport by rail is two to three times more energy efficient per metric ton of cargo than by road, the continuing decline of the rail freight market share will need to be addressed (especially in the new Member States) to facilitate a shift toward multimodal transport.

R&D and technology will be at the heart of greening the transport sector. On the one hand, technologies will need to be tested. On the other, only deployment ensures decreasing costs. The new transport and climate package should thus introduce technology deployment targets, for example in the area of advanced car technologies. This could relate to the vehicles themselves (e.g., a certain share of the vehicle fleet needs to be carbon neutral), as well as to innovative infrastructure projects (e.g., minimum requirements for electricity infrastructure for cars). To stimulate technological innovation, a number of demonstration or 'flagship' projects may be considered, aimed at using state-of-the-art technologies, including advanced telematics technology in urban transport to reduce greenhouse gas emissions and other harmful environmental effects, to reduce congestions, to increase efficiency and generally to increase competitiveness. Such systems can now be based on the GALILEO global navigation satellite system. Mandatory large-scale demonstration projects can be justified because they play an important role in bringing down costs of the equipment.

The contributions from technology should be complemented by those from other stakeholders, including users, government, and associated industries. Technology alone will not be enough to bring down emissions and demand side management, including infrastructure pricing, will also need to be given consideration in the proposed transport and climate package. Internalizing the full environmental and social costs according to the polluter pays principle together with better data and information will be crucial in influencing consumer's behavior.

Similarly, efficiency standards should be the backbone of any sensible climate change policy. Fuel efficiency standards have been introduced for cars with the revised fuel quality directive in the context of the energy and climate change package. These should be extended to vans and trucks. Standards for aviation and shipping should also be taken into consideration.

The transition toward a low-carbon EU transport system is a European task. Despite the fact that transport policy is still largely determined by national and commercial interests rather than European considerations, one or several Member States alone will not be able to achieve this transition on their own. Greening the transport sector will require an integrated approach from all stakeholders, including the automotive industry, the fuel industry, different governmental institutions, and consumers. Europe will need to develop the most viable pathways toward decarbonizing the transport sector in different modes and to come up with cost-effective, incremental solutions to achieve this vision.

Policy Conclusions

With almost 80 percent of the European energy mix based on fossil fuels in 2007 (European Commission 2010), Europe's energy systems are still far from sustainable levels of greenhouse gas emissions. Given the substantial emissions reductions that will need to be achieved by 2050 in order to stay below the 2 degrees Celsius threshold, the strategic decisions of the coming years will be decisive. With its ETS strengthened through the adoption of the energy and climate change package, the EU has attempted to start addressing the issue of climate change domestically. Internationally, the EU continues to push for a legally binding global agreement for the post-2012 period. This reflects the fact that Europe's transition toward a low-carbon energy system will be greatly facilitated in the context of global greenhouse gas emissions reductions.

Domestically, the EU will need to do more to speed up this transition. The financial and economic crises have substantially reduced the ambitiousness of the EU emissions reduction target (–20 percent by 2020 compared to 1990) by leading to accumulated output losses that will impact greenhouse gas emissions in 2020. The 20 percent EU target is thus already within easy reach even without much further action. Although more robust figures are currently being gathered, it can be said that the equivalent of a 20 percent reduction effort precrisis is close to a 30 percent reduction target postcrisis. In addition, it is not credible that anything less than a EU 30 percent reduction target (or possibly even more) by 2020 can realistically keep the option open to reach the envisaged 80–95 percent reduction for industrialized countries by 2050 (as reaffirmed by the European Council, for example, in October 2009).

While an increase of the greenhouse gas reduction target to -30 percent may prove politically difficult in the current economic situation, other alternatives may be more plausible. Targeting specific sectors such as transport, buildings or agriculture with integrated policies could be a politically more realistic strategy to tighten EU climate change policy. Similarly, it should be considered to make the energy efficiency target legally binding and to tighten the ETS cap in order to ensure that EU climate change policy sets the right incentives for low-carbon energy investments. However, there is a risk that governments in the end might take the easy way out, that is, by favoring policies to postpone action in the hope that new back-stop technologies such as carbon capture and storage or new nuclear will become available, which will reduce costs for climate change mitigation. Relying primarily on such a technology push is a convenient short-term strategy but will ultimately increase costs and the risk that Europe could fail to achieve broad-based incremental technology improvement.

The EU's leading role in combating climate change and in increasing energy efficiency offers opportunities for a worldwide advance in related technologies and patents, and for new domains of excellence and export worldwide. The European Strategic Energy Technology Plan (SET-Plan) is a step in the right direction aimed at boosting a clean technology sector currently characterized by high costs, market barriers, and underinvestment. However, various challenges still need to be solved. One of them is the level of financing. With substantial EU funding required for a low-carbon future in Europe, the budget review in 2011 is a unique chance to reallocate funding toward SET-Technologies. To take into account the technology specialization of Member States/regions and thus to increase efficiency, it should be considered to create clusters of EU Member States for each European Industry Initiative. But EU support will not be enough, and Member States will need to contribute substantial amounts of public money to SET-Plan funding.

The EU technology policy is emerging only very gradually. To date, the EU's contribution typically is low —focusing on EU added value, and dwarfed by Member-States' payments. Similar but longer-term and greatly scaled up programs are most likely needed also for other low-carbon technologies, for example, in the European transport sector. In addition, a principal EU role is to ensure better coordination of industry and Member States' R&D programs and dissemination of results. The SET-Plan aims at facilitating these coordination efforts. Another effective means to support industry R&D has been EU support for industry commitments such as industry technology platforms.

Finally, there is a clear case for aligning transport and energy policies. Clean power will be a prerequisite for a low-carbon transport system. However, due to the slow pace of change based on major infrastructure investment, "decarbonizing the energy sector needs to be even higher on the agenda than the development of low-carbon vehicle technologies" (Netherlands Environmental Assessment Agency 2009).

Notes

1. The energy and climate change package contains six elements: The renewable energy directive, a directive improving and extending the EU ETS, an effort-sharing decision covering greenhouse gas emissions outside of the EU ETS, a regulation on reduced CO2 emissions from cars, a revised fuel quality directive, and a directive setting up an EU-wide regulatory framework for CCS.
2. Directive 2009/29/EC of the European Parliament and of the Council of April 23, 2009 amending Directive 2003/87/EC so as to improve and extend the greenhouse gas emission allowance trading scheme of the Community.
3. Decision No 406/2009/EC of the European Parliament and of the Council of April 23, 2009 on the effort of Member States to reduce their greenhouse gas emissions to meet the Community's greenhouse gas emission reduction commitments up to 2020.
4. Directive 2009/28/EC of the European Parliament and of the Council of April 23, 2009 on the promotion of the use of energy from renewable sources and amending and subsequently repealing Directives 2001/77/EC and 2003/30/EC.
5. Directive 2009/28/EC of the European Parliament and of the Council of April 23, 2009 on the promotion of the use of energy from renewable sources and amending and subsequently repealing Directives 2001/77/EC and 2003/30/EC.
6. European Commission, *Summary of the Member State Forecast Documents* (Brussels: European Commission, 2010).

7. Communication from the Commission to the European Parliament, the Council, the European Economic and Social Committee and the Committee of the Regions, Second Strategic Energy Review: An EU Energy Security and Solidarity Action Plan.
8. All figures include international bunkers, that is international traffic departing from the EU.

Work Cited

Amann, M., J. Cofala, P. Rafaj., and F. Wagner. 2009. *GAINS—The Impact of the Economic Crisis on GHG Mitigation Potentials and Costs in Annex I Countries.* International Institute for Applied Systems Analysis. Luxemburg.

Behrens, A. 2010. Renewables in the Interaction between Climate Change Policy and Energy Security. *Renewable Energy Law and Policy Review.* RELP 1/2010 5–15. Lexxion: Berlin.

Behrens, A., A. Georgiev., and M. Carraro. 2010. *Future Impacts of Climate Change in European Regions.* CEPS Working Document. Centre for European Policy Studies. Brussels.

Council of the European Union. 2007. *Presidency Conclusions of the Brussels European Council (8/9 March).* Brussels.

Council of the European Union. 2009. *Presidency Conclusions of the Brussels European Council (29/30 October).* Brussels.

Egenhofer, C. 2010. A Closer Look at the EU Climate Change Leadership. *Intereconomics.* 45(3): 167–170.

Egenhofer, C., S. Kurpas., and L. van Schaik. 2009. *The Ever-Changing Union—An Introduction to the History, Institutions and Decision-Making Processes of the European Union.* CEPS Paperback. Centre for European Policy Studies. Brussels.

European Commission. 2009a. *Regions 2020—the Climate Change Challenge for European Regions.* Background document to Commission staff working document SEC (2008). March 2009.

European Commission. 2009b. *Toward a Comprehensive Climate Change Agreement in Copenhagen.* Communication from the Commission to the Council, the European Parliament, the European Economic and Social Committee, and the Committee of the Regions. COM(2009)39 final, January.

European Commission. 2009c. *A sustainable future for transport: Towards an integrated, technology-led and user friendly system.* Communication from the Commission. COM(2009): 279/4.

European Commission. 2010. *EU Energy and Transport in Figures.* Statistical Pocketbook 2010. Brussels.

European Environment Agency. (EEA) 2008. *Impacts of Europe's Changing Climate—2008 Indicator-Based Assessment.* Joint EEA-JRC-WHO report. Copenhagen.

Gros, D. and C. Egenhofer in collaboration with N. Fujiwara, S. Guerin and A. Georgiev. 2010. *Climate Change and Trade: Taxing Carbon at the Border?* CEPS Paperback. Centre for European Policy Studies (CEPS). Brussels.

International Energy Agency. (IEA) 2008.*Energy Technology Perspectives 2008*.OECD/IEA. Paris.

International Energy Agency. (IEA) 2009a. How the Energy Sector can Deliver on a Climate Agreement in Copenhagen. Special Early Excerpt of the World Energy Outlook 2009 for the Bangkok UNFCCC meeting.

International Energy Agency. (IEA) 2009b. Presentation of Fatih Birol at the 4th Annual CEPS/Epsilon Energy Conference. Brussels.

Intergovernmental Panel on Climate Change. (IPCC) 2007a.*Climate Change 2007: Synthesis Report*. An Assessment of the Intergovernmental Panel on Climate Change. Geneva.

Intergovernmental Panel on Climate Change, Working Group 2. (IPCC) 2007b.*Contribution of Working Group 2 to the Fourth Assessment Report of the Intergovernmental Panel on Climate Change: Summary for Policy-Makers*. Geneva.

Netherlands Environmental Assessment Agency. 2009.*Getting into the Right Lane for 2050*. Bilthoven.

Chapter Eleven

The Role of EU Institutions in Energy Policy Formation

Vicki L. Birchfield

A basic puzzle underlying any effort to understand energy policy formation within a complex transnational decision making arena like the European Union (EU), where both national and supranational level interests are simultaneously represented and preferences continuously negotiated, is why there is any semblance of a common energy policy in the first place. Such an achievement, albeit limited and fragmented in its current state, is quite remarkable given the sheer complexity of the energy sector, the range of import dependencies, and the varying energy mixes among the 27 Member States. Coupled with these challenges is the multiplicity of crosscutting pressures inherent in the EU's three-pronged policy objectives of energy security, economic competitiveness, and environmental sustainability. As the preceding chapter highlighted, problems emerging from environmental degradation, rapidly diminishing resources, and the increasing reliance on energy imports have necessitated the development of a more integrated approach to energy and climate change and the move to a more sustainable and secure energy supply. Despite the fact that large majorities of European citizens embrace the goals of environmental sustainability and show strong support for EU and domestic efforts to combat climate change, there nonetheless remains a complex array of core and often competing national interests that would seem to bedevil a more comprehensive, transnational approach to energy policy. How have EU level institutions and supranational processes operated thus far to transform such national and intergovernmental barriers to a common energy policy?

Although many of the contributing chapters to this volume have demonstrated how the complex and varied dimensions of a common European energy policy are being negotiated in less than coherent ways due to the influence of narrow interests of industry lobbies and the competing agendas of various Member States, less attention has been paid to the nature and role of the specific EU institutions and the actual processes of policy formation at the community level. Therefore, this chapter offers an analysis of the policy-making process within the EU institutional landscape with a goal of teasing out how each of the core EU institutions contributes to energy policy formation and its relative coherence (or lack thereof), given the varying degrees of competence and authority possessed by each institution, the interinstitutional rivalry inherent in the EU policy process, and the elements of both intergovernmentalism and supranationalism that characterize how European energy policy is being shaped at this stage. Each of these three factors will be addressed here as we seek to understand the prospects for a common energy policy in this new era of EU institutional development under the Treaty of Lisbon.

The chapter is organized into three sections. The next section "Theoretical and Conceptual Models for Understanding EU Institutions and the Policy-Making Process" provides an overview of the most prevalent conceptual or theoretical frameworks that are typically employed to explain policy outcomes in the EU context and argues that the multilevel governance approach is the most useful and analytically appropriate for our examination of energy policy and the role of EU institutions in its formulation thus far. Following this discussion, the second section "The Role of EU Actors and Inter-Institutional Rivalry and Coordination in Shaping Energy Policy Development" employs the multilevel governance framework to trace key policy developments in recent years and to analyze the role and specific actions of each institution therein. Whereas many of the preceding chapters in this volume have highlighted the various tensions between the European Commission's (hereafter: the Commission) approach vis-à-vis the Council and Member States, very little attention has been paid to the third actor in the EU institutional triangle, the European Parliament. Therefore, more effort is made here to elucidate the role of the Parliament in advancing EU energy policy through its various responses to the key actions and proposed legislation of the Commission as well as its interaction with the other decision making body, the Council of the European Union (formerly known as the Council of Ministers in the pre-Lisbon period). Addressing the fundamental questions at the heart of this book, the final section of the chapter "EU Institutional Interactionand Impact in the Formation of the EU Energy Policy" attempts to answer to what extent the EU's institutional actors can lay some claim to the success and progress made so far in the effort to formulate a common and more comprehensive energy policy and to identify the major obstacles and institutional barriers that might impede further movement toward a truly common EU energy policy.

Theoretical and Conceptual Models for Understanding EU Institutions and the Policy-Making Process

The scholarly literature on the EU has evolved significantly since the early days of the functionalist/neofunctionalist debates when European integration was almost exclusively studied from the lens and theories of International Relations. As the Union itself has developed politically and institutionally over the course of more than half a century, the concepts and analytical tools of Comparative Politics have been increasingly applied to understand and explain decision making processes and policy outcomes in the EU setting. Since its inception, the EU[1] has had the institutional characteristics of a domestic political system, that is, legislative, executive, and judicial organs, and as Simon Hix (1994, 1999) argued, has by now acquired most of the policy-making attributes possessed by national governments. In fact, he suggests that approximately 80 percent of the laws and rules governing the flow of goods, services, and capital in the Member States now emanates from the European level (Hix 1999, 3). Whether or not the EU functions like a state or is rather a *sui generis* political entity is a central question that continues to drive a great deal of theoretical and methodological debate, but perhaps the more contentious division is between state-centric and nonstate-centric approaches to understanding European integration. The former largely rejects supranationalist or federalist perspectives or interpretations of developments in EU history and generally draws insights from realist theories of international relations to explain those developments as products of interstate bargaining and compromises reached through intergovernmental negotiations. Moravcsik's seminal text *The Choice for Europe* (1998) is perhaps the defining work of this approach and the central tenet articulated therein is (unsurprisingly) that European integration can be best understood "as a series of rational choices made by national leaders" (1998, 18).

In contrast, those applying nonstate-centric approaches are much more willing to acknowledge the autonomy of action and power of supranational institutions and elites. These approaches can be loosely seen as descendants of the neofunctionalist school whose founding text was Haas's 1958 classic, *The Uniting of Europe,* wherein the critical concept of political spillover was elaborated. Political spillover refers to the gradual convergence of interests and beliefs of national elites in response to the integration process. Haas asserted that: "Political integration is the process whereby political actors in several distinct national settings are persuaded to shift their loyalties, expectations and political activities toward a new centre, whose institutions possess or demand jurisdiction over the pre-existing national states" (1958, 16). In no way discounting the role of Member States and their elites in the integration process, there is, nonetheless, recognition that the supranational institutions and the leaders within them are independent actors in their own right. Thus, this phenomenon of supranationalism—community level actors, ideas, and interests—could be seen as the primary object of inquiry and locus of analysis of those working in the nonstate-centric tradition. One such example is the Sandholtz and Zysman (1989) analysis of the instrumental role the Commission played under the leadership of its president, Jacques Delors, in revitalizing the European project and relaunching political integration through its introduction of the Single European Act in 1986. In their study, the authors asserted the notion of policy entrepreneurship to describe the leadership initiative taken by the Commission to galvanize national governments and enlist industry support for achieving a unified internal market. As others have noted and the authors readily acknowledge, their argument was reminiscent of Haas's depiction of institutions as "agents of integration" (1958, 29).

Understanding the functions of the EU institutions and how they shape policy development is therefore directly linked to the larger interest in or broader goal of explaining integration and how policy formation can be seen as a key variable in that enterprise. As such is the primary objective of this chapter, it is important to bring these theoretical debates into focus and particularly to underscore how scholarship seems to have moved beyond the facile intergovernmentalist versus supranationalist debates. Sandholtz in particular rejected the dichotomy between what he referred to as the intergovernmentalist and institutionalist approaches recognizing that some decisions are made within intergovernmental institutions and therefore require analysis of intergovernmental bargaining, but he also emphasized that the formation of government preferences are "themselves influenced by EC institutions and law" (1993, 3). This more symbiotic perspective was further developed by Sandholtz and Stone Sweet in *European Integration and Supranational Governance* (1998) where the authors sought to explain why lawmaking competences tended to migrate from the national to the EU level more rapidly in some policy domains than in others. Their question bears directly on our attempt in this volume to understand the emergence of and the prospects for continued and deeper development of a common energy policy. They argued that increasing cross-national exchanges would encourage public authorities to develop modes of supranational governance undermining and making national modes of governance more costly to maintain. Thus, once these supranational rules were in place and new policy spaces created, institutions and EU organizations would structure further expansion of cross-border exchanges, transnational policy networks and the EU's authority to govern. The authors called this process one of "institutionalization" and further argued that it is this dynamic that has essentially transformed the integration process, shifting it away from negative integration that focuses on eliminating national barriers to exchange to one of positive integration of forging common European policies that now extend beyond agriculture, trade, and monetary policy to include areas such as environmental protection, consumer health and safety, gender equity, foreign policy, and justice and home affairs, and so on.

Included in these institutionalist approaches are also scholars who have applied the insights of historical institutionalism to the study of the EU, arguing that while national governments are key actors responsible for making most EU decisions, the rationale and motivations for their decisions and preferences are shaped by the history of their past involvement in the EU ("path dependency"). These scholars also refuse to treat EU-level institutions as black boxes or mere arenas within which interstate bargaining takes place and view institutions as shapers of values and norms.[2] Mirroring broader debates in international relations and comparative politics, constructivist approaches are also on the rise in EU studies.[3] Sharing with historical institutionalists the notion that ideas and identities matter, constructivists explore how integration processes are transforming the nature of the state system and the political, social, and cultural identities therein. While important, such approaches are not as relevant for understanding why and how certain policies evolve upward to the EU level and what specific roles are played by the EU institutions in creating and sustaining that legal and policy migration.

The framework that seems best suited for that task and the aims of this project is what may be broadly referred to as the governance approach. This growing literature examines the functioning of the EU as a system of governance and emphasizes not only the process of institutional change but also the day to day functioning of the EU as a normal polity. There is a plethora of studies employing some form of governance approach[4] but one of the earliest and most influential is the multilevel governance approach formulated by Marks (1992) and Hooghe and Marks (2001). Their approach emphasizes the open-ended nature of the EU system within which a diverse range of actors operates at different levels from the local to the international where all have the potential to wield influence.

Theories of multilevel governance attempt to go beyond traditional analyses, which focus on competing national and EU level interests. Rather, multilevel governance scholars insist that EU policy is shaped by cross-national and cross-institutional actors/alliances that work together toward common objectives in issue areas and reflect a "melding" of states "into a multi-level polity" (Hooghe and Marks 2001, 27). As Warleigh has pointed out, new theories and approaches to studying the EU must "address what appears to be a rather different world of policymaking, in which not only the range of actors involved, but also the very ways they produce policy, have changed. This shift is often thought of as one from "government" to "governance..." (2006, 78). Interestingly Warleigh advocates combining multilevel governance with concepts of policy networks, which he says can be either policy communities or issue networks. He argues that taken separately each approach can elucidate only so much about the nature of the EU polity or the process of decision making but employed together we can understand both issues. However, alone the policy-based literature and related concepts seem analytically inadequate to fully explain why new policy formation such as that of the energy field is emerging in the first place. Ironically, as Richardson points out, policy communities and network analysis are the dominant models for explaining EU policy making despite the fact that most radical policy changes did not emanate from either but rather in response to exogenous changes (see Richardson 2001, 12). Indeed, as Jean Monnet famously opined, "Europe will be forged in crises, and will be the sum of the solutions adopted for those crises." One way of interpreting the recent flurry of activity and attempts to formulate a common energy policy in Europe could in fact be related to the threat of an already real and looming crisis over energy security problems as well as the growing evidence of global warming. Such conjecture would not give us much analytical purchase here, but the crisis thesis will be revisited in the concluding chapter.

Ironically, one of the limitations of the purely policy oriented studies includes the failure of describing the actual workings of the EU institutions. In addressing this problem, Richardson explores the relationship between epistemic communities and EU institutions and the influence that knowledge-based communities can wield in the policy-making process. The role of epistemic communities, which are in fact a variant of a policy network, is certainly critical in shaping EU energy and environmental policy, yet applying this conceptual framework only brings in a single dimension of the policy process—the initial phases of discerning the technical nature of problems and how they contribute to policy formation. For example, the Commission often convenes panels of experts to study problems and produce reports that subsequently form the basis of a policy initiative.[5] Certainly these approaches are superior to the "garbage can" model where analysts assert that "decision situations" arise under three conditions: problematic preferences, unclear technology, and fluid participation. Here the key decision making organization is viewed as "a collection of choices looking for problems, issues, and feelings looking for decision situations in which they might be aired, solutions looking for issues to which they might be the answer, and decision-makers looking for work." (Cohen, et al. 1972, 2) This is a much less structured approach to describing the policy-making process, and therefore has been employed to analyze the EU policy-making process, but it tends to imply that policy agendas are somewhat random, which is certainly not reflective of what has transpired in the 2000s with regard to EU-level energy policy innovation.

Likewise, the "Policy Soup" approach (Kingdon 1984) argues that policy agendas emerge out of a process stream of problems, policies, and politics, which converge at certain opportune "policy windows" to allow for policy formation, depending on compelling outside circumstances. Again, the vagueness and lack of analytical focus on nonstate oriented institutional actors like the Commission and the European Parliament render this policy approach ineffective and largely inapplicable to the analysis of EU energy policy formation. Finally, Richardson's work on policy making in the EU traces how game theorists have attempted to explain EU policy formation through rational choice models. However, there are many critiques of this approach (Busch 1999, Hechter 1990, Garrett and Weingast 1993, Sabatier 1988), particularly given the repeated social interactions within the EU, the ideational factors around which actors may converge, and shared normative beliefs, all of which can significantly influence cooperative efforts. Thus it appears that the frameworks conventionally employed to understand EU policymaking too often offer only partial explanations and are inadequate to the deeper aim of understanding how the institutional architecture within the EU fundamentally shapes the process. Instead, many studies are now combining various polity- and policy-oriented explanatory frameworks in efforts to more fully understand EU policy-making. Notable among these are the combination of multilevel governance and policy network theory as advocated by Warleigh (2006) and Bache (2008). Per Ove Eikeland (2010) employs this synthetic approach to powerful effect in a recent analysis of the EU's third internal energy market package. As he frames it: "The *supranationalist* perspective inspires our long-term analysis of the power of EU institutions vis-à-vis Member-State governments, while a *policy network* perspective underlies our analysis of influence by nonstate agents on the Commission proposal" (2010, 3). It is interesting to note that while only attempting to explain a single dimension of EU energy policy—efficiency and competitiveness elements concerned with creating free and fair internal energy markets—there was nonetheless a need to utilize a more complex analytical apparatus. Specifically, what Eikeland sought to explain were the logic behind and the implications of the Commission proposals in the 2007 package, which included revised electricity and gas directives as well as new regulations of access conditions for electricity and gas networks, the establishment of a new EU-level energy regulatory agency, and last but not least, the highly contested mandatory ownership unbundling proposal.

Eikeland's study powerfully illustrates the crosscutting and complex nature of EU energy policy formation. As the author notes, even within this singular focus on the internal market and the economic efficiency drive, strong degrees of "high politics" are present due to the role of energy supply as a strategic security asset. Furthermore, strong control traditionally exercised by national governments, and even by some sub-state levels of political administration, would lead one to predict Member-State government reluctance to yield control in favour of the EU level. On the other hand, the decision to include energy in the single market policy framework back in the 1990s had already created the potential for EU institutions to play a greater role in energy policy, which incidentally validates the insights and arguments made by historical institutionalists. In trying to answer whether or not the Commission through its third internal energy market package exerted more independence and ability to influence Member States than had previously been the case, Eikeland's analysis also brought into focus the roles of the other institutions such as the Parliament and the European Court of Justice (ECJ) as well as the critical role of industry-related policy networks. While the study answered this affirmatively with solid empirical evidence, it was also concluded that the various coordination linkages between the EU institutions and external policy actors are far from approximating a strong policy community. As the author sums up: "With the traditionally strong policy network between the Commission and energy producers now appearing weaker than before, the larger picture to emerge from this study is clearly in line with Richardson (2000, 1008): policy networks in Europe have become less stable and more issue-specific, making policy predictions less certain than before" (Eikeland 2010, 14).

Thus, if the energy policy networks are too disparate to systematically impact the policy process even within a narrow domain, it is not necessary or appropriate to integrate such concepts here for this broader level of analysis. Nonetheless, this lengthy digression on Eikeland's study serves to accentuate the tensions and complexities involved even when isolating the analysis to one single dimension of EU energy policy. Although this chapter is concerned with more fully exposing the policy-making process, the primary aim is to discern the scope of action of the EU institutions in energy policy formation, and therefore the more general theoretical framework of multilevel governance seems better equipped to this descriptive and analytic task.

The multilevel governance approach does not deny that the state is an important feature in decision making (perhaps even the most important), but asserts that the EU represents a new type of polity where the state no longer monopolizes European-level policy making or, for that matter, even the aggregation of domestic policy interest. A second and related assumption is that decision making at this level necessarily results in some loss of control at the national level. A final claim of the approach is that subnational actors do not necessarily operate within one national arena, but rather can create transnational associations. In summing up their approach, the authors insist that, "supranational institutions...have independent influence in policy making that cannot be derived from their role as agents of national executives.... National governments play an important role but, according to the multilevel governance model, one must analyze the independent role of European-level actors to explain European policy making." (Hooghe and Marks 2001, 3) Invoking the analytical concepts and theoretical assumptions of the multilevel governance framework, the independent role of EU institutions in energy policy formation will now be assessed.

The Role of EU Actors and Inter-Institutional Rivalry and Coordination in Shaping Energy Policy Development

As is well understood by students of EU politics, three actors form what is known as the "institutional triangle" in the European Union (See Egenhofer et al. 2008). These core institutions are the European Commission, the Council of the EU and the European Parliament. Although the ECJ is a critical institution that undeniably shapes integration through its rulings and is perhaps the most supranational of all the EU institutions, it does not form part of the policy-making triangle per se and thus will not be considered here. The core competence and authority of each of institution have been defined and transformed through the treaties with the most noteworthy changes being the ever expanding role of the parliament from an appointed and relatively powerless assembly in the first decades of its existence (1950s to the 1970s) to a directly elected body in 1979 and now a nearly equal co-legislative partner with the Council resulting from changes brought forth in the Single European Act (1986), Maastricht (1993), Amsterdam (1999), and Lisbon (2009) treaties. The Council, long considered the main decision making body and the chief mechanism of representing the Member States, has also been somewhat transformed through the sheer expansion of the Member States (from 6 at its founding to 27 today) and the accompanying changes in its voting procedures—namely the shift toward more qualified majority voting thereby making this most intergovernmental of the institutions slightly less so with the national veto possibilities significantly curtailed. Still, the Council undoubtedly remains the champion of the Member States' interests and the least supranationalist of the institutional actors. The Commission, since its origins with the European Coal and Steel Community (ECSC) High Authority, continues to play the dominant and indeed monopoly role in policy initiation and such has been the case with recent innovations in energy policy and, as will be emphasized below, the Lisbon Treaty further enhances this capacity.

Though a full-scale textbook explanation of the powers and functions of these institutions is beyond the scope of this chapter,[6] it is necessary to sketch out the conventional trajectory of policy formulation in the EU context to better understand the critical role of each institution in shaping EU energy policy thus far. In its role as the executive body and its sole authority to propose legislation, the

Commission will be briefly analyzed first followed by a short discussion of the Council, and a fuller description of the role and newly expanded powers of the Parliament. Once these roles, functions and internal organizations are clearly understood, we can more readily trace specific examples of individual action of these key institutions as well as their relative degree of coordination in shaping energy policy formation. The multilevel governance framework specifies four distinct, sequential phases of the policy-making process in the European Union: (1) policy initiation; (2) decision making; (3) implementation; and (4) adjudication (Hooghe and Marks 2001, 12). For our purposes, only the first two will be considered as the implementation phase is nascent at best for most aspects of energy policy and the Court is not a part of our present analysis.

The Commission

Hooghe and Marks refer to the Commission as the "conditional agenda setter" in its power to initiate and draft legislation (2001, 12). As such it has been one of the most powerful institutions in shaping the evolution of integration, but it is also quite restrained in its financial and administrative resources. The Commission is led by a president, a set of vice presidents, and a College of Commissioners divided into various functional units and policy portfolios at the ministerial level with the total number comprising 27—one representative from each of the Member States. The corresponding Directorates-General (DGs) are predominantly sectoral in nature and generally provide technical and administrative support for each of the policy sectors. Approximately 23,000 officials comprise the bureaucracy or administrative services making this the largest institution, yet its expenditures represent a mere 5 percent of the total EU budget. With this in mind it is quite remarkable that the Commission has operated as effectively as it has, particularly as its policy remit has expanded dramatically from a few limited fields to now include almost every policy sector imaginable. Part of this stems from the character of the Commission as a collegial body. There are elaborate mechanisms to ensure this principle of collegiality, with the real key to this being the Secretariat-General (SG). The SG serves as a sort of clearing house and a nerve center as it monitors legislation, chairs meetings of the DGs and generally facilitates the horizontal coordination of the Commission. This is a crucial element in policy fields like energy and the environment where crosscutting issues involve multiple DGs in the drafting of policy proposals.

Also, it should be noted that Commission decisions are collectively taken by simple majority, and once a common Commission policy has been articulated and approved, all of the Commissioners must support that policy even it is not a part of their own portfolio and, of course, even if their own national government opposes it. In the context of formulating policy initiatives, many of the Commission's core competences derive from its role in the regulation of the internal market, but as Andersen (2000) has illustrated, the Commission has been effective in exploiting institutional rules to redefine the energy sector to the environment and foreign policy areas as well. DG Tranport and Energy (DG TREN) has taken the lead in drafting actual legislation that has been the bulk of analysis in this volume but the environment, enterprise, competition, and in some instances two or three other DGs have all followed the dossiers very closely. In fact, as we will see below, the Commission has recently and quite aggressively invoked its authority in the external dimension of energy policy, by directly addressing the security of supply issue and putting concrete strategies and a proposed new organization into place to ensure diversification and to coordinate energy supply. This aspect of energy policy has, of course, historically been the jealously guarded prerogative of Member States, so if this policy direction progresses, it is a clear validation of the multilevel governance assertion that national governments are indeed increasingly losing traditional decision making authority. To further illustrate the crosscutting nature of the energy sector just in terms of the Commission's authority, whereas DG TREN and others have actually crafted the legislation, DG Competition intervenes in the implementation phase when Member States have not fully transposed internal energy market rules or implemented other energy regulations (van Shaik 2006, 181).

The Council of the European Union

Until the ratification of the Lisbon Treaty, the Council was always characterized as the main decision making body of the Union but as previously mentioned, the Parliament has now become a veritable co-legislator. The Council is an interesting institution in that it is composed of both permanent representation from each Member State, the Coreper I and II, as well as the important (non-permanent) ministerial formations that are convened in semi-regular sessions with the delegated Ministers coming from national capitals in order to deliberate and take decisions on legislative proposals from the

European Commission or amendments proposed by the Parliament. These meetings of national ministers take place in the composition of different sectoral Councils, the two most politically significant ones being the General Affairs comprised of foreign ministers and the ECOFIN Council composed of national economics and finance ministers, both of which incidentally, have some aspects of energy issues on their agendas. In the context of formal energy policy proposals, the leading Council formation is the Transport, Telecommunications and Energy (TTE), but as energy has become more of a political priority since 2006, other Council formations have been convened such as GAERC (security of supply, Russia, external relations and development issues), ECOFIN (energy markets), and Competitiveness and Agriculture Council (biofuels) (van Schaik 2006, 178–179). Once again, this range of Council formations underscores the cross-cutting complexity and multifaceted nature of the energy policy area.

In contrast to the various Council ministerial formations that convene only semi-regularly, the Working Party (WP) on Energy within the Council typically meets on a weekly basis. Coreper I led by deputy permanent representatives from the Member States acts as the main clearing house between the WP and the Council and Coreper II, led by ambassadors, is involved only with the issues related to foreign policy, development and nuclear aspects. As noted above, the competences on which much of the energy policies or proposals have been based are predominantly that of the internal market and the environment, and both of these areas are subject to the co-decision procedure (meaning an equal legislative role for the Parliament) with Qualified Majority Voting (QMV) used as the voting method within the Council. The QMV essentially means Member States do not exercise veto power, thus again strengthening the argument of the multi-level governance approach in that even in this strategic issue area, where horizontal competence has been absent until the Lisbon Treaty and where EU Member States have such diverse interests and needs (i.e., producers versus nonproducers, cross-national diversity in the structures of energy sectors, varying energy mixes, different conceptions of energy as a tradable commodity or a public service, etc.), the decision patterns and policy making trends are decidedly less intergovernmental than might otherwise be expected. Nonetheless, as we examine specific examples of Council action below, it is clear that it is definitely the Member States and their negotiations within the Council that put the brakes on or otherwise limit the ambitions of a coherent, common approach to energy policies, particularly in the areas of competitiveness and security of supply.

The European Parliament

Turning to the third actor in the institutional triangle, the European Parliament, it is critical to underscore again the extent to which its powers have expanded dramatically over the past decades in order to appreciate how these may be increasingly deployed to exert more influence in shaping energy policy. As this institution has been the least discussed in this volume, we should first briefly examine the basic composition and internal organization of the institution before analyzing its role in the policy-making process. Directly elected in EU-wide elections since 1979, the European Parliament (EP hereafter) presently comprises 736 members for fixed, renewable five-year terms. Although the elections are organized nationally, once elected, the MEPs (Members of the European Parliament) do not sit as national delegations but rather in political-ideological blocs.[7] Representing on average over 100 different political parties, the political groups are now reduced into seven core formations on the left-right dimension with an eighth grouping representing the "non-attached" members. Never has a single party group had enough seats to form a majority, so groups must work together to achieve a majority. Three groups have developed a rather consistent grouping over the EP's history—the Socialists on the left, the Liberals in the center-right, and the European People's Party on the right.

The 2009 European elections resulted in a clear victory for the European People's Party (EPP) and a defeat for the Party of European Socialists (PES) grouping. The EPP group currently has 265 members against 184 MEPs for the Socialists. In the outgoing 2004 European Parliament, the former EPP-European Democrats (EPP-ED) group had 284 MEPs to the PES's 215. The Alliance of Liberal and Democrats for Europe (ALDE) obtained 84 seats, down from 103 in the previous legislature. The Greens/European Free Alliance group won 55 MEPs, increasing from 42 the last time around, which is a positive development in terms of prospects for greater pressure on sustainability and climate change issues.[8] In terms of Member-State representation, the number of seats is based roughly on the size of population, meaning that Germany, the most populous EU Member State, has 99 seats whereas Malta, the least populous, is allocated five seats. Such a formula results in the smaller countries being overrepresented while larger ones are underrepresented. This is not a particularly salient factor however given that most scholarly research has shown that party or political affiliation is the stronger predictor of voting behavior, not national identity (See for instance, Hix and Lord (1997) and Kreppel (2000)). The president is elected by the MEPs and thus is typically from the largest political group, and he or she serves a two-and-a-half year renewable term. The president plays a powerful role in this most unique of unicameral, transnational legislative bodies, where his or her responsibilities include presiding over plenary sessions, working with leaders of party groups to draw up the agenda, and overseeing the work of the parliamentary committees.

Just as in normal parliamentary bodies, the bulk of the real legislative work is done in committees, so for two to three weeks each month MEPs work in Brussels and typically convene full plenary sessions only three or four days each month in Strasbourg. The committees range in size from 28 to 86 members, reflecting the EP's own hierarchy and influence over certain policy areas with the environment and budget among the most powerful. In the case of energy policy, the Committee on Industry, Research, and Energy (CIRE) is the key actor, but other committees such as environment and foreign affairs are also engaged, depending on the particular content of legislation under consideration (van Schaik 2006, 181).

As noted, the EP's decision making authority has incrementally expanded from an advisory and consultative (Treaty of Paris 1952 and Treaties of Rome 1957) to a cooperative role (Single European Act 1986) giving the EP the right to a second reading for certain laws being considered by the Council, to its current role as a full legislative actor initiated with the co-decision procedure and rights to a third reading introduced by the Maastricht Treaty in 1993, extended in the Amsterdam Treaty in 1997, and further strengthened with the 2009 Lisbon Treaty. In addition to these legislative powers, the Parliament also exercises joint powers with the Council over fixing the EU budget and enjoys supervisory authority over other EU institutions, including the right to approve the College of Commissioners, and with a two-thirds majority, to force the resignation of the Commission through a vote of censure. Because the EP functions in a political system that is partly supranational and partly intergovernmental, there are nonetheless significant constraints on its power, in particular its inability to introduce legislation and raise revenue—the classic instruments of power wielded by traditional legislatures. However, in an empirical analysis of the EP's relative policy-making authority vis-à-vis national parliaments, Bergman and Raunio concluded that "MEPs probably have a more direct impact on policy outputs at the EU level than many national MPs have on national-level policy" (2001, 123). This assessment is further validation that the EU political system is becoming more reflective of a multilevel governance structure as opposed to a state-centric, intergovernmental one. While not dismissing entirely the notion that states continue to matter and are vigilant in their attempt to safeguard sovereignty and policy-making authority, the multilevel approach allows us to move beyond the rigid intergovernmentalist versus supranationalist dichotomy and appreciate the multiactor, multilevel governance mechanisms in place that are melding a new kind of polity. The way in which national parliaments and the EP interact is a primary case in point. All Member States' parliaments now have standing European Affairs committees and subcommittees that institutionalize their coordination and relations with the European Parliament. Therefore, rather than seeing power shifts in zero sum ways, the multilevel governance perspective emphasizes the intermeshing of competencies and shared authority across EU level institutions and between national governments and supranational actors.

The EP's role in actual policy formation is substantially affected by the ways in which it acts in concert or in tension with its co-legislator, the Council. The Lisbon Treaty has now made virtually all policy areas subject to the co-decision procedure, which means that the EP has essentially obtained veto power. If a piece of legislation ends up being negotiated in a conciliation committees comprised of members from both institutions with a Commission and the Council does not accept the EP amendments, a proposal dies. Thus, the fate of and the actual policy content of the EP's agenda and the way in which they try to shape proposals are largely determined by this interinstitutional procedure. Undoubtedly, then, there is an element of institutional rivalry that characterizes the policy-making process in the EU context, where the Parliament plays an increasingly independent and powerful role as opposed to its past experience as a junior legislative partner and an ineffectual and weak counterpart to the Commission. Now we will examine how this unique policy-making process and these key EU institutions have shaped the development of an emerging common energy policy.

EU Institutional Interaction and Impact in the Formation of EU Energy Policy

Figure 11.1 displays the timeline of the most significant actions taken by the EU since the mid-2000s. What is missing from this trajectory

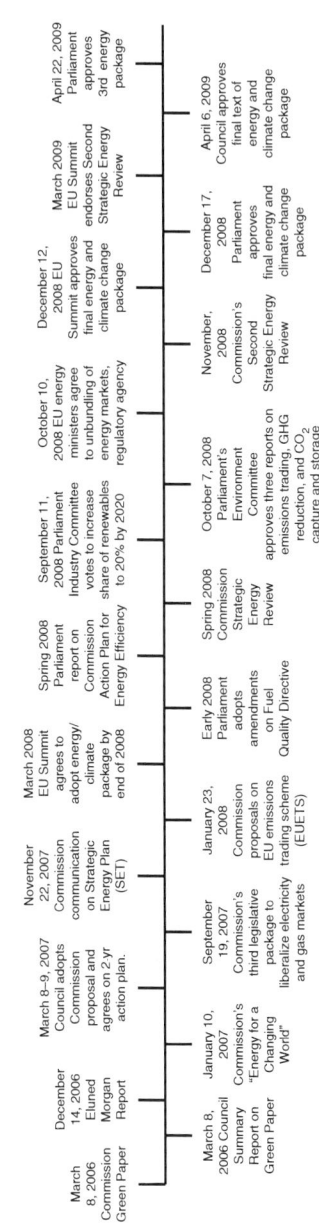

Figure 11.1 Key developments in EU policy formation

is the politically momentous decision taken by the European Council at the 2005 Hampton Court summit, where under the leadership of the UK presidency of the EU, the heads of state and government of the 25[9] Member States acknowledged the need for a more coherent EU energy policy to reconcile the three primary objectives of competitive energy choices for European consumers, security of supply, and environmental sustainability. This pronouncement paved the way for the Commission Green Paper in the spring of 2006 that in turn laid the groundwork for the EU's new strategic energy policy proposed by the Commission. It is worth highlighting this event as it illustrates that ultimately the decision to push policy and governance upwards to the EU level still ultimately resides with the Member States. The Commission is obviously a key driver of the future policy developments, but the initial political will that precipitates and is necessary to sustain it should not be underestimated. This final section will trace some of the key developments of energy policy formation with a goal of elucidating how these three core institutional actors can take some credit for the progress made so far in the effort to formulate a common and more comprehensive energy policy but it will also identify the major obstacles and institutional barriers that might impede further movement toward a truly common EU energy policy.

Table 11.1 highlights key elements contained in the early communications regarding energy policy and illustrates many of the institutional tendencies discussed in this chapter. Displayed in the first column, the Commission Green Paper, "A European Strategy for Sustainable, Competitive and Secure Energy," published March 8, 2006, laid the foundations of a renewed effort to construct a common energy policy by outlining general policy areas and overarching goals. The paper focused on the completion of an internal energy market but also included proposals for responding to disruptions in supply, such as compulsory gas and oil stocks and a new regulatory European Energy Observatory, as well as the development of a common external energy policy to coordinate relations with external suppliers. The Commission paper also addressed diversification of supply as well as a road map for renewable energy and a strategic energy technology plan to promote research into new energy technologies. Goals proposed by the Commission remained broad, however, as reflected in the table, with the exception of a target 15 percent reduction in greenhouse gas emissions after 2025.

The Council responded favorably to the Green Paper on March 24, 2006, adding several of its own concrete energy targets as well as text addressing Member State sovereignty, external relations, and security

Table 11.1 Energy policy initiatives and legislative actions

Commission Green Paper (Mar. 8, 2006)	Council (Mar. 24, 2006)	Parliament—Eluned Morgan Report (Dec. 14, 2006)	Commission: An Energy Policy for Europe (Jan. 10, 2007)	Parliament (Feb. 14, 2007)	Council (Mar. 8–9, 2007)
CO_2 reduction by 15% (as much as 50%) after 2025	Diversification of energy sources	30% CO_2 reduction by 2020	20% CO_2 reduction by 2020	30% CO_2 reduction by 2020	20% CO_2 reduction by 2020
Internal energy market	Electricity interconnections	60–80% CO_2 reduction by 2050	Int'l negotiations for 30% co_2 reduction by 2020	60%–80% reduction by 2050	30% reduction by 2020 if other developed countries also commit, should aim for 60% by 2050
European Energy Observatory	20% energy saving by 2020	Binding target for 25% renewables in primary energy by 2020	50% reduction by 2050	25% renewables by 2020	Binding 20% renewables by 2020
Diversify energy mix	Increase renewables to 15% by 2015	Roadmap for 50% renewables by 2040	binding 20% renewables by 2020	12.5% biofuels by 2020	10% binding target for biofuels by 2020
Strategic Energy Review	Increase biofuels to 8% by 2015	Target for energy efficiency improvements by 20% by 2020	10% target for biofuels by 2020	60% carbon-neutral electricity by 2020	Strategic Energy Reviews
Roadmap for renewable energy with targets for 2020 and beyond (including heating and cooling directive)	Common approach to address crisis situations	Set binding target for car emissions	20% energy consumption reduction by 2020	50% increase in spending on energy research	ETS review
Review of ETS	Common external energy policy	ETS revision	ETS revision	ETS revision	enable increased energy efficiency requirements on office and street lighting by 2008 and in private households by 2009
Strategic energy technology plan	Internal energy market	Make EU most energy efficient economy in the world by 2020	Supply crisis response development (strategic stocks)	Make eu most energy efficient economy in the world by 2020	
Common external energy policy	Review of ETS	Heating and cooling directive	Internal energy market ("unbundling," regulation)	Partnership with Africa but also other world regions	
Promote international agreement	toward 3rd countries		Common external energy policy		
Crisis response mechanism			Africa-Europe Energy partnership		
			Strategic Energy Technology Plan		

of supply. The Council approved of measures to further the internal energy market and proposed the first concrete goals for energy saving and renewable energy usage, calling for a 20 percent savings in energy by 2020, an increase in the percentage of renewable energy in overall energy consumption to 15 percent and biofuels to 8 percent by 2015. Most notably, the Council document, while proposing targets for Europe as a whole, reasserted the sovereignty of Member States in determining the composition of their own energy usage and focused on the need for solidarity in external relations as well as a crisis response mechanism to address disruptions in supply. The Council justified its proposals for renewable energy targets as necessary for the diversification of supply and the promotion of energy security.

A less favorable response came from the Parliament on December 14, 2006, in the form of the Eluned Morgan Report.[10] The report asserted the need for more action, specifically in the realm of climate change policy, with the goal of making the EU "the most energy efficient economy in the world by 2020" (Eluned Morgan Report). To reach this end, the Parliament argued for higher binding targets in nearly every area. It proposed cutting greenhouse gas emissions by 30 percent by 2020, with a 60–80 percent reduction by 2050, increasing energy efficiency improvements to 20 percent by 2020, and requiring a higher percentage of renewable energy usage (25 percent by 2020, 50 percent by 2040). At times, the Parliament's report took a harsh, scolding tone toward the Commission for its lack of ambition in goal setting, such as when it stated that the Parliament "regrets that the Commission has enormous problems linking transport with the energy question; recalls that the transport sector is the cause of Europe's biggest security of supply problem and intense oil dependency, and that climate changing emissions from the transport sector are rising steeply, notably from aviation" (Eluned Morgan Report).

The Commission responded with its first proposals on January 10, 2007, in "Energy for a Changing World" (An Energy Policy for Europe), which outlined more concrete goals for a common energy policy. Proposals included a 20 percent reduction in greenhouse gas emissions from primary energy sources by 2020, with up to a 50 percent reduction by 2050, and a minimum target of 10 percent for the use of biofuels by 2020. The communication also focused on the "unbundling" of energy companies and distribution networks to increase competition in energy markets and the development of a European Strategic Energy Technology (SET) Plan to support technology growth in areas related to energy efficiency. In the realm of external relations, the Commission suggested developing an Africa-Europe

Energy partnership to assist the continent in developing as a sustainable energy supplier.[11]

Once more, the Parliament responded with a request for more aggressive measures, specifically to address climate change and environmental issues. While the Parliamentary resolution welcomed efforts to harmonize markets and echoed security of supply concerns, the largest section of the document focused on "making energy policy environmentally sound."[12] The Parliament once more encouraged the Commission and the Council to make the EU the most energy efficient economy in the world by 2020 and proposed higher targets in every area, calling for 25 percent renewables in the EU energy mix, 30 percent greenhouse gas reduction by 2020, 60–80 percent reduction by 2050, and a 60 percent carbon neutral electricity supply by 2020. In arguing for these goals, the Parliament acknowledged the need for security of supply, but took most of its justification from the need to combat climate change. The Parliament also displayed some impatience with Member States' progress in implementing older policies noting that, "if Member States were to fully implement existing EC legislation, half the EU target of a 20 percent energy saving by 2020 would already be met" (European Parliament resolution on the input to the 2007a Spring Council in relation to the Lisbon Strategy).

An additional resolution on climate change, approved by the Parliament on the same day, reiterated this impatience with the other two institutions' reluctance to act decisively on environmental issues. For example, the resolution states that the Parliament "regrets the lack of clarity of the Commission's 'energy and climate package' with regard to the target for greenhouse gas emission reductions for 2020; emphasises that an overall 30 percent reduction for all industrialised countries is necessary to have a reasonable chance of attaining the EU objective of limiting the average temperature increase to 2°C," and then "insists" that the Commission impose binding targets on CO_2 emissions reduction.[13] The Parliamentary document also admonishes Member States that had not taken appropriate measures to meet building energy efficiency standards and urges the Commission to take action against them. (European Parliament resolution on climate change)

The Council's response to these communications reflects a compromise between the Commission and Parliamentary proposals. A meeting of the Council on March 8–9, 2007, debated and approved proposals including the original 20 percent reduction in CO_2 emissions by 2020. It did, however, include a provision for a 30 percent reduction goal if other developed countries agreed to comparable measures. The Council also accepted the Commission's original goals of

20 percent renewable energy and 10 percent biofuel usage by 2020. It invited the Commission to publish updated Strategic Energy Reviews to serve as the basis for new action plans in the future. From these specific examples, as well as some of the other interventions highlighted in Table 11.1, we can discern a pattern of coordination and push-back that is largely reflective of the identity and the interests of each institution and their native competencies. The Commission, long an advocate of liberalization and completion of the single market, has been most eager to push through measures that deliver on that aspect of the EU's energy policy priorities—competitiveness. In contrast, the Council, the negotiated summation of Member State interests, is most defensive of each country's sovereign right to choose between different energy sources and the structure of its own energy supply, thus privileging the energy security priorities.

Finally, the Parliament is in a sense the most unencumbered of the institutions in that its main motivations and actions stem from overarching environmental commitments and the priority of sustainability and combating climate change. In this vein, we might even characterize the Parliament's role thus far in energy policy formation as perhaps the conscience of the Union.

These characterizations may be a bit oversimplified, but the general pattern is not altogether unsurprising and seems likely to continue in the Lisbon era where Community level competence has been expanded in the area of energy policy. The expansion is explicit with the inclusion of the Energy Chapter and implicit by virtue of its granting to the EU a single legal personality, allowing it to act in a more unified and decisive way in its external relations and in signing international agreements.

The majority of text regarding energy in the Lisbon Treaty falls under Article 2, which lays out Union versus member authorities in certain policy areas. While it lists energy as a shared competence area in Article 2C, the Treaty reserves more authority for the EU in instances of difficulties in supply of energy, with an amendment to the Treaty on the European Union Article 100. The biggest section on energy, though, appears under Article 2, 147, replacing the old language in Title XX (which concerned the environment) with the more specific language that forms the basis of the new chapter on energy policy. The new Title XX, Article 176A stipulates that European Union energy policy will ensure the functioning of an internal energy market, guarantee security of supply, and promote efficiency and interconnection. Paragraph 2 gives responsibility for these goals to the Council and Parliament, with consultation of the Economic and Social Committee and the Committee of the Regions. The Title then asserts that such authority will not hamper an individual Member-State's ability to structure its own energy supply and resources and then in paragraph 3 reasserts the authority of the Council and Parliament over energy matters within the fiscal realm.[14]

Also noteworthy is the fact that the Lisbon Treaty does away with the comitology procedure, under which the European Commission had to consult with committees made up of Member-State experts as part of the implementation process. The Parliament had been critical of the comitology procedure as undemocratic, as it gave a very limited role to the elected body and allowed the Commission to push through important implementing measures without its endorsement. The Lisbon Treaty now puts the Parliament on the same footing as the Council, as the delegating acts come under parliamentary control. With the new legislation, the Member States wanted to ensure that the EU executive must still consult national experts in the process and establish a mechanism for any institution to revoke an implementation measure. The Parliament, on the other hand, appears satisfied that it will have more powers under the new rules. It can revoke delegations or object to changes made by the Commission to an annex, for example.

In conclusion, it is evident that the EU institutions and supranational processes will likely play an ever greater role in shaping EU energy policy in the future vis-à-vis national governments and intergovernmental bargaining, given the new found powers of the Parliament, the shift toward Community methods and voting procedures even within the most intergovernmental institution, the Council, as well as the growing entrepreneurial drive and assertiveness of the Commission. However, the scope of their action and the relative coherence of the emerging common energy policy will likely be conditioned by the existing interinstitutional rivalries and the policy preferences and biases therein. Thus, even in the face of new found political will and momentum and a stronger legal basis from which to exercise authority, the obstacles to a more coherent energy policy may ironically lie as much with the fragmented, competitive nature of the EU institutions and policy process as it does with the purported intergovernmental barriers.

Notes

1. Note that this chapter follows the conventional practice of using the EU to refer not only to its proper name post-Maastricht, but also its former iterations as the ECC and the EC.

2. See for instance the collected volume edited by Sophie Meunier and Kathleen McNamara, (2007) *The EU at Fifty*.
3. In fact, the *European Journal of Public Policy* in 1999 devoted a special issue to *The Social Construction of Europe*.
4. Richardson (2001) provides an excellent overview of the various approaches that apply concepts of governance and suggests how such studies have contributed to better understanding of the complex system of governance within the EU including clearer analysis of the various actors (state, nonstate, supranational institutions and interest groups) and their mechanisms of coordination.
5. This approach is extremely useful and applicable when it comes to environmental policy making. In the EU context, he, Mazey, and Richardson's (1992) study revealed how the Commission worked with an epistemic community to process the CFC problem.
6. See the following for such expositions: (Peters 1991; Nugent 1999 and McCormick 2010; Dinan 2011).
7. According to EP rules, a group must have at least 20 members, elected from at least one-fifth of Member States.
8. EurActiv June 25, 2009. (http://www.euractiv.com/en/eu-elections /2009-2014-centre-right-european-parliament/article-183383 (accessed September 30, 2010).
9. 25 as opposed to the current 27 because the summit preceded the accession of Romania and Bulgaria in 2007.
10. The Eluned Morgan Report was an own-initiative report drawn up by Eluned Morgan, British member of the Industry, Research and Energy Committee, and later adopted by other committees and the Parliament as a whole.
11. Illustrating even further the cross-cutting policy perspectives that get folded into the EU's energy policy agenda, the GAERC adopted Council Conclusions in April 2006 for the first time linking energy concerns with development policy. For more discussion, see van Schaik (2006) pp. 182–185.
12. http://www.europarl.europa.eu/sides/getDoc.do?type=TA&language=E N&reference=P6-TA-2006-0603 (accessed October 5, 2010).
13. http://www.europarl.europa.eu/sides/getDoc.do?type=TA&language=E N&reference=P6-TA-2006-0603 (accessed October 5, 2010).
14. In Article 100, paragraph 1 shall be replaced by the following:
    "1. Without prejudice to any other procedures provided for in the Treaties, the Council, on a proposal from the Commission, may decide, in a spirit of solidarity between Member States, upon the measures appropriate to the economic situation, in particular if severe difficulties arise in the supply of certain products, notably in the area of energy."
    (replaced: The Council shall, acting unanimously on a proposal from the Commission and after consulting the European

Parliament and the Economic and Social Committee, issue directives for the approximation of such laws, regulations or administrative provisions of the Member States as directly affect the establishment or functioning of the common market." (147) **Title XX shall be replaced by the following new Title and new Article 176 A: "TITLE XX ENERGY** Article 176 A

1. In the context of the establishment and functioning of the internal market and with regard for the need to preserve and improve the environment, Union policy on energy shall aim, in a spirit of solidarity between Member States, to:

   (a) ensure the functioning of the energy market;
   (b) ensure security of energy supply in the Union; and
   (c) promote energy efficiency and energy saving and the development of new and renewable forms of energy; and
   (d) promote the interconnection of energy networks.

2. Without prejudice to the application of other provisions of the Treaties, the European Parliament and the Council, acting in accordance with the ordinary legislative procedure, shall establish the measures necessary to achieve the objectives in paragraph 1. Such measures shall be adopted after consultation of the Economic and Social Committee and the Committee of the Regions. Such measures shall not affect a Member State's right to determine the conditions for exploiting its energy resources, its choice between different energy sources and the general structure of its energy supply, without prejudice to Article 175(2)(c).

3. By way of derogation from paragraph 2, the Council, acting in accordance with a special legislative procedure, shall unanimously and after consulting the European Parliament, establish the measures referred to therein when they are primarily of a fiscal nature."

Work Cited

Bache, Ian. 2008. *Europeanization and Multi-level Governance: Cohesion Policy in the European Union and Britain.* New York: Rowman and Littlefield.

Busch, Andreas. 1999. *From "Hooks" to "Focal Points": The Changing Role of Ideas in Rational Choice Theory.* In Public Policy and Political Ideas, Ed. Dietmar Braun and Andreas Busch. Cheltenham: Edward Elgar.

Cohen, Michael D., James G. March, and Johan P. Olsen. 1972. A Garbage Can Model of Organizational Choice. *Administrative Science Quarterly.* 17(1). (March 1972): 1–25.

Council of the European Union. 2006. *2717th Council Meeting Transport, Telecommunications and Energy.* (March 24) Available at http://europa

.eu/rapid/pressReleasesAction.do?reference=PRES/06/67&format=HTML&aged=0&lg=en&guiLanguage=en (accessed November 8, 2010).
Council of the European Union. 2007. *Presidency Conclusions*. (March 8/9). Available at http://www.consilium.europa.eu/ueDocs/cms_Data/docs/pressData/en/ec/93135.pdf (accessed November 8, 2010).
Dinan, Desmond. 2011. *Ever Closer Union: An Introduction to European Integration*. Boulder: Lynne Rienner.
Egenhofer, Christian, Sebastian Kurpas, and Louise van Schaik. 2008. *The Ever Changing Union: An Introduction to the History, Institutions, and Decision-Making Processes of the European Union*. Center for European Policy Studies. Brussels.
Eikeland, Ove. 2010. The Third Internal Energy Market Package: New Power Relations Among Member States, EU Institutions and Non-State Actors? *Journal of Common Market Studies*. Article forthcoming in March, 2011.
European Commission. 2006. *A European Strategy for Sustainable, Competitive and Secure Energy*. (March 8). Available at: http://ec.europa.eu/energy/green-paper-energy/doc/2006_03_08_gp_document_en.pdf (accessed November 8, 2010).
European Commission. 2007. *Energy For a Changing World (An Energy Policy for Europe)*. (January 10). Available: http://eur-lex.europa.eu/LexUriServ/LexUriServ.do?uri=CELEX:52007DC0001:EN:NOT. (accessed Nov. 8, 2010).
European Parliament. 2006. *European Parliament resolution on a European strategy for sustainable, competitive and secure energy—Green paper. (Eluned Morgan Report)*. Available at http://www.europarl.europa.eu/sides/getDoc.do?type=TA&language=EN&reference=P6-TA-2006-0603 (accessed November 8, 2010).
European Parliament. 2007a. *European Parliament resolution on the input to the 2007 Spring Council in relation to the Lisbon Strategy*. (February 14). Available at http://www.europarl.europa.eu/sides/getDoc.do?type=TA&reference=P6-TA-2007-0040&format=XML&language=EN (accessed November 8, 2010).
European Parliament. 2007b. *European Parliament Resolution on Climate Change*. (February 14). Available at http://www.europarl.europa.eu/sides/getDoc.do?pubRef=-//EP//TEXT+TA+P6-TA-2007-0038+0+DOC+XML+V0//EN&language=EN (accessed November 8, 2010).
European Union. *Treaty of Lisbon*. 2007. Available at http://eur-lex.europa.eu/JOHtml.do?uri=OJ:C:2007:306:SOM:EN:HTML (accessed November 8, 2010).
Garrett, G. and Weingast, G. 1993. *Ideas, Interests and Institutions: Constructing the European Community's Internal Market*. In Ideas and Foreign Policy: Beliefs Institutions and Political Change. Ed. Judith Goldstein and Robert Keohane.

Haas, Ernst B. 1958. *The Uniting of Europe: Political, Social, and Economic Forces, 1950-1957 (Contemporary European Politics and Society)*. Stanford: Stanford University Press.

Hechter, Michael. 1990. Comment: On the Inadequacy of Game Theory for the Solution of Real-World Collective Action Problems. In *The Limits of Rationality*. Ed. Karen Schweers Cook and Margaret Levi. Chicago: University of Chicago Press.

Hix, Simon. 1999. *The Political System of the European Union*. London: Palgrave.

Hix, Simon. 1994. The Study of the European Community: The Challenge to Comparative Politics. *West European Politics*. 17(1): 1–30.

Hooghe, Liesbet and Gary Marks. 2001. *Multi-Level Governance and European Integration*. New York: Rowman & Littlefield Publishers, Inc.

Kingdon, John W. 1984. *Agendas, Alternatives and Public Policies*. New York: HarperCollins.

Marks, Gary. 1992. Structural Policy in the European Community. In *Euro-Politics: Institutions and Policy-Making in the "New" European Community*. Ed. Alberta Sbragia. Washington, DC: Brookings, 191–224.

Moravcsik, Andrew. 1998. *The Choice for Europe: Social Purpose and State Power from Messina to Maastricht*. Ithaca: Cornell University Press.

McCormick, John. 2010. *Understanding the European Union: A Concise Introduction*. New York: Palgrave.

Nugent, Neill. 1999. *The Government and Politics of the European Union*. Durham: Durham University Press.

Peters, B. Guy. 1991. "The Institutions of the European Community: Movement and Resistance on the Road to 1992", in Alberta Sbragia, ed., Europolitics: Politics and Policymaking in the "New" Europe. Washington, DC: The Brookings Institution.

Richardson, Jeremy. 2000. Government, Interest Groups, and Policy Change. *Political Studies*. 48(5):,1006–1025.

Richardson, Jeremy. 2001. Policy-Making in the EU: Interests, Ideas and Garbage Cans of Primeval Soup. In *European Union: Power and Policy-Making*. Ed. Jeremy Richardson. New York: Routledge. 3–26.

Sabatier, Paul. 1998. An Advocacy Coalition Framework: Revision and Relevance for Europe. *Journal of European Public Policy*. 5(1): 93–130.

Sandholtz, Wayne and John Zysman. *1989:* Recasting the European Bargain. *World Politics* 42/1989 (October).

Sandholtz, Wayne. 1993. Choosing Union: Monetary Politics and Maastricht. *International Organization*. 47: 1–39.

Sandholtz, Wayne and Alec Stone Sweet. 1998. *Integration, Supranational Governance, and the Institutionalization of the European Polity*. In European Integration and Supranational Governance, Ed. Wayne

Sandholtz and Alec Stone Sweet. Oxford: Oxford University Press. 1–26.

Van Schaik, Louise. 2006. Fiche on EU Energy Policy. In *Policy Coherence for Development in the EU Council; Strategies for the Way Forward.* Ed. Christian Egenhofer. Brussels: Center for European Policy Studies. 177–186.

Warleigh, Alec. 2006. Conceptual Combinations: Multilevel Governance and Policy Networks. In *Palgrave Advances in European Union Studies.* Ed. Michelle Cini and Angela K. Bourne. 77–95.

Conclusion

Taking Stock of EU Energy Policy: Problems, Progress, and Prospects

Vicki L. Birchfield and John S. Duffield

> Energy has become an issue of integration and disintegration of the EU and perhaps will turn out to be the ultimate litmus test of political and economic unity in the EU.
>
> Jacques de Jong and Coby van der Linde (2008)

This volume has brought together a broad range of expertise in energy policy and European integration to assess the current state of one of the most complex policy challenges facing the European Union (EU) today. European energy policy is a vexing subject to understand comprehensively due in part to its relatively nascent state, but also because of the multifaceted-objectives and policy-priorities. These include energy security, efficiency and economic competitiveness, and environmental sustainability, all of which encompass or impinge upon various dimensions of both the internal and external affairs of the European Union. The goals of this concluding chapter are to summarize briefly the key insights and findings of the individual chapters, to evaluate how much progress has actually been made toward the achievement of a common EU energy policy, and to identify the main problems that might hinder its further development. Synthesizing the analyses of the preceding chapters, we also seek to offer an overall assessment of why progress has been more substantial in some areas than in others and what the implications of this uneven development are for moving toward a truly coherent and effective common energy policy in Europe.

The Context

As acknowledged throughout this volume, energy in some ways has been at the heart of the European integration project from its very inception in the form of the European Coal and Steel Community (1952), which fostered economic and technical cooperation through the pooling and collective regulation of these two basic resources essential to the reconstruction of Europe after the destruction of World War Two. That a supranational authority was first put into action as early as the 1950s to monitor production and prices in the critical and strategic area of energy belies the reality that it took nearly six decades before a more comprehensive EU energy policy would begin to crystallize. Despite the creation of European Atomic Energy Community (Euratom) with the Rome Treaty of 1957 and subsequent attempts to mount a community-level approach to energy, sustained movement toward a common energy policy began only with the adoption in the late 1980s and early 1990s of the agenda to complete the internal market, as contained in the Single European Act and the Maastricht Treaty on EU. Deepening integration was intended to increase efficiency in sectors that had been largely under national control, which still included most aspects of energy policy.

Earlier efforts to develop a common energy policy had mostly failed due to the diverse mixes of energy in Member States and the range of national interests invested in them. In the 1990s, EU energy policy discussions were predicated on the twin assumptions that energy markets would remain or become ever more globalized and that a market oriented approach with Russia and other energy-producing former Soviet bloc countries would be successful. Both of these assumptions turned out to be problematic. Instead, the attempted European Energy Charter and its associated treaty were frustrated by Russia's refusal to ratify, and the focus on an internal market strategy became increasingly problematic, as volatility in international energy markets resulted in a shift from a buyer's to a seller's market. Thus, rather than being driven by companies and market forces, energy policy discussions became increasingly dominated by national political interests (de Jong and van der Linde 2008, 2–3). Global energy demand rose rapidly, particularly with the accelerated growth of emerging economies in China and India, while production capacity struggled to keep up. The lack of expected liberalization in Russia's gas markets also caused problems, as did the divergence of views within the EU regarding a strategic relationship with Russia (see Grätz, this volume). Furthermore, political instability in other supplier countries contributed to rising prices and fears about supply disruptions.

As a result of these developments, national political concerns appeared to be trumping globalizing economic and European regional interests. Relations with Russia have become central in the EU's quest for a common energy policy, particularly given the recent membership of former communist countries with lingering fears toward Russia and greater exposure to security of supply concerns. Furthermore, many of these newer Member States did not have the benefit of liberalizing their markets when supplies seemed abundant and prices were lower. Crisis management has arisen as another important issue to be addressed, along with external relations with supplier and transport countries, but it is exceedingly difficult to arrive at a consensus in these areas. As many of the preceding chapters have elucidated, the EU is poorly equipped to play the usual governmental regulator role in energy, since it is not a state in itself with a direct and decisive capacity to act and the Member States that comprise it have such divergent interests and varying import dependencies.

Thus it has become increasingly evident that viewing energy policy primarily as an internal market issue is no longer adequate. Political concerns have moved to the forefront, with the tighter global market, the politicization of energy issues, and growing fears over security of supply taking precedence. And, it is precisely Member-States' varying levels of exposure to supply issues, differing energy mixes, and divergent views toward external relations (particularly with Russia) that make this critical policy area one for which it is ever difficult to reach consensus among 27 Member States. Furthermore, the challenge of addressing all aspects of energy in one coherent policy—of combining environmental concerns with security of supply issues and internal market goals—is proving to be exceptionally difficult. The imperative to create an energy policy for the whole of EU in the face of such obstacles has resulted in what Jacques de Jong and Coby van der Linde have aptly described as a "litmus test of economic and political integration in the EU (2008, 3)." Bearing this in mind, we now offer a brief overview of the key insights of the various chapters in this volume to gauge the status of such a litmus test at this point in EU energy policy development.

EU Energy Policies: Progress and Problems

The chapters in part one of the book examine recent developments in six key policy areas: market liberalization, external energy policy, EU energy relations with Russia, emissions trading, renewable energy, and energy efficiency. Each chapter seeks to identify the key proposals and actions taken by the EU and Member States, and to explain why such particular policies were proposed and what considerations motivated EU bodies and Member States in both furthering and/or impeding the creation of a common policy in the specific area of concern. The chapters may loosely be grouped according to whether the specific areas analyzed deal with the internal or the external dimensions of the EU policy efforts. Emissions trading, renewable energy, efficiency, and market liberalization all fall under the general guise of the EU's internal policies, whereas relations with Russia and external energy policy issues such as security of supply are more bound up with the EU's foreign policies and external relations.

One common theme among the disparate chapters in this volume, however, is that this bifurcation of internal versus external policies is a considerable hindrance to the development of a more coherent energy policy. Many of the contributing authors have observed that this rigid conception and binary classification of internal versus external policy is actually quite misleading. Richard Youngs provides an explicit example of why this distinction is a rather dubious one:

> EU competition laws condition foreign policy positions. For example, they have required non-EU oil producing countries to drop traditional "destination clauses," through which they traditionally prevented a buyer passing on surplus supplies to other states. Removing such provisions undermines the exclusivity of bilateral contracts. Supplies are better able to flow to where they are needed within the European Union. And national EU governments gain leverage over producer states. Europeanised internal rules are what provide foreign policy leverage and unity. European policy-makers have readily acknowledged that completing the internal market in energy is necessary for external influence and unity. **The rules and regulations of the internal market are defined as the key foundation to the EU's international projection in energy matters** (Emphasis added. See Youngs page 48, this volume.).

Nonetheless, as Youngs' analysis reveals, there is still a considerable degree of political maneuvering as Member States pursue bilateral strategies that ultimately undermine the more "communautaire" approach. This problem is also pinpointed by Grätz in his chapter on the EU's relations with Russia. The challenge of a common energy policy toward Russia has been aggravated by the fundamentally different perceptions of and widely divergent foreign policies toward Russia held by the Member States. Whereas the European Commission (hereafter: the Commission) and a few smaller and new Member States from Central and Eastern Europe have been wary of relying heavily on Russia to meet their energy needs, some older Member States such as Germany have preferred instead to endow energy policy with the broader goal of binding Russia closer to Europe by integrating their respective energy sectors. Thus it would appear that the external dimensions of the EU's energy policy will continue to pose the most difficulty with respect to forging a more coherent and unified position with Russia and also with other suppliers and third countries.

Ironically, even in areas where specific policies appear to be clearly within the internal domain of EU policy-making, the external dimension is often directly implicated. We see this, for example, in Jørgen Wettestad's examination of the development of the EU Emissions and Trading System (ETS). While he acknowledges that insufficient time has passed to effectively and comprehensively evaluate this program, he does take stock of some preliminary progress and challenges. Among the achievements of the ETS, Wettestad points to the development of an unprecedented international marketplace for carbon emissions trading, the growth of important infrastructure to support and regulate the ETS, and the beginnings of change in the mindset of corporate leaders with regard to climate change issues. He also acknowledges several criticisms of the ETS, however, including charges of too many allowances in the initial stages, wide fluctuations in price, internal market anomalies benefiting energy producers, and external market anomalies involving carbon leakage. Overall, Wettestad assigns a "mixed performance" to the ETS, citing the reservations and mixed reviews of non-state actors as well as Member States and EU institutions. For the future, Wettestad sees prospects for a much more centralized ETS with tighter caps, less flexibility for Member States, and more auctioning. Importantly, he also notes that the ETS came about not only as a direct response to climate change, but also in an effort to influence and encourage climate change action on the international level. Thus, once again we see how EU internal policies are often motivated by external as well as internal factors and not easily interpreted or explained by a single theoretical framework, a point that was also made by Birchfield in her overview of EU institutions and policy making.

In an adjacent policy area, Jørgen Henningsen tackles issues related to energy efficiency. He argues that while there have been many opportunities in this area—what he terms "low-hanging fruit," especially with the entrance of new Member States, and in spite of the fact that energy efficiency has been given a prominent place in the 20-20-20 scheme, there has been in fact little progress thus far, and energy efficiency has remained a secondary priority. This is the case, Henningsen asserts, because the EU has found it much easier to identify energy efficiency potential than to prescribe measures to improve it, as seen in the 2005 Green Paper on energy efficiency and the 2006 Energy Efficiency Action Plan, which merely restated previous measures or mentioned plans to review existing policies without advancing much of anything new. The lack of progress stems partially from the difficulty in addressing an issue that spans literally nearly all sectors of society, from appliances, buildings, energy production, and transportation, to the ETS, and the very different energy usage within Member States. As a result of this enormous scope, a focused policy has been difficult to achieve and progress has been very limited. Furthermore, as Henningsen puts it, energy efficiency lacks the "glamour" of other priorities, such as renewables and security of supply. Henningsen does regard progress as likely in the future, although he predicts that the same problems will persist and that many of the energy efficiency "low-hanging fruit" will remain to be picked due to the limitations of ETS, the lack of a legally binding efficiency target, and the greater sense of urgency surrounding other issues.

Similarly pessimistic, Måns Nilsson discusses the less than stellar development of renewable energy sources (RES) as well as the challenges and successes seen in attempts to promote a common RES policy on the European level. He asserts that RES policy has long been an area of Member-State dominance, with several states developing successful programs such as Tradeable Renewable Electricity Certificates (TREC) and feed-in tariffs (FIT). Not much progress has been made in harmonizing these efforts under the European umbrella, however, particularly before 2006, largely because of differences in Member-State interests. Recently, though, due to growing concerns over security of supply and stronger links to climate change, which has become an increasingly important consideration in European energy policy, RES policy has seen movement on the European stage, with the setting of binding national target levels. Nilsson asserts, however, that the EU is still far from having a real common RES policy. Furthermore, he argues that the future of RES is highly dependent upon the evolution of institutional relationships and agendas within the EU and does not view a true common RES policy as a step likely to be taken soon.

Underlying motivations for a more unified approach to energy policy at the European level is the implicit, but fundamental recognition that this sector is one that is inherently linked to the basic needs and welfare of society, yet also determinative of how competitive a domestic economy is. When that domestic economy is enmeshed in a larger regional economy like the EU, it is imperative that the energy systems not operate in isolation, but rather that national markets be regionally coordinated to tap the full efficiency potential as well as to ensure consumer choice and lower prices—both of which are purported benefits of economic integration.

How has the EU fared in achieving the internal energy market? Eikeland's assessment is somewhat mixed. On the one hand, the Commission has been aggressive in its three policy packages replete with various regulations and directives designed to create free and fair markets for electricity and gas. On the other hand, the ultimate success of this legislation has been contingent on the proper transposition of these energy rules and regulations into the 27 national systems. Eikeland's study shows the gap between these two forces at work in EU policy-making efforts. The Commission has repeatedly, and as recently as 2009, had to initiate infringement procedures against many Member States for deficiencies in their implementation of improperly implementing internal market provisions for both electricity and gas. Despite these setbacks, he also reveals that the Commission's benchmarking report for 2009 shows that most Member States have finally transposed the legal provision guaranteeing all consumers the right to shift suppliers in the national electricity and gas markets, with just a few still lagging behind. So, the pattern of very mixed success seems to prevail, even in an area where the Commission has exercised clearer competence. A critical but often overlooked factor when assessing EU policy innovation is the extent to which Member States actually follow through on the implementation front. It appears this will remain a key challenge in the area of energy policy.

National Perspectives: The Role of the Big Three

As we have seen, the sheer range of initiatives and the complexity of both the internal and external dimensions of energy policy make it difficult to offer definitive assessments of the EU's relative success in achieving a common energy policy. The picture becomes even more complicated once we begin addressing the specific positions and influence of the Member States in either pushing a EU policy forward or inhibiting its further development. In no way intending to discount the significance of other Member States, this volume nonetheless focuses on the experience and perspectives of the three most influential Member States: Germany, France, and the United Kingdom (UK). Although some chapters touch on the role of other Member States and underscore the diverse interests and policy-prerogatives underlying various aspects of energy policy as it gradually moves upward to the European level, the prime movers and resisters have arguably been the largest and most powerful states. Analyses like those presented by Sophie Méritet, Francis McGowan, and John Duffield and Kirsten Westphal sufficiently illustrate that energy policy formation at the EU level is still very much a Member State driven enterprise, even though the intergovernmental restraints have been lessened with the Lisbon Treaty and the Commission has become increasingly proactive in promoting a common energy policy (Eikeland 2010).

Meritet's chapter closely examines the challenges in aligning national energy policies with EU energy policy goals. She provides a detailed account of the French situation, unique for its lack of natural fossil fuels, strong governmental role, longstanding movement toward energy independence, and emphasis on its nuclear program, and analyzes how the country navigates its relationship with EU energy policy. While France is a founding and powerful member of the EU with a significant voice in EU policy, it has been considered a "black sheep" in energy policy because of its unique situation, and thus it too has had to adjust its traditionally state-centric energy sector in order to comply with EU energy requirements and policy goals. While this requirement has presented challenges for both France and the EU, Méritet sees much commonality in the overarching goals of Member States. All share a desire for environmental protection, reduced dependence on oil, the development of renewables to achieve diversity and security of supply with efficient market mechanisms, but national interests pose continual problems in achieving these EU level goals. Méritet points to the widespread acknowledgement of the need for a common EU energy policy throughout Europe and the development of stronger European foreign policy as promising indicators of future progress in this area. With these goals in mind, Méritet suggests that France itself may shift from a "black sheep" to a role model for future EU energy intensity, independence, and efficiency, if it can overcome its propensity toward heavy government intervention.

Similar to Meritet's chapter, McGowan highlights the uniqueness and specificity of the relationship of the UK with EU energy policy. Like France, the UK viewed itself as an exceptional case initially when it came to energy issues—France because of its unusually high use of nuclear power and large government control of the energy sector, and Britain because of its unique position as a net fossil fuel exporter. Over recent years, however, both countries have recognized the need for a stronger common European stance in this area, due to supply security concerns and increased awareness of climate change issues. McGowan details the shift in the British case, focusing on the importance of market-based solutions in the UK. Britain was initially hesitant, if not hostile, toward transferring authority to the EU in energy areas, with the exception of market liberalization, which has traditionally been the area of EU integration most acceptable to Britain. However, as the UK has shifted from an energy producer to an energy consumer and has become increasingly concerned with climate issues, the country has grown more open to the idea of European involvement and cooperation within the energy sector and more willing to consider solutions other than those that are market based and dominated by liberalization. As a result, the UK has become an influential actor in energy policy making on the EU level.

In contrast to the British case, Duffield and Westphal remind us that Germany has been a much more consistent champion of EU integration generally, yet when it comes to energy, it displays a similar ambivalence. The areas in which it has traditionally opposed cooperation, however, are unique. It has tended to back policy initiatives concerning climate change, renewable sources of energy, and energy conservation, but it has resisted a number of others, such as the creation of a common external energy policy and the liberalization of the gas and electricity markets, toward which Britain has been more supportive. This chapter examines in detail the specific context of German energy policy, which has been consistently in favor of energy efficiency and renewables, and less so toward nuclear energy and market opening. German policy has been strongly influenced by the interests of a small number of powerful domestic energy companies, which dominate the internal market and retain very close ties with Russian suppliers. As a result, Germany has expressed rhetorical support for the internal energy market and a common external energy policy, but has been much more reluctant to back its words with actions. In other areas, however, Germany has backed EU measures because of strong societal support for renewables and action to improve energy efficiency, particularly where it concerns climate change and the environment. Despite this record of mixed support for a common European energy policy, the authors do see some hope for future progress as a result of recent political developments in Germany.

Energy, Climate Change, and the Role of EU Institutions

The chapters in the third part of the book operate from a more macro perspective, addressing the role that the EU has played in promoting climate change policies, particularly as a global leader in pressing for stronger reductions of greenhouse gas emissions and sustainable energy policies leading up to the Copenhagen summit, and assessing the overall nature of EU institutions and policy-making in the energy field. Both chapters attempt to situate the developments in EU energy policy in terms of the crosscutting pressures and perspectives inevitably associated with policy-making at multiple levels of governance—the global, regional, and national. Each chapter also confronts head on the challenges of policy-making in an area where intergovernmental interests and institutional mechanisms coexist with supranational policy ambitions and community level competence and authority.

Arno Behrens and Christian Egenhofer offer an assessment of the EU's approach to combating climate change by first tracing how the European community will likely be impacted. They show that the consequences will in all probability vary considerably across regions, with northern Europe likely to experience some positive effects and the southern regions, already comparatively economically disadvantaged, very likely to be more negatively impacted and perhaps even devastated by extreme weather patterns and rising temperatures. The authors provide a detailed summary of these projected impacts in order to contextualize more properly EU policy responses and to show that the EU is ultimately falling behind in constructing a more comprehensive and integrated approach to energy policy. In particular, they suggest that the EU needs a clearer strategy on how to address more effectively increasing transport emissions not only from rail and automobiles, but also aviation and maritime transport. At the global level, they argue that the EU needs to regain leadership and proffer options of both a "soft" approach (e.g., the United Nations (UN) negotiation tracks) and a "hard" one (e.g., by introducing carbon border taxes).

While the focus on the EU actions in the climate change area demonstrate how the EU's rise as a global actor can help legitimize and shape its policy efforts, Birchfield's chapter shows how the EU institutional and policy-making landscape itself has propelled a new policy dynamic within which each of the three core institutions can be seen to be championing specific aspects of the EU's overall energy policy goals. The Parliament appears to be the strongest advocate of a more ambitious approach to sustainable energy and fighting climate change, while the Commission, also proactive in this area, nonetheless tends to take a more market oriented approach consistent with its original competence to pursue economic integration through liberalization strategies, but also pushing regulatory processes upwards to the EU as opposed to national levels. The Council of Ministers, of course, is predictably more concerned with energy security and supply questions and related issues that go to the heart of national sovereignty, geostrategic interests and independence in its foreign relations. Taken as a whole, we might then conclude that energy policy making at the EU level ultimately revolves around the classic push and pull of what the proper scope of action is for the supranational versus intergovernmental level, how individual Member States are negotiating this question, and how the various EU institutions themselves are shaping the multilevel governance and policy-parameters of an emerging, albeit fragmented and incomplete, common energy policy.

The Implications of the Lisbon Treaty and the Future Prospects for a Common European Energy Policy

After years of institutional impasse and intergovernmental negotiations, the Treaty of Lisbon finally entered into force on December 1, 2009. Characterized as the new institutional foundation for a more democratic, transparent, and streamlined EU, the treaty provides the EU with a new legal basis and specific mechanisms to tackle complex policy challenges such as energy and the environment. It consists of amendments to the Union's two main treaties, Treaty on European Union (TEU) and Treaty establishing the European Community (TEC), with the latter being renamed as the Treaty on the Functioning of the European Union (TFEU). As the Birchfield chapter highlights, the Lisbon Treaty places the European Parliament more or less on an equal footing with the Council of the European Union (formerly the Council of Ministers) in deciding the vast majority of EU laws and subjects 40 new fields to the co-decision procedure. Key areas of increased European Parliament power include energy security. The Parliament's budgetary powers are also extended to the entirety of the EU budget. Although the main principles and objectives of EU environmental policy remain largely unchanged, the treaty explicitly reinforces the EU's commitment to sustainable development, the fight against climate change, and development of renewable energy sources.

Article 3.3 of the amended TEU states that the Union "shall work for the sustainable development of Europe based on balanced economic growth and price stability, a highly competitive social market economy, aiming at full employment and social progress, and a high level of protection and improvement of the quality of the environment" (Treaty of Lisbon, Article 3.3).The change of emphasis brought by the amendment underlines the different dimensions of sustainable development (economic, social, and environmental). The same article also introduces specific reference to the promotion of scientific and technological progress, which could also have implications for environmental protection. In its relations with the wider world, the EU shall uphold and promote its values and contribute to the "sustainable development of the Earth." To this end, the union will work toward the adoption of "international measures to preserve and improve the quality of the environment and the sustainable management of global natural resources (Art. 21.2 TEU)." The treaty also introduces a single legal personality for the European Union, enabling it to conclude international agreements and be formally represented in international organizations. Furthermore, the treaty ensures consistency of EU policies on the global stage, by connecting the different strands of EU external action, such as diplomacy, security, trade, development, humanitarian aid, and international negotiations. Of course, all of these legal changes must be proven through concrete measures and actions taken by the EU and then fully implemented at the national level, so only time will tell if the political will of the Member States matches the treaty's aspirations.

Of particular relevance to the development of a common EU energy policy are those provisions specifically concerned with the subject. Article 4 of the TFEU formally establishes energy, for the first time, as an area in which competence is shared between the EU and Member States. Article 194 of the TFEU goes on to elaborate four concrete aims for EU energy policy:

1. to ensure the functioning of the energy market;
2. to ensure the security of energy supplies;
3. to promote energy efficiency and energy saving and the development of new and renewable forms of energy; and
4. to promote the interconnection of energy networks.

Measures intended to achieve these aims may be established by the Parliament and the Council acting under the co-decision procedure. The treaty nevertheless contains an important caveat that could significantly constrain the ability of the community institutions to forge a common energy policy. It formally confirms each Member-State's "right to determine the conditions for exploiting its energy resources, its choice between different energy sources and the general structure of its energy supply." How and when this reservation of state sovereignty is invoked will do much to shape the future course of EU energy policy. At the same time, there are reasons to expect that this obstacle is not insuperable. To be sure, a connecting theme of many of the chapters of this volume is that, while some impressive strides have been made, many obstacles stand in the way of a more coherent and truly common energy policy in Europe. Nevertheless, as invoked in the Birchfield chapter, the father of European integration, Jean Monnet, surmised that fundamental change and deeper integration would likely result not through incremental treaty changes or intergovernmental bargains but from profound crises and the solutions or responses put forward to deal with such crises.

It remains to be seen whether the natural gas conflicts of 2006 and 2009, or the growing evidence of global environmental degradation and potential devastation caused by climate change constitute the sort of crises that will propel the EU and its Member States into the kind of action that will be necessary to overcome the barriers of narrow national interests flowing from geopolitical and domestic economic concerns as well as traditional foreign policy strategies in securing national energy needs. But when Russia's gas deliveries through Ukraine were interrupted and some EU Member States went weeks without power, thus invoking calls for solidarity and community-level action, the EU responded. Likewise, the global environmental crisis related to the effects of climate change or, for that matter, the crisis-like nature of the rapid deletion of fossil fuels coupled with instability and crisis in the global economic system have formed the backdrop for the EU's justification to take aggressive measures in pursuing greater energy efficiency and renewable, alternative and "green" sources of energy. Thus, it could be argued that these various crises do indeed constitute a political call to action or the foundation upon which a common EU energy policy can be forged.

Yet, it is also well to acknowledge that even before the financial crisis of 2008, the incipient pressures of the 2009 UN conference on climate change, and the most recent Russian-Ukraine gas crisis, the EU had acted in an ambitious and progressive way in first articulating the 2006 Green Paper, adopting a comprehensive action plan in 2007, and then developing a detailed climate and energy package in 2008, Even with its noted limitations, this approach seemed positioned only to expand and deepen. Many factors, ranging from the internal (e.g., Member-States' varying energy mixes, different economic structures, public attitudes etc.) to the external (e.g., regional and global energy markets, relations with suppliers, and transit countries) will shape the ways in which EU Member States and EU institutions work in concert to establish policies that will be more effective, efficient and sustainable. Thus, the prospects for a future common energy policy within the EU will depend on both the degree to which energy issues in the 21st century are marked by crises and the institutional and economic logic of operating within a complex policy landscape (supranational, intergovernmental, and multilevel) that itself reflects the interdependencies of a policy area like that of energy and the environment.

Works Cited

De Jong, Jacques and Coby van der Linde. 2008. EU Energy Policy in a Supply-constrained World. *European Policy Analysis*. Swedish Institute for European Policy Studies. (October, Issue 11).

Eikeland, Ove. 2010. The Third Internal Energy Market Package: New Power Relations Among Member States, EU Institutions and Non-State Actors? *Journal of Common Market Studies*. Article forthcoming in March, 2011.

European Union. *Treaty of Lisbon*. 2007. Available at http://eur-lex.europa.eu/JOHtml.do?uri=OJ:C:2007:306:SOM:EN:HTML (accessed November 8, 2010).

Contributors

Arno Behrens is Head of Energy and Research Fellow at the Unit for Energy and Climate Change of the Centre for European Policy Studies (CEPS). Before that, he worked as Second Secretary at the German Federal Foreign Office in the context of the 2007 German Presidency of the European Union. Other main cornerstones of his career include the European Commission, the Sustainable Europe Research Institute (SERI), and the United Nations Development Program (UNDP). His main research areas include European responses to energy and climate change issues as well as policy options in support of sustainable development. Mr Behrens is an economist with training in environmental economics and management, as well as in international development. His Ph.D. is near completion with a dissertation focusing on the sustainability of current patterns of global natural resource and energy use.

Vicki L. Birchfield is Associate Professor and Director of the European Union Center of Excellence in The Sam Nunn School of International Affairs at Georgia Tech. She received a DES from the Institut Universitaire de Hautes Etudes Internationales, University of Geneva, Switzerland and her Ph.D. in Political Science from the University of Georgia. Her research and teaching specializations are comparative politics, international political economy, and European integration. She is the author of *Income Inequality in Capitalist Democracy: The Interplay of Values and Institutions* (Penn State University Press 2008) and has published in *International Studies Quarterly*, the *European Journal of Political Research*, the *Review of International Studies*, *Globalizations*, and the *Review of International Political Economy*.

John S. Duffield is Professor of Political Science at Georgia State University in Atlanta. He is the author of *Over a Barrel: The Costs of U.S. Foreign Oil Dependence* (2008), *World Power Forsaken: Political Culture, International Institutions, and German Security Policy After Unification* (1998), and *Power Rules: The Evolution of NATO's Conventional Force Posture* (1995) as well as numerous other publications on international politics, institutions, and security, and he is coeditor of *Balance Sheet: The Iraq War and U.S. National*

Security (2009). His current research focuses on the politics of energy security in the United States and other industrialized countries.

Christian Egenhofer is Senior Fellow and Head of the Energy and Climate Change Programme at the Centre for European Policy Studies (CEPS). He is also Senior Research Fellow and Jean-Monnet Lecturer at the Centre for Energy, Petroleum and Mineral Law and Policy at the University of Dundee (UK) and a Visiting Professor at the College of Europe. As Head of the CEPS energy and climate change programme, he has developed the CEPS multi-stakeholder programme that regularly brings together policy makers from EU and Member States with different stakeholders and researchers. Mr Egenhofer is member of several editorial boards and has published extensively in energy and climate change issues. In addition, he is heading his unit's input to several large European and international projects.

Per Ove Eikeland is specialized in policy analysis and industrial strategic management, with emphasis in studies of environmental affairs, energy and innovation. He is Research Fellow with the European Studies Program at the Fridtjof Nansens Institute and head of the institute's Energy Studies Group. Per Ove has published a number of articles in academic journals related to policy analysis and environmental affairs. In 1995, he was visiting scholar with the Division of Energy and the Environment at the Lawrence Berkeley National Laboratory, California, USA. He received his Cand. Polit. Degree in Economics from the University of Oslo, Norway and has since 2002 worked part time on his dissertation for the Dr. Oecon degree at BI—The Norwegian School of Management. Defense of the dissertation "Environmental innovation in the electricity industry—Explaining differences across national industrial innovation systems" is scheduled for autumn 2006. Per Ove is experienced in research project management with clients including the Norwegian Government, the Norwegian Electricity Industry Association and the Research Council of Norway.

Jonas Grätz specializes in Russian and EU energy policies and strategies of energy companies. For his PhD thesis at Goethe-University Frankfurt he focuses on the global strategies of Russian energy companies and compares them to the strategies of other actors. Mr. Grätz is a member of the Russia/CIS Division at the German Institute for International and Security Affairs (SWP) since 2008. From January to July 2010 he was guest researcher with the Norwegian Institute for Defense Studies. He has published articles and book chapters on

EU-Russian energy relations, as well as Russian-Ukrainian relations. Mr. Grätz holds an M.A. degree in Political Science, Law and Slavonic Studies from Goethe University Frankfurt, following his studies in Greifswald, St. Petersburg and Frankfurt.

Jørgen Henningsen has almost 20 years of experience working in the European Commission, first as the Director of DG Environment and from 2001 as the Principal Advisor of DG Energy and Transport. He was head of the Commission's negotiations on the UN Climate Convention and the subsequent Kyoto Protocol. Mr. Henningsen retired from the European Commission in 2006 and currently acts as a senior consultant for the European Policy Centre think tank. He was assistant/associate professor at the Department of Chemical Engineering (DTU—Technical University of Denmark) before he moved to the Ministry of the Environment, first as Head of Division responsible for planning and development, and from 1976 as Deputy Director General of the Environmental Protection Agency. From 1980 to 1983, Mr. Henningsen was responsible for the oil trade activities of Danish Oil & Natural Gas (DONG A/S). He was a member of the Danish Natural Science Research Council (1973–1977), the first board of Risø (the National Laboratory for Sustainable Energy (1976–1980)), and had two one-year sabbaticals at Stanford University (1971–1972) and Harvard (2004–2005).

Francis McGowan is Senior Lecturer in Politics, University of Sussex. His research interests include the political economy of regulation, policy making in the European Union, and government industry relations. His publications include *The struggle for power in Europe* (Royal Institute for International Affairs, London. 1993), and European energy policy in a changing environment (ed). (Springer-Verlag 1996).

Sophie Méritet, after earning her PhD in Economics in 2000, worked for two years in Houston, Texas, as energy economist at the French Consulate and lecturer at the University of Houston. Since 2002, she has been Associate Professor in Economics at the Université Paris-Dauphine and researcher at Centre de Géopolitique de l'Energie et des Matières Premières (CGEMP). She teaches microeconomics, industrial organization, antitrust, European economics, and energy economics. Responsible of a seminar at Ecole Nationale des Ponts et Chaussées and College of Europe in Bruges, she also teaches at the American University in Paris and manages continuing education seminars. Her teaching experience abroad includes, for example, the University of

Chicago, CIDE in Mexico City, and Hautes Etudes Marocaines in Morocco. Invited to seminars (FGV in Rio de Janeiro, CEEM in Sydney, etc.) and author of several articles, her research is linked to the reorganization of energy markets and the geopolitics of energy.

Måns Nilsson is Deputy Director at the Stockholm Environment Institute and Visiting Professor in Environmental Strategies Research at the Royal Institute of Technology (KTH) in Stockholm. He is interested in energy and climate policy, innovation, European politics, and international governance. He has slipped over 20 papers past unsuspecting editors of academic journals. Måns combines academic achievement with extensive management experience, overseeing staff within SEI as well as managing multiple research and policy projects and programs including advisory and capacity building projects in Europe, Southeast Asia and Africa. Clients have included the World Bank, the Asian Development Bank, the African Development Bank, the European Commission, the Swedish government, bilateral development agencies and the private sector. Prior to joining SEI, he worked with the United Nations Development Program in New York and Vattenfall Energy Systems in Sweden. He received his MSc in International Economics from University of Lund, Sweden, and his PhD degree in Policy Analysis from Delft University of Technology, Netherlands.

Kirsten Westphal is based at the Stiftung Wissenschaft und Politik, the German Institute for International and Security Affairs in Berlin. She is assigned for International Energy Relations and Global Energy Security. Previously, she was Assistant Professor for International Relations at the Department for Political Science at the Justus Liebig University of Giessen, Germany. She has been a consultant and scholarship holder in the energy industry and has been working in several EU and OSCE missions in Latin America, Eastern Europe, the CIS, and Asia. She has published widely on international energy relations and EU external energy relations with the most recent publications on *Global Energy Governance in a Multipolar World* (with Dries Lesage and Thijs van de Graaf), Aldershot/ Burlington Ashgate 2010, *The Energy Charter Treaty Revisited* SWP Comments 2011, *Internationale Energiebeziehungen (International Energy Relations)*, in: Wichard Woyke (Hrsg.), Handwörterbuch Internationale Politik, 12. Auflage, Opladen & Farmington Hills: UTB, 2011, pp. 186–197; *Solar Power from North Africa* (with Isabelle Werenfels) SWP Research Paper 2010; *Energy Policy in the USA* (with Stormy-Annika Mildner) in: World Energy Council, Energy for Germany 2010, pp. 16–44; and

Russian Gas, Ukrainian Pipelines and European Supply Security, SWP Research Paper 2009.

Jørgen Wettestad is Senior Research Fellow and Director of European Program at the Fridtjof Nansen Institute in Oslo, Norway. He has been Coordinator of the EU-financed Concerted Action Program on the Effectiveness of International Environmental Agreements and EU Legislation (1999–2000), Associate Fellow, International Institute for Applied Systems Analysis (IIASA) (1994–1996), and Visiting Scholar, Institute for International Studies, Berkeley (1993). He has been Editorial Advisory Board Member of the *Climate Policy* journal since 2001. His main research interests are EU energy, environmental and resource politics, with a specific empirical focus on climate politics and air pollution politics at the domestic, European/EU and global levels; the design and functioning of emissions trading systems; and regime theory, with specific focus on questions related to the effectiveness and design of international environmental institutions, including the science-politics relationship. His most recent book is (together with Jon B.Skjærseth) *EU Emissions Trading: Initiation, Decision-making and Implementation* (Aldershot, Ashgate, 2008).

Richard Youngs is Director of FRIDE. He also lectures at the University of Warwick in the UK. Prior to joining FRIDE, he was EU Marie Curie Research Fellow from 2001 to 2004. He studied at Cambridge (BA, Hons) and Warwick (MA, PhD) universities, and previously worked as Analyst at the Foreign and Commonwealth Office, United Kingdom. He is the author of six books and editor of eleven volumes on different aspects of EU foreign policy. One of his recent publications is *Energy Security: Europe's New Foreign Policy Challenge* (Routledge, 2009).

Index

20-20-20 goals, 22-23, 88, 90-91, 93-94, 96-97, 99, 102, 106, 132, 139-140, 152, 177, 267

Agency for the Cooperation of Energy Regulators (ACER), 24-25, 37

Barroso Commission, 27, 131-132, 141
benchmarking report, Commission, 16, 20, 33-35
bilateral contracts, energy, 48-51, 53, 57, 66, 71, 266
biofuels, 5, 114, 117, 152, 155, 222, 227, 247, 253-254
biogas, 114, 152
biomass, 114, 122, 152
Blair, Tony, 193, 204-205
Brown, Gordon, 205

carbon
  border taxes, 225
  prices, 94, 97, 101, 104, 106, 136, 139, 226
  tax, 202-203, 206, 225
Carbon Capture and Storage (CCS), 94
Carbon Disclosure Project, 90
carbon leakage, *see* emission trading scheme (ETS), carbon leakage
Carbon Trust, 100, 104
Central Asia, 57, 63
Champsaur Commission, 160, 166
Clean Development Mechanism (CDM), 88, 101, 226

climate change, 31, 120, 125, 128, 139, 194, 255-256, 267
  impacts, 218-220, 223, 272
  multilateral negotiations, 220
  package, 22-23, 131
  policy, 22, 87, 98, 117, 125, 139-140, 203, 206-207, 220-222, 224-225, 227, 231, 272, 280-281
CO_2, 93, 136-137
  emissions, 131, 134, 136, 138, 152, 164-165, 171, 255
  prices, 136-137, 140
  reduction, 203
coal, 2-3, 136-137, 140, 152, 158, 162, 169-170, 177, 189, 191, 193, 196
Commission (European), 18-20, 29-30, 236, 238, 241, 243-246, 252, 254-257, 269, 272
  College of Commissioners, 245
  ETS, 100
  Single Market initiative, 200
"common carrier" system, 13, 17, 19
competition, 15-16, 19, 30, 72, 125, 181, 192, 254
Copenhagen Accord, 226
Copenhagen climate talks, 217, 224-225
Council (of the European Union), 4, 17, 19, 21, 30-31, 236, 244, 246-247, 254-255, 257, 273

decarbonization, 227-229, 232
destination clauses, 48
Directive on Energy End-Use Efficiency and Energy Services, 135

Directorates-General (DGs), 245
DG-ENV, 99
DG-TREN, 26–29, 37, 246
diversification of energy supply, 45,
  51, 71, 73–74, 150, 246, 254
electricity
  grids, 29, 178, 222, 228
  industries, 15, 34, 201
  market, 22, 27, 66, 75, 167
  production, 31, 170, 173, 177
  renewable, 5, 114, 127
  supply, 14, 121, 156
Electricity and Gas Directives, 20,
  24, 158
Eluned Morgan Report, 254
emission rights, *see* emmission
  trading scheme (ETS),
  allowances
emission trading scheme (ETS)
  allowances, 87–88, 91, 94, 99,
    102, 106
  Directive, 88
  effects on company practices,
    93–95
  and energy efficiency, 134,
    136–140
  and ENGOs, 97
  and EU institutions, 100, 103
  import credits, 88
  and industry, 91, 94, 96, 102, 105
  international regime, 103
  and member states, 91, 96,
    98–99, 105
  NAPs (National Allocation
    Plans), 88, 91, 96, 98,
    100–101
  revised directive, 221
  surplus allowances, 91
  windfall profits, 91–92, 94, 97,
    104
emissions, 104, 106, 137, 139, 153–
  155, 177, 202, 227, 229, 253
  cap, 88
  reduction, 87, 93, 98, 221, 230

trading, 5, 7, 91, 96–100, 105,
  131, 203
Energie Baden-Wuerttemberg
  (EnBW), 181
energy
  companies, 50, 182
  consumers, 15, 21, 27, 34, 271
  consumption, 131–136, 138, 140,
    148, 150–152, 170, 172,
    253–254
  correspondents, 43, 45
  dependence, 64–65, 71, 148–149,
    206
  imports, 46, 65, 146, 150, 172,
    174, 222, 235
  infrastructure, 6
  mix (EU), 24, 146–150, 162–163,
    230, 247, 255, 264
  prices, 17, 137, 173
  security of supply, 23, 26, 30–32,
    77, 113, 187, 228, 246, 259
Energy and Climate Change
  Package, 6, 22–23, 131, 221,
    223, 230, 255
Energy Charter Treaty (ECT),
  64–68, 70, 77, 175
Energy Community of South East
  Europe (ECSEE), 42
Energy Community Treaty, 53
Energy Council, 24–25, 27
Energy Customers' Charter, 23
energy efficiency, 5–6, 72, 106,
  131–132, 138–139, 141, 162,
  172–173, 223, 231, 253,
  267–268, 271, 274–275
  appliances, 132–133, 139
  buildings, 133–134
  climate policy, 140
  ETS, 136–137
  Lisbon Treaty, 139–140, 256, 259
  new member states, 135
  power production, 134
  and security of supply, 140
  technology, 139–140, 254
  transport, 134–135

Index

Energy Efficiency Action Plan (EEAP), 132, 135–136, 268
Energy Efficiency Action Plans (EEAPs), 135–136
Energy End-Use Efficiency and Energy Services Directive, 2006, 135
energy intensity, 153, 155, 164, 166
Energy Labeling Directive, 223
energy market, *see* internal energy market
Energy Performance of Buildings Directive, 2002, 133, 223
energy policy
  British, *see* UK, energy policy
  European, *see* EU, energy policy
  French, *see* France, energy policy
  German, *see* Germany, energy policy
Environmental Non-Governmental Organizations (ENGOs), 97, 100–101, 103–104
environmental policy, 20, 106, 202, 241, 258, 273
Euro-Mediterranean Partnership (EMP), 42, 53, 57–58
European Atomic Energy Community (Euratom), 2, 264
European Coal and Steel Community (ECSC), 2–3, 6, 64, 145, 195, 244, 264
European Court of Justice (ECJ), 18, 28, 51, 243–244
European Development Fund (EDF), 30, 146, 156, 158–161, 167
European Economic Community (ECC), 17–18, 145
European Energy Charter, 264
European Energy Observatory, 252
European Environment Agency (EEA), 124
European Neighbourhood Policy (ENP), 42, 44, 57

European Network for TSOs (ENTSO), 25
European Regulators' Group for Electricity and Gas (ERGEG), 21, 23, 36
European Renewable Electricity Federation (EREF), 121
European Renewable Energy Council (EREC), 29, 121
European Strategic Energy Technology (SET), 231, 254
European Union (EU)
  climate change policy, 217, 225
  energy policy, 43, 145–146, 162, 235, 271, 273
    common external, 5, 42, 179–180, 269
    comprehensive, 4, 196, 236, 252
    formation, 1, 235, 241–243
    national priorities, 152
    study of, 6–7
  external relations, 61, 75, 79, 254, 256, 265–266
  institutions, 236, 238–239, 242–245, 249–250, 257, 271-272
  integration, 237, 275
  policy formation of, 236, 241
  policy making, theoretical approaches, 237–240, 242–243

feed-in tariffs (FIT), 116, 119, 121–123, 127, 268
Florence Forum, 36
France, 4, 15, 24, 27, 30, 32, 48, 54, 66, 120, 146–166, 169, 179, 269–270
  climate change, 161
  CO_2 emissions, 152–153
  Commission actions against, 158
  dirigisme, 158
  Electricité de France (EDF), 146

France—*Continued*
Energy Act of 2005, 154–155
energy consumption, 148–154
energy dependence, 57, 146, 148, 156
energy mix, 148, 157
energy policy, 145, 147–149, 152–157, 159–161, 163, 165, 167, 270
EU presidency, 120
GDF Suez, 55
nuclear program, 146–147, 149–152, 156–157, 159, 162
renewable energy, 156
transport sector, 149
within EU energy policy, 146, 157–159, 161, 163–164
French Energy Regulatory Commission, 160
functionalism/neofunctionalism, 237

Gas and Electricity Directives, 13, 18–20
Gazprom, 29, 32–33, 47–48, 50–52, 57, 62–63, 67, 70–71, 73, 77–78, 173, 181–183
Gazprom clause, 50, 179
geopolitics, 41, 49, 52–53
Germany, 8, 14–15, 24, 27, 30–32, 40, 53, 55, 70, 80, 98, 165, 169–172, 174–181, 271
BASF Wintershall, 181
climate change, 180
Electricity Feed Law, 173
energy consumption, 169–170, 172–173
energy efficiency, 172–173, 180
energy market liberalization, 179, 183
energy mix, 169–171, 174, 180, 183
E.On Ruhrgas, 181–182
EU Emissions Trading Scheme (ETS), 177
EU presidency, 175, 178
external energy relations, 174, 179, 183
Federal Ministry of Economics (BMWi), 182
Green party, 174
IECP (Integrated Energy and Climate Programme), 172
import dependence, 170
nuclear power, 174, 180
relations with Russia, 174–175, 179, 181–182
renewable energy, 173, 180
role in EU energy policy, 169, 175–181, 183
Ruhrgas, 173, 181
Social Democratic Party (SPD), 174, 182
Union parties (CDUCSU), 174, 182
governance approach, 239–240
Green Paper, 13, 72
Green Paper (2000), 72
Green Paper (2005), 131–132, 268
Green Paper (2006), 5, 43, 145, 154, 157, 162–163, 251, 275
Green Paper on the Internal Energy Market (1998), 13
greenhouse gas, 132
emissions, 6, 139–140, 218, 220, 223–224, 228, 252, 254
reduction, 5, 231

High Authority, 2–3, 244
hydroelectricity, 150, 152

Independent System Operator (ISO), 23–24, 179
institutional triangle, 244, 248
institutionalism, 238–239
Inter-Executive Working Party on Energy, 3
intergovernmentalism, 8, 236, 238, 250

Index

internal energy market, 5, 20, 47–48, 71, 75, 123, 128, 163, 203, 242, 266
   Commission, 246
   creation, 17, 19–20, 35
   and energy security, 47, 56
   Lisbon Treaty, 259
internal energy policy package
   first, 13, 17–19, 31
   second, 13, 19–21, 33
   third, 13, 21–23, 35–36
International Energy Agency (IEA), 46, 198, 222
issue networks, 240
Italy, 31, 55, 57

Kyoto Protocol, 88, 97, 220

Lawson, Nigel, 192
liberalization, 200, 256
liquified natural gas (LNG), 53, 163
Lisbon Treaty, 1, 5–6, 46, 164, 176, 204, 236, 244, 246–247, 249–250, 256–257, 270, 273–274
   energy chapter, 256

Members of the European Parliament (MEPs), 248–249
Merkel, Angela, 172
Messina conference, 3
Middle East, 32, 38, 57, 65
monopolies, 19, 69, 78, 200
multilevel governance, 236, 240, 242–243, 250, 273

National Renewable Energy Action Plan, 222
nationalization, 191, 196
natural gas, 14, 73, 189, 193
Netherlands, 32, 57
North Africa, 53, 57–58
nuclear energy, 146, 151–152, 156, 159, 162–163, 180, 194, 270

Office of the Energy Observatory, 23
oil, 2–3, 47, 63, 113, 149, 170, 189
   demand, 47
   dependency, 46, 148, 228, 270
   markets, 62
   prices, 32, 171
   shocks, 4, 172, 191
   supply, 51, 62
Organisation for Economic Co-operation and Development (OECD), 66, 196
Organization of Petroleum Exporting Countries (OPEC), 43, 164

Parliament (European), Committee on Industry, Research, and Energy (CIRE), 30, 249
photovoltaics, 114, 116, 152, 222
Piëbalgs, Andris, 24, 27, 54, 131
pipeline diplomacy, 54
pipeline politics, 53–54
pipelines
   Nabucco, 54–56, 72–73
   Nord Stream, 50, 55, 71, 73, 146, 151–152, 159, 162–163, 180, 182, 194, 270
   South Stream, 55
   Trans–Adriatic, 72
pipelinles, Trans-Saharan gas, 54
Poland, 46, 99, 103
policy communities, 240
policy networks, 240–241, 243
privatization, 15, 192–193, 207
Prodi Commission, 67, 131
public service obligations (PSOs), 23, 31

reciprocity clause, 50, 77, 179
reciprocity laws, 159
renewable energy, 5, 31, 115, 117, 131–132, 138, 163–164, 222, 252, 254, 256
renewable energy directive, 222

renewable energy sources (RES), 113–115, 120, 222, 228, 268
  binding targets, 119, 128, 162, 205
  and energy security, 120
  and member states, 113, 116, 119, 121, 124, 126, 128
  policy, 117–120, 123, 125–128, 268
  technologies, 122
  transport, 117
Russia, 29, 53–54, 63, 67–68, 70, 181–182, 264, 267
  EU energy relations, 7, 50, 53, 55, 57, 61–62, 64, 66–68
  Soviet Union, 65
  Russia-Georgia conflict, 52, 54–55
  Russia-Ukraine gas disputes, 32, 44, 47, 53–54, 120, 172, 180, 183, 204, 275

Schröder, Gerhard, 70, 174
Schuman Plan, 2
SET Plan, see European Strategic Energy Technology (SET)
Shore, Peter, 198
Single European Act (SEA), 4, 17, 75, 183, 238, 244, 249, 264
solar power, 113–114, 121
Spain, 15, 48
Steinmeier, Frank-Walter, 175
Suez Gulf Power Company, 51
supranational institutions, 238, 243
supranationalism, 237–238, 250

"third-country clause", 29
third-party access (TPA), 20, 66, 77, 158, 178
Tradable Renewable Electricity Certificates (TREC), 115–116, 122, 268

transmission system operators (TSOs), 16, 19, 21, 30, 32, 34–36
transport, 65, 114, 117, 134–135, 227, 230, 232, 272
transport and climate package, 228–229
Treaties of Rome, 249
Treaty of Paris, 249
Treaty on European Union (TEU), 4
Turkey, 44, 53

UK (United Kingdom), 15, 27, 31–32, 187, 196, 202, 269
  coalition government, 188, 194, 206
  Conservative Party, 193, 202, 206
  energy policy, 48, 92, 187–195, 197–200, 202–205, 270–271
  energy supply, 187, 189–190, 195, 198, 206
  and the internal energy market, 199
  and International Energy Agency (IEA), 198–199
  Labour Party, 187–188, 191, 193–194, 206
  and oil shocks, 191
  role in EU energy policy, 187–188, 196, 199–207
Ukraine, 32, 42, 47, 53–54, 63, 172, 204, 275
UN Intergovernmental Panel on Climate Change (IPCC), 218
unbundling, ownership (see also: MOU), 5, 15, 20–21, 24, 26–27, 30, 32, 35, 47, 49–50, 77, 178, 181, 201, 254
United Nations Framework Convention on Climate Change, 125

United States (US), 49, 66, 70, 101, 105, 161, 195, 220, 226

vertical integration, 22, 77
vertically integrated companies, 14, 21, 179, 181, 201
vertically integrated energy groups, 30

White Paper on renewable energies (1997), 20, 115
wind power, 113–114, 116, 121–123, 138, 152, 173, 222
windfall profits, 91–92, 97, 104, 110, 123